D1606528

THE
FOURTH
DIMENSION

SPECIAL COMBINED EDITION — VOLUMES ONE AND TWO

THE
FOURTH
DIMENSION

SPECIAL COMBINED EDITION — VOLUMES ONE AND TWO

DR. DAVID YONGGI CHO

BRIDGE LOGOS

Newberry, FL 32669

The Fourth Dimension
by Dr. David Yonggi Cho

Bridge-Logos
Newberry, FL 32669

The Fourth Dimension

by Dr. David Yonggi Cho

©1979 and 1983 by Bridge-Logos Publishers

All Scripture quotations are from the King James Bible unless otherwise stated.

Quotes marked NKJV are taken from the New King Janes Version. Copyright © Thomas Nelson. Used by permission. All rights reserved.

Printed in the United States of America.

Library of Congress Catalog Card Number: 2016949003

ISBN: 978-1-61036-999-2

Dedication

This book is dedicated to the many people who are seeking, searching, and struggling to find and walk a consistent road of faith in their Christian lives.

Table of Contents

Foreword

I count it a great honor to write these words as a foreword to this exciting book by my brother in Christ, David Yonggi Cho. I am personally indebted to him for spiritual strength, and for insights I have received from God through this great Christian pastor.

I was ministering to his huge congregation in Seoul, Korea, when we received a telephone call that our daughter was tragically injured in a horrible traffic accident in Iowa. Accompanying us to the plane as my wife and I left in haste was our dear friend, David Yonggi Cho, prayerfully supporting and sustaining us. And when I arrived some hours later to sit through the black night hours at the pain-wracked side of my daughter, whose left leg had just been amputated and whose life had just been snatched from death, I found myself reading page after page of the unpublished manuscript of this book for which I now, with enthusiasm, offer a word or two.

I discovered the reality of that dynamic dimension in prayer that comes through visualizing the healing experience. Line after line of the original manuscript was underlined by this travel-weary pastor, this suffering father. I can only hope and pray that many Christians—and unbelievers too!—will find this book coming into their hands and drawing from it the amazing spiritual truths that its pages contain.

Don't try to understand it. Just start to enjoy it! It's true. It works. I tried it. Thank you—David Yonggi Cho—for allowing the Holy Spirit to give this message to us and to the world. God loves you and so do I!

— Dr. Robert Schuller

Preface

LIFE FULL AND FREE

In the chaos that followed the Korean Conflict, I was among the many struggling for existence. Poor but persistent, I held several jobs in the course of a single day.

One afternoon I was working as a tutor. Suddenly I felt something oozing up from deep inside my chest. My mouth felt full. I thought I would choke.

As I opened my mouth, blood began to gush out. I tried to stop the bleeding, but blood continued to flow from my nostrils and mouth. My stomach and chest soon filled with blood. Severely weakened, I fainted.

When I returned to consciousness everything seemed to be spinning. Shaken, I barely managed to travel home.

I was nineteen years old. And I was dying.

GO HOME, YOUNG MAN

Frightened, my parents immediately sold enough of their

possessions to take me to a famous hospital for treatment. The doctor's examinations were careful, their diagnosis: incurable tuberculosis.

When I heard their assessment, I realized how badly I wanted to live. My desires for the future were to end before I even had the chance to start fully living.

Desperate, I turned to the physician who had pronounced the grim diagnosis. "Doctor," I plead, "isn't there anything you can do for me?"

His reply was to resound often in my mind. "No. This type of tuberculosis is very unusual. It is spreading so fast that there is no way to arrest it.

"You have three, at the most four, months to live. Go home, young man. Eat anything you want. Say good-bye to your friends."

Dejected, I left the hospital. I passed hundreds of refugees on the streets, and felt a kindred spirit. Feeling totally alone, I was one of the hopeless.

I returned home in a dazed condition. Ready to die, I hung a three month calendar on the wall. Raised a Buddhist, I prayed daily that Buddha would help me. But no hope came, and I grew continually worse.

Sensing that my time to live was shortening, I gave up faith in Buddha. It was then that I began to cry to the unknown God. Little did I know how great an impact His response would have on my life.

TOUCHING TEARS

A few days later a high school girl visited me, and began to talk about Jesus Christ. She told me about Christ's virgin birth, His death on a cross, His resurrection, and salvation through grace. These stories seemed nonsense to me. I neither accepted her stories, nor paid much attention to this ignorant young female. Her departure left me with one emotion: relief.

But the next day she returned. She came again and again, every time troubling me with stories about the God-man, Jesus. After more than a week of these visits, I became greatly agitated, and roughly rebuked her.

She did not run away in shame, nor retaliate in anger. She simply knelt down, and began to pray for me. Large tears rolled down her cheeks, reflecting a compassion foreign to my well-organized and sterile Buddhist philosophies and rituals.

When I saw her tears, my heart was deeply touched. There was something different in this young girl. She was not reciting religious stories to me; she was living what she believed. Through her love and tears I could feel the presence of God.

"Young lady," I entreated, "please don't cry. I am sorry. I now know about your Christian love. Since I am dying I will become a Christian for you."

Her response was immediate. Her face brightened into a glow, and she praised God. Shaking hands with me, she gave me her Bible.

"Search the Bible," she instructed. "If you read it faithfully you will find the words of life."

That was the first time in my life I had ever held a Bible. Constantly struggling to gasp air into my lungs, I opened to the Book of Genesis.

Turning the pages to Matthew, she smiled: "Sir, you are so sick that if you start from Genesis, I don't think you will last long enough to finish Revelation. If you start from the Book of Matthew, you will have enough time."

Expecting to find deep moral and philosophical religious teachings, I was shocked at what I read. "Abraham begat Isaac; Isaac begat Jacob; and Jacob begat Judas and his brethren."

I felt very foolish. I closed the Bible saying, "Young lady, I won't read this Bible. This is only a story of one man begetting another. I would rather read a telephone directory."

"Sir, she replied. "You don't recognize these names right now. But as you read on, these names will come to hold special meaning for you." Encouraged, I began reading the Bible again.

THE LIVING LORD

As I read I did not find any systematized philosophies, any theories of medical science, or any religious rituals. But I did find one striking theme: The Bible constantly talked about Jesus Christ, the Son of God.

The imminence of my death had brought me to the realization that I needed something greater than a religion, greater than a philosophy, and even greater than sympathy for the trials of human existence. I needed someone who could share my struggles and sufferings, someone who could give me victory.

Through reading the Bible I discovered that someone to be the Lord Jesus Christ:

The Person Jesus Christ was not bringing a religion, a code of ethics, nor a series of rituals. In a profoundly practical way, Jesus was bringing salvation to humanity. Hating sin, Christ loved the sinner, accepting all who came to Him. Deeply aware of my sins, I knew I needed His forgiveness.

Christ healed the sick. The ill and infirm came to Him, and He healed all He touched. This put faith in my heart. I became hopeful that He might heal me, too.

Christ gave peace to the troubled. He urged, "Have faith in God! Don't be troubled! There is no reason to fear!" Christ hated fear, showing man that he was born to live by faith. Christ gave confidence, faith and peace to those who came to receive help. This tremendous message thrilled my heart.

Christ raised the dead. I never found one incident in the Bible where Christ conducted a funeral service. He brought the dead to life, changing funeral services into magnificent resurrections.

Most outstanding in my mind was Christ's mercy to the demon possessed. During the Korean War many people lost their families and businesses. Suffering from nervous breakdowns, many became completely possessed by the devil. Bereft of shelter, they wandered aimlessly around the streets.

Christ was even ready to meet this challenge. He cast out demons and restored the possessed to a life of normalcy. Christ's love was powerful, touching the lives and needs of all who came to Him.

Convinced that Jesus Christ was alive and moved by the vitality of His ministry, I knelt down. I asked Christ to come into my heart, to save, heal and deliver me from death.

Instantly the joy of salvation and the peace of Christ's forgiveness surged over me. I knew that I was saved. Filled with the Holy Spirit, I stood up and shouted, "Glory be to the Lord!"

From that time on I read the Bible like a starving man eats bread. The Bible supplied foundation for all the faith I needed. Despite the prognosis and old feelings of fear, I soon knew I was going to live. Instead of dying in three months, I was out of my deathbed in six.

Since that time I have been preaching the dynamic Gospel of Jesus Christ. The girl whose name I never knew taught me the most precious name I will ever know.

Through the years God has helped me to understand several important principles of faith. These are the principles I share with you in the chapters that follow, in order that you can enter a deeper dimension and more abundant life.

Christ is unchanging. He is the same yesterday, today and forever.

Christ wants to bear your burdens. Jesus can forgive and heal you. He can cast out Satan, and give you confidence, faith and peace.

Christ wants to give you life eternal and be a present part of your daily living. While thieves come to kill and destroy, Jesus Christ comes to give you life, life full and free.

Through the presence of the Holy Spirit, Jesus is with you right now. Christ desires to heal you, and to deliver you from death. He is your living Lord. Put your faith in Jesus Christ, and expect a miracle today.

CHAPTER 1

Incubation: A Law of Faith

God will never bring about any of His great works without coming through your own personal faith. It is taken for granted that you have faith, for the Bible says that God has dealt to each and every one of us a measure of faith. You have faith whether you feel it or not. You may try to feel faith, but when you need faith, then faith is there. It is there for your use, like having two arms; when you need to use them, you just reach out your arms and move them. I do not need to feel that my two arms are hanging on my shoulders to know that I have them.

There are, however, certain ways your faith works, and links you to the Heavenly Father who dwells within you. The Bible says that faith is the substance of things hoped for, a substance which first has a stage of development—of incubation—before its usage can be full and effective. You might now ask, "What are the elements needed to make my faith usable?" There are four basic steps to the process of incubation.

ENVISION A CLEAR-CUT OBJECTIVE

First, to use your faith you must be able to envision a clear-cut objective. Faith is the substance of things, clear-cut things, hoped for. If you have only a vague idea about your goal, then you are out of touch with the One who could answer your prayer. You must have a clear and defined faith goal. I learned this lesson in a very peculiar situation.

I had been in the ministry for quite a few months, and was so poverty-stricken that, as far as material things are concerned, I had nothing. I was not married, and was living in one small room. I had no desk, no chair, and no bed and was eating on the floor, sleeping on the floor and studying on the floor, but walking miles and miles everyday to carry out soul winning.

But one day while reading my Bible, I was tremendously impressed by God's promises. The Bible said that if I would just put my faith in Jesus, praying in His name, that I would receive everything. The Bible also taught me that I was the son of God, a child of the King of kings, and of the Lord of lords!

So I said, "Father! Why should a child of the King of kings, and of the Lord of lords, live without a desk, chair and bed, and walk mile after mile everyday? At least I should have a humble desk and chair to sit on, and a humble bicycle to ride on to do my home visitation." I felt that according to Scripture I could ask for these kinds of things from the Lord. I knelt down and prayed, "Father, now I am praying. Please send me a desk, chair and bicycle." I believed and praised God.

From that moment on I was waiting for the delivery of each thing I had prayed for. A month passed with no answer. Then two months, three, four, five, six, and still I was waiting; but nothing happened. Then one rainy day I was really depressed, and not having any food by that evening was so hungry, tired and depressed I started complaining, "Lord, I asked you to supply me with a desk, a chair, and a bicycle several months ago, but you have not supplied me with any of those things. Now you see me as I am here preaching the Gospel to the poverty stricken people of this slum area. How can I ask them to exercise faith when I cannot even practice it myself? How can I ask them to put their faith in the Lord, and truly live by the Word, and not by bread?

"My Father! I am very discouraged. I am not sure about this, but I do know I cannot deny the Word of God. The Word must stand, and I am sure that you are going to answer me, but this time I'm just not sure when or how. If you are going to answer my prayer after my death, what kind of profit will that have for me? If you are ever going to answer my prayer, please speed it up. Please!"

Then I sat down and began to cry. Suddenly I felt a serenity, and a feeling of tranquility come into my soul. Whenever I have that kind of feeling, a sense of the presence of God, He always speaks; so I waited. Then that still, small voice welled up in my soul, and the Spirit said, "My son, I heard your prayer a long time ago."

Right away I blurted out, "Then where are my desk, chair and bicycle?"

The Spirit then said, "Yes, that is the trouble with you, and with all my children. They beg me, demanding every kind of request, but they ask in such vague terms that I can't answer. Don't you know that there are dozens of kinds of desks, chairs and bicycles? But you've simply asked me for a desk, chair and bicycle. You never ordered a specific desk, chair or bicycle."

That was a turning point in my life. No professor in the Bible college ever taught me along these lines. I had made a mistake, and it was an eye opener for me.

I then said, "Lord, do you really want me to pray in definite terms?" This time the Lord led me to turn to Hebrews, the eleventh chapter: "Faith is the substance of things," clear-cut things, "hoped for."

I knelt down again and said, "Father, I'm sorry. I made a great mistake, and I misunderstood you. I cancel all my past prayers. I'll start all over again."

So I gave the size of the desk, which was to be made of Philippine mahogany. I wanted the best kind of chair, one made with an iron frame, and with rollers on the tips, so that when I sat on it I could push myself around like a big shot.

Then I came to the bicycle, and I really gave much consideration to the matter, because there were so many kinds of bicycles: Korean, Japanese, Formosan, German. But in those days bicycles made in Korea or Japan were usually quite flimsy. I wanted to have a very strong, sturdy bicycle; and since any machine made in the U.S. was the best, I said, "Father, I want to have a bicycle made in the U.S.A., with gears on the side so that I can even regulate speed." I ordered these things in such articulate terms that God could not make a mistake in delivering them. Then I felt faith flowing up and out of my heart, and I was rejoicing in the Lord; that night I slept like a baby.

But when I awoke at 4:30 the next morning to prepare for the early morning prayer meeting, I suddenly found that my heart was empty. The evening before, I had all the faith in the world, but while I slept faith took wing and left me. I could not feel anything in my heart. I said, "Father, this is terrible. It is one thing to have faith, but it's entirely different to keep that faith till I receive your answer."

This is a problem common to all Christians. They have a special guest speaker, and are filled with faith when he ministers to them, but before they reach their homes they have lost it all. Their faith takes wing and flies away.

On that morning while I was reading the Bible, and looking for a particular scripture to speak on, suddenly my eyes fell upon Romans 4:17, "God raises the dead, and calls those things which be not as if they were." My heart fastened to that scripture, and it began to boil in my heart. I said to myself, "I might as well just call those things which are not as if they were, as if I already had them." I had received the answer to the problem of how to keep one's faith.

I rushed out to our tent church where the people had already begun praying, and after a few songs I started preaching. I expounded that scripture, and then said, "Folks, by the blessings of God I have a desk made of Philippine mahogany, a beautiful chair with an iron frame and rollers on the tips, and a bicycle made in the U.S.A. with gears on the side. Praise God! I've received all these things."

The people just gasped, because they knew that I was absolutely poverty stricken. I was bragging about these things, and they could not believe their ears. In faith I was really praising God, doing just as the Word of God told me to do.

After the service, as I was walking out, three young fellows followed me and said, "Pastor, we want to see those things."

I was taken aback and frightened, because I had not counted on having to show any of those things. These people were living in a slum area, and once they knew I had lied, it would be my last time to minister there. They would never come back. I was in a terrible situation, so I began to pray to the Lord, "Lord, from the beginning this wasn't my idea. It was your idea for me to tell it like that. I just obeyed you, and now I'm in a terrible situation. I said it as if I had it, and now how can I explain this? You've got to always help me."

Then the Lord came and helped me, and an idea floated up from my heart. I said, "You come over to my room and see."

They all came, and they looked around to find the bicycle, chair and desk. I said, "Don't look around. I'll show you later."

I pointed my finger at Mr. Park, who is now pastor of one of the largest Assemblies of God churches in Korea, and said, "I'll ask you a few questions. If you can answer my questions, I'll show you all of those things. How long were you in your mother's womb before you were born into this world?"

He scratched his head and said, "Well, nine months."

I then replied, "What were you doing for nine months in your mother's womb?"

"Oh, I was growing."

"But," I said, "no one saw you."

"No one could see me because I was inside of my mother."

Then I said, "You were as much a baby inside your mother's womb as you were when you were born into the world. You gave me the right answer. Last evening I knelt down here and prayed to the Lord for that desk, chair and bicycle, and by the power of the Holy Spirit, I conceived that desk, chair and bicycle. It is as if they're inside me, growing right now. And they are as much a desk, chair and bicycle as when they will be seen by people at the time of their delivery."

They started laughing and laughing. They said, "This is the first time we've ever seen a man pregnant with a bicycle, chair and desk." Rushing out of my room they began to spread the rumor all over town that the minister was pregnant with a bicycle, chair and desk. I could hardly walk through that town because women would gather to look at me and giggle. Mischievous youngsters would come to me on Sunday, touch my stomach and say, "Pastor, how big you are becoming!"

But all those days I knew that I had every one of those things growing in me. It just takes time, as a mother takes time to give birth to a child. It takes time for you, too, because you become pregnant with all of your clear-cut objectives.

I was praising the Lord, and sure enough, when the time came, I had every one of those things. I had exactly all the things I had asked for—a desk made out of Philippine mahogany; a chair made by the Japanese Mitsubishi Company, with rollers on the tips so that I could roll around when I sat on it; and a slightly used bicycle, with gears on the side, from an American missionary's son. I brought that desk, chair and bicycle into my house and was completely changed in my prayer attitude.

Until that time I had always prayed in vague terms, but from that time until now I have never prayed in vague terms. If God were ever to answer your vague prayers, then you would never recognize that prayer as being answered by God. You must ask definitely and specifically.

The Lord never welcomes vague prayers. When the son of Timaeus, the blind Bartimaeus came running after Jesus Christ, he cried, "Oh, thou Son of David, be merciful to me." Although everybody knew that Bartimaeus was asking for the healing of his blindness, Christ asked, "What do you want me to do for you?" Christ wants very specific requests. Bartimaeus said, "Sir, I want to see." Jesus replied, "It shall be done unto you as you believe." Bartimaeus opened his eyes.

But before he asked specifically for the healing of his blindness, Christ never pronounced the healing. When you bring your request to the Lord, come with a specific request, with a definite objective, with a clear-cut goal.

Once when I was the visiting preacher in a church, the pastor's wife invited me to the pastor's office. The pastor asked, "Cho, would you please pray for a lady here?"

I asked, "For what?"

"Well, she wants to get married, and she still hasn't found a husband."

"Ask her to come in."

So in she walked, a nice spinster over thirty years old. I asked her, "Sister, how long have you been praying for a husband?"

She answered, "For more than ten years."

"Why hasn't God answered your prayer for these more than ten years?" I asked. "What kind of husband have you been asking for?"

She shrugged her shoulders, "Well, that's up to God. God knows all."

"That's your mistake. God never works by Himself, but only

through you. God is the eternal source, but He only works through your requests. Do you really want me to pray for you?"

"Yes."

"Okay, bring me some white paper and a pencil, and sit down in front of me." She sat down and I said, "If you write down the answers to my questions, then I'll pray for you. Number one: now, you really want a husband, but what kind of husband do you want—Asian, Caucasian, or Black?"

"Caucasian."

"Okay. Write it down. Number two: do you want your husband to be as tall as six feet, or as small as five feet?"

"Oh, I want to have a tall husband."

"Write that down. Number three: do you want your husband to be slim and nice looking, or just pleasantly plump?"

"I want to have him skinny."

"Write down *skinny*. Number four: what kind of hobby do you want your husband to have?"

"Well, musical."

"Okay, write down *musical*. Number five: what kind of job do you want your husband to have?"

"Schoolteacher."

"Okay, write down *schoolteacher*." I went through ten points with her, and then said, "Please read aloud your list." So she read each point, one through ten with a loud voice. Then I said, "Close your eyes. Can you see your husband now?"

"Yes, I can see him clearly."

"Okay. Let's order him now. Until you see your husband clearly in your imagination you can't order, because God will never answer. You must see him clearly before you begin to pray. God never answers vague prayers."

So she knelt down and I laid my hands on her, "O God, now she knows her husband. I see her husband. You know her husband. We order him in the name of Jesus Christ."

"Sister, take this written paper to your home and paste it on a mirror. Every evening before you go to sleep read those ten points aloud, and every morning when you get up read those ten points aloud, and praise God for the answer."

One year passed, and I was through that area again when the wife of the minister called me on the telephone. She said, "Pastor, would you come and have lunch with us?"

"Of course I will," so I went to eat lunch.

As soon as I arrived at the cafeteria she said, "Oh, she got married! She got married!"

"Who got married?"

"Do you remember that girl you prayed for? You asked her to write down those ten points? She got married!"

"Yes, now I remember. What happened?"

"That particular summer at the church one high school music teacher came in with a quartet, staying in that church for a week to carry out a singing revival. He was a single man, and all of the young girls were crazy about him; they wanted to date him, but this guy was nonchalant to the young girls. Yet he was fascinated with this older spinster. He was always hanging around her, and before he left he asked her to marry him. Eventually she not so reluctantly gave her consent.

They were happily married in that church, and on their marriage day her mother took that paper written with the ten points, and read it publicly before the people, then tore it up."

It sounds like a story, but it really works like that. I want to remind you of one thing: God is within you. God never works anything independently of you that concerns your life. God is only going to work through your thinking, through your beliefs; so, whenever you want to receive answers from the Lord, bring out that clear-cut objective.

Do not say, "O God, bless me, bless me!" Do you know how many blessings the Bible has? Over 8,000 promises. If you say, "O God, bless me," then God might ask you, "What kind of blessing out of over 8,000 promises do you want?" So be very definite. Take out your notebook, write it down, see it clearly.

I always ask God to give a revival to my church according to a definite number. In 1960 I began to pray, "God, give us one thousand more members each year." And until 1969, one thousand members were added to my church every year.

But in 1969, I changed my mind and thought, "If God could give one thousand members per year, why shouldn't I ask God to give one thousand members per month?" So since 1970 I started praying, "Father, give us one thousand members per month."

At first God gave 600, then He began to give more than 1,000 per month. Last year we received more than 12,000 members in our church. I lifted my goal higher this year, and we are now going to have 15,000 additional members; next year I can easily ask for 20,000. If you have a definite request, and if you really see it, then you can have it.

When I was building the present church structure, which seats 10,000, even before they poured the concrete, I saw it clearly in my imagination. I walked hundreds of times in that building, and I felt the magnificent presence of the Holy Spirit there. I felt the magnitude of that church, a thrill to my heart. You must see your objective so vividly and graphically that you can really feel it in your emotions. If you do not exercise this law of faith you can never really get an answer to everything you request.

Now in my prayers I always try to see clearly. I want to see my objective so vividly that I feel a thrill in my heart. It is then that this first condition is completed.

HAVE A BURNING DESIRE

Secondly, if you have a vivid picture, you should have a burning desire for those objectives. Many people just pray casually, "God, answer my prayer," and before walking out of the church have forgotten all the things they prayed for. That kind of attitude will never bring the faith and touch of God. You need to have a burning desire.

Proverbs 10:24 reads, "The desire of the righteous shall be granted." Psalms 37:4 says, "Delight thyself also in the Lord; and He shall give thee the desires of thine heart." You should have a burning desire for a goal, and you must keep on seeing that goal accomplished.

When I started my ministry in 1958, I had a burning desire in my soul, a burning goal to build the largest church in Korea. That desire was burning in me so much that I was living with it, sleeping with it, and walking with it. Now after twenty years it has been said that my church is the largest church in the world.

You have to have a burning desire in your heart. If you do not have a burning desire, then wait and ask God to impart His desire to your heart. God does not like the lukewarm, for He specializes only in the red-hot; if you have that red-hot burning desire, then you are going to have results.

PRAY FOR ASSURANCE

Third, you must have the substance, or assurance. "Substance" in the Greek language is *hupostasis*. In the English language this can be translated "title deed, or legal paper." When you have a clear goal, and you have this desire burning in your heart to a boiling point, then you should kneel down and pray until you receive the substance, the assurance.

When I was conducting a meeting in Hawaii, one Japanese woman came and asked me how long she should pray to receive assurance. I told her that sometimes it takes only a minute, and if she would have peace and assurance in her heart in that instant, she would not need to pray any longer. "But," I told her, "it could sometimes take two minutes, two hours, two weeks, two months, or two years; but whatever the length of time, you should pray through until you have this substance."

Westerners are often wrapped up in the problem of trying to live according to schedules. Everything is rush, rush, rush. Soon they start losing the time to have fellowship with family and friends, and even the time to wait upon the Lord. Everything seems instant: instant breakfast, T.V. dinners, fast food counters—all is ready in five minutes. So when going to church they seem to pray, "O God, answer me. I have no time—five minute—and if you don't answer me quickly, forget about it." They are not waiting upon the Lord.

Americans have often turned churches into a place for lengthy entertainment. In Korea we have gotten rid of all that entertainment. We make our announcements very short, with the Word of God taking preeminence. After preaching the Word of God we have two or three specials—then we conclude. But the Word of God is always uppermost.

I had been invited to speak in an evening service at a church in Alabama. The service opened at seven o'clock, and the announcements and musical preliminaries took almost two hours; I got sleepy just sitting there. The people also began to feel tired, and the preacher came to me and said, "Cho, please speak only ten minutes tonight. We have a wonderful television program coming on tonight, so I want you to preach for only ten minutes." I had come all the way from Korea, by his invitation, to speak ten minutes that evening.

In such a church you cannot have the Lord's full blessings. In a church there needs to be a long time of waiting upon the Lord, and of praising Him, as well as a solid preaching of the Word of God; that builds faith. And you must wait upon the Lord until you get the assurance.

When we needed five million dollars to build the church already contracted, I had a clear-cut vision, a clear-cut goal, and a burning desire to build this church which would seat 10,000 people. But my heart was full of fear. I was shaky, fearful, and I had no assurance. I was like a frightened rabbit, and that five million dollars looked like Mount Everest. To rich foreigners a million dollars may mean relatively little; but to Koreans a million dollars means a great deal of money. So I began to pray like a person dying. I said, "Lord, now they've started working. But still I have no assurance. I don't know where we can get all this money."

I began travailing. A month passed, and still I had no peace and no assurance. A second month passed and I was praying into the middle of the nights. I would roll out of the bed and go to the corner and cry, sobbing my heart out. My wife thought that I was losing my mind, but I was mentally blinded. I would just stand, without thinking, worrying about the five million dollars.

After I prayed incessantly like that for three months, one morning my wife called, "Honey, breakfast is ready." As I was walking out of my study, just about to sit in the chair, suddenly the heavens opened up and the tremendous blessings of the Lord poured into my heart! And this great title deed, the substance and the assurance, were imparted into my soul. Suddenly I jumped out of my chair like a shot and I began to shout, "I've got it, I've got it, oh, I've got it!!"

My wife rushed out of the kitchen and when I looked at her I saw that her face was absolutely pale. She was frightened, and taking me, said, "Honey, what's happened to you? Are you all right? Sit down."

"I've got it!" I, replied.

"What do you have?"

"I have five million dollars," I strongly asserted.

Then she said, "You are really crazy now. Really crazy."

"But Honey, I've got all these five million dollars inside of me. They're growing now! Oh, inside me it's growing!!" Suddenly those five million dollars had turned into a small pebble on my palm. I prayed with assurance. My faith reached out, and I grabbed hold that five million dollars; it was mine.

I got the substance, and once you have the substance—the title deed, the legal paper—whether you see those things or not, legally those things are bound to come to you because legally those things belong to you. So pray through until you have this assurance.

I prayed through the early part of this year and God gave me the assurance of a total of 50,000 members in my church. So I claimed it, and in my heart I saw 50,000 members. Those members are inside of me, growing, and as the vision grows inside of me, the same is growing outside. This is the secret: pray until you get the substance, the assurance.

SPEAK THE WORD

Fourth, you should show evidence of your faith. The Bible says God raised the dead. That means that God performed miracles, calling "those things which be not as if they were."

Abraham was one hundred years old, and Sarah was ninety. They had a clear-cut goal—to have a son. They had a burning desire to have this son, and they prayed for twenty-five years. Eventually God gave them a promise, and when they received the assurance, God immediately changed their names: "You are no more Abram, but Abraham, the father of many nations; and you should not call your wife Sarai, but Sarah, the princess."

Abraham protested to God, "Father, people will laugh at us. We don't even have a puppy in our home, and you mean you want us to change our names to 'father of many nations,' and 'princess?' My, all the people in town will call us crazy!"

But God might have said, "If you ever want to work with me you should do as I do. I call those things which be not as if they were, and if you don't speak boldly as if you already had what now is not, then you are out of my category."

So Abraham changed his name. He came to his wife and said, "Wife, now my name is changed. I am no more Abram, but Abraham, 'the father of many nations,' for God changed my name. Your name is no more Sarai; but Sarah."

Evening came and Abraham was walking far down in the valley. Sarah prepared a meal and she called to her husband, "Abraham! The supper is ready," those phrases reverberating throughout all of the village.

The village people stopped working. They probably said, "Listen! She is calling her husband Abraham, 'the father of many nations!' Oh, poor Sarah! She wanted to have a child so badly in her ninetieth year that she's started calling her husband 'the father of many nations!' She's lost her mind. Oh, we feel sorry for her."

Then suddenly they heard a big baritone sound from the valley. "Sarah, I'm coming."

"What?!" they probably murmured, "Sarah, 'the princess, the mother of many children?' Oh, he's in the same boat! They're crazy together."

But Abraham and Sarah ignored the criticism of the villagers. They talked back to each other: "the father of many nations," and "the princess." And exactly as they called each other, exactly as they gave affirmation, they had a beautiful child, Isaac, meaning "smile."

Brothers and sisters, do you like to see a smile? Do you like smiles in your home? Do you like to have a smile in your businesses and churches? Use the law of faith! Then you can see the birth of Isaac again and again in your life.

Miracles come not by blindly struggling. There are laws in the spiritual realm, and you have endless resources in your heart. God is dwelling within you; but God is not going to do anything for you without coming through your own life. God is going to cooperate with you to accomplish great things. God is the same, for Jehovah never changes; but before a person changes, God cannot manifest himself to them. God used Moses and Joshua, and other men of giant faith; but when they passed away and people began to backslide, God stopped manifesting His power.

God wants to manifest Himself through you today, just as He manifested Himself through Christ 2,000 years ago. He is just as powerful as He was before, and He is depending upon you. I claim that I could build a church which has more than 10,000 members very easily in the States, as well as in Germany or in Tokyo, for the vision for a church is not built in the external world, but inside a man or woman.

What becomes pregnant in your heart and mind is going to come out in your circumstances. Watch your heart and your mind more than anything else. Do not try to find the answer of God through another person, for God's answer comes to your spirit and through your spirit the answer comes to your circumstances.

Claim and speak the word of assurance, for your word actually goes out and creates. God spoke and the whole world came into being. Your word is the material which the Holy Spirit uses to create.

So give the word, for this is very important. The church today has lost the art of giving commands. We Christians are becoming perennial beggars, for constantly we are begging. On the bank of the Red Sea Moses begged, "O God, help us! The Egyptians are coming." God rebuked him saying, "Moses, why are you crying to me? Give the command and the Red Sea shall be divided."

There are times for you to pray, but there are also times for you to give the command. You must pray through in your prayer closet, but when you come out to the battlefield, you are coming to give the word of creation. When you read the life of Jesus Christ you see that He always gave the command. He prayed all night, but when He came out to the front lines He commanded that the people be healed. He commanded the sea to be calm. He commanded the devil to leave.

And His disciples did exactly the same thing. To the beggar Peter commanded, "Silver and gold have I none, but what I have, give I unto you. Rise up in the name of Jesus Christ!" To the body of a dead woman Peter commanded, "Dorcas, rise up!" To the cripple at Lystra Paul commanded, "Stand on your feet!" He gave the word of creation.

The Bible says to heal the sick. In James the Bible says, "The prayer of faith shall save the sick." God clearly asks us to heal the sick; so in my church I heal the sick as the Holy Spirit guides me. I plainly stand before them and claim, "You are healed! Rise and stand up!" And I call the different healings out, and by the dozens and by the hundreds people have received healing.

A few months ago I was holding a meeting in a Western country. One evening in the meeting we had about 1,500 people packed into this one place, and right in front of me was one lady in a wheelchair. She was so badly twisted that I felt depressed. I asked, "Lord, why did you put her in front of me? I can't exercise faith after seeing her." So I tried to avoid looking at her while I was preaching. I would look one way, and then suddenly turn around and look the other way; for the sight of her poured cold water on my heart.

At the close of the sermon the Holy Spirit suddenly spoke in my heart, "Walk down and lift her up."

I replied, "Dear Spirit, you really mean that I should go down and lift her up? She is so twisted, I wonder if Jesus Christ Himself could lift her up. I can't do it. I'm scared."

But the Holy Spirit said, "You go and lift her up."

I refused, saying, "Oh, no, I'm afraid."

So I started calling out the types of healing that the Holy Spirit showed me taking place in people other than this woman. First a blind lady was healed. She was so frightened when I called out her healing she shrieked and fainted, just after her eyes had suddenly opened. Then people began to be healed all over the auditorium. I kept calling out healings continuously but the Holy Spirit kept saying to me, "Go down and lift her up."

I replied, "Father, she is too twisted, and I'm scared."

In the last moments of the service I gave in, and when the pastor asked all the people to stand up and sing the concluding song, I slipped down and spoke with a whisper so people would not hear me. "Lady, if you wish, you could come out of that chair." Then I stood up and began to rush away.

When I turned around all the people had started shouting and clapping their hands, for that woman had stepped out of her wheelchair and started walking around the platform. I was foolish, for if I had lifted her up in the beginning I could have brought heaven down to that service; but I was scared.

Many people come and ask me whether I have the gift of faith, or the gift of healing. But I've searched through my heart and so far I have not found any gift in me. I believe that is because it is the Holy Spirit who has the gifts, all nine of them. He dwells within us, and within me. The Holy Spirit manifests Himself through me; I do not have any of the gifts, only the Holy Spirit, and I just obey Him, and believe in Him.

What kind of gift do I have? I will tell you the one gift I have—the gift of boldness. With this gift of boldness we just launch out by faith; then the Holy Spirit is going to follow after us. The Bible does not say that a sign shall go ahead of you; the Bible says that a sign shall follow you. Abide by the law of incubation, and throughout your life watch as sign after sign follows your path of faith.

You have the resources within you, and now you know the elements needed in incubation to make your faith usable. Get a clear-cut goal and objective. Have a desire that burns to the boiling point, then pray until you have the substance, the assurance. Then begin to speak the word about which you have been given assurance.

CHAPTER 2

The Fourth Dimension

As there are certain steps that we must follow in order for our faith to be properly incubated, there is also a central truth concerning the nature of faith's realm that we need to understand. The most important lessons that I have learned about the nature of the realm of faith began as a result of what was at first an unpleasant experience.

In America ministers do not have this kind of problem, but in the Orient I have real trouble in preaching about the miraculous power of God, for in Buddhism monks also have performed fantastic miracles. Just recently in Korea one woman was dying from a case of terminal cancer, and no doctor could cure her. She went to many churches, then to a Buddhist monk. He took her to a grotto where many were praying, and she was completely healed and cleansed, and the cancer disappeared.

In Korea many people involved in yoga are healing the sick by yoga meditation. When attending meetings of the Japanese Sokagakkai, many are healed—some of stomach ulcers, the deaf and dumb hearing and speaking, and the blind seeing. So naturally we Christians, especially Pentecostal Christians, have real difficulty in explaining these occurrences. You cannot put these things away simply as a manifestation of the devil. But if the devil could do these things, why should not the Church of Jesus Christ do all the more?

I was quite troubled one day, for many of our Christians were not considering God's miracles to be of importance. They said, "Oh, how can we believe in God as an absolutely divine being? How can we call the Jehovah God the unique creator in heavenly places? We see miracles in Buddhism, miracles in yoga, and miracles in Sokagakkai. We see many miracles in the Oriental religions. Why should we claim Jehovah God as the only creator of the universe?"

But I knew that our God was the unique God, the only God, and the creator of the universe. So I made their questions a matter of prayer before God. I fasted and prayed, seeking the faith of the Lord, and His answers. Then a glorious revelation came to my heart, and I received a clear explanation. And from that time on I began to explain these things through my lectures in my church in Korea. Now I can give a satisfying reply to any of those questions, and I can easily give explanations, explanations as clear as a sunny day. Let me explain it to you.

THE FOUR DIMENSIONS

In the universe there are three types of spirit—the Holy Spirit of God, the spirit of the devil, and the human spirit. When you study geometry you put up two points, one here, and one there, and if you draw a line between the two you call it one dimension. It is just one line between the points, one dimension. But if you add line upon line by the hundreds of thousands, then one dimension naturally creates a second dimension, a plane. And if you stack up planes one upon another then it becomes cubic; this is called the third dimension. The material world and the whole earth belong to the third dimension.

This first dimension, a line, is contained in, and therefore controlled by, the second dimension, a plane; and the second dimension is included in, and therefore controlled by, the third dimension, the cube. Who then creates, contains, and controls the third dimension, the cubical world? You have the answer when you open the Bible and read in Genesis 1:2: "And the earth was without form, and void; and darkness was upon the face of the deep. And the Spirit of God moved upon the face of the waters."

But if you look into the original language of that scripture, it carries the meaning that the Spirit of the Lord was incubating over the waters, brooding over the waters. This chaotic world belonged to the third dimension, but the Holy Spirit, who is pictured here incubating on the third dimension, belongs to the fourth dimension. So the spiritual kingdom of faith belongs to the fourth dimension.

Since the spiritual world hugged the third dimension, incubating on the third dimension, it was by this incubation of the fourth dimension on the third dimension that the earth was recreated. A new order was given out of the old, and life was given from death; beauty from ugliness; cleanliness from those things dirty; and abundance from poverty. Everything was created beautiful and wonderful by the incubation of the fourth dimension.

Then God spoke to my heart, "Son, as the second dimension includes and controls the first dimension, and the third dimension includes and controls the second dimension, so the fourth dimension includes and controls the third dimension, producing a creation of order and beauty. The spirit is the fourth dimension. Every human being is a spiritual being as well as a physical being. They have the fourth dimension as well as the third dimension in their hearts." So men, by exploring their spiritual sphere of the fourth dimension through the development of concentrated visions and dreams in their imaginations, can brood over and incubate the third dimension, influencing and changing it. This is what the Holy Spirit taught me.

So naturally these yoga people and Buddhist believers could explore and develop their human fourth dimension, their spiritual sphere; with clear-cut visions and mental pictures of health they could incubate over their bodies. By natural order the fourth dimension has power over the third dimension, and the human spirit, within limitations, has the power to give order and creation. God gave power to human beings to control the material world and to have dominion over material things, a responsibility they can carry out through the fourth dimension. Now unbelievers, by exploring and developing their inner spiritual being in such a way, can carry out dominion upon their third dimension, which includes their physical sicknesses and diseases.

Then the Holy Spirit said to me, "Look at the Sokagakkai. They belong to Satan; the human spirit joins up with the spirit of the evil fourth dimension, and with the evil fourth dimension they carry out dominion over their bodies and circumstances." The Holy Spirit showed me that it was in this manner that the magicians in Egypt carried out dominion over various occurrences, just as Moses did.

God then taught me that since we can link our spirit's fourth dimension to the fourth dimension of the Holy Father—the Creator of the universe—we can have all the more dominion over circumstances. Praise God! We can become fantastically creative, and we can exercise great control and power over the third dimension.

After receiving this revelation from the Lord I began to easily explain the happenings and miracles of other religions. People would come and challenge me, "We can do the same miracles."

I would say, "Yes, I know you can. It's because you have the fourth dimension in your spirit. You are developing your spirit and carrying out dominion over your body and circumstances. But that spirit is not a spirit with salvation, even though you can exercise those kinds of miracles.

"You are linked to the evil fourth dimension. The fourth dimension has the power to carry out dominion over the third dimension. You do have certain limited powers to carry out dominion over the third dimension, influencing your circumstances."

THE ROLE OF THE SUBCONSCIOUS

In America I saw a lot of mind-expanding books, and I see similar things happening everywhere because of all this emphasis on the subconscious. What is the subconscious? The subconscious is your spirit. The Bible calls the subconscious the inner man, the man hidden in your heart.

Before psychology found the subconscious, Apostle Paul had already discovered it 2,000 years before, writing of the inner, hidden man. The Bible had that truth 2,000 years ago. Now scientists and psychologists make a great affair of this discovery, digging into the ideas of the subconscious and trying to direct its energies. Though the subconscious is in the fourth dimension, therefore having certain limited power, however, a great amount of deception is involved in what these people claim.

I was amazed coming to America and reading the books some

American ministers gave me, for these books had almost made the subconscious into an almighty god, and that is a great deception. The subconscious has certain influence, but it is quite limited, and cannot create like our Almighty God can. I have begun to see in America the Unitarian Church try to develop the subconscious, the fourth dimension of the human spirit, and put that human spirit in the place of Jesus Christ; this indeed is great deception, and a great danger.

While we do recognize certain realities and truths in these teachings, it is also important to realize that the devil occupies an evil fourth dimension. God, however, is holy, unique, and almighty. The fourth dimension is always creating and giving order, and carrying out dominion over the third dimension by the means of incubation. In Genesis the Spirit of the Lord was incubating, brooding over the water; He was like a hen sitting on her eggs, incubating them and hatching chickens. In much the same manner as the Holy Spirit incubates the third dimension, so does the evil spirit incubate.

I was watching the television news in the U.S., and there was a great controversy in one area because a man was murdered, the lawyer claiming that this young murderer was intoxicated by violent television programs. There was a certain truth in that, for this boy, after watching television, began to exercise his fourth dimension. He was incubating on those acts of violence, and naturally he hatched the same sin.

THE LANGUAGE OF THE FOURTH DIMENSION

My ministry has been revolutionized by discovering the truth of the fourth dimension, and you can revolutionize your life with it. You may wonder how we can incubate our subconscious. We dwell in limited bodies, whereas the Holy Spirit in His omnipresence can simply incubate over the whole earth. But we are so limited in space and time, and the only way for us to incubate is through our imaginations, through our visions and our dreams.

This is the reason the Holy Spirit comes to cooperate with us—to create, by helping young men to see visions, and old men to dream dreams. Through envisioning and dreaming dreams we can kick away the wall of limitations, and can stretch out to the universe. That is the reason that God's Word says, "Where there is no vision the people perish." If you have no vision, you are not being creative; and if you stop being creative, then you are going to perish.

Visions and dreams are the language of the fourth dimension, and the Holy Spirit communicates through them. Only through a vision and a dream can you visualize and dream bigger churches. You can visualize a new mission field; you can visualize the increase of your church. Through visualizing and dreaming you can incubate your future and hatch the results. Let me substantiate this with scriptural examples.

Do you know why Adam and Eve fell from grace? The devil knew that the fourth dimension visions and dreams in a person's mind could create a definite result. The devil used a tactic based on this premise; he invited Eve saying, "Eve, come over and look at that fruit on the forbidden tree. Looking at it is harmless, so why don't you come over and just look at it?"

So since simply looking at the fruit seemed to be harmless, Eve went and looked at the fruit of the tree. She looked at that tree not only once, but she kept looking. The Bible says in Genesis, the third chapter, verse six, "And when the woman saw that the tree was good for food ... she took of the fruit thereof, and did eat." Before she partook she saw the tree, also seeing this fruit in her imagination. She played with the idea of eating the fruit, and brought that to her fourth dimension.

In the fourth dimension either good or evil is created. Eve brought that picture of the tree and fruit deep into her imagination, seeing the fruit clearly, imagining that it could make her as wise as God. Then she felt so attracted to that tree, it was as if she were being pulled toward it; next she took the fruit of the tree and ate, then gave some to her husband. And with that action, she fell.

If seeing is not important, why did the angel of God give such a grievous judgement to the wife of Lot? In Genesis 19:17 the Bible reads, "Escape for thy life; look not behind thee." It is a simple command: do not look behind you. However, when you read Genesis 19:26, you discover that Lot's wife looked back and became a pillar of salt. She received that grievous judgement just because she looked back.

You might say that the judgement was too harsh, but when you understand this law of the Spirit, it is not, for when she looked back, she did not only see with her physical eyes; when she looked, that sight came to her innerself, and gripped hold of her imagination. Lust for her former life began to take hold of her, and God carried out His just judgement upon her.

God has been using this language of the Holy Spirit to change many lives. Look carefully when you read Genesis 13:14-15, "And the Lord said unto Abraham, after that Lot was separated from him, 'lift up now thine eyes, and look from the place where thou art, northward, southward, and eastward, and westward: For all the land which thou seest, to thee will I give it, and to thy seed forever.' "

God did not say, "Oh, Abraham, I'll give you Canaan. Just claim it." No, very specifically, God told him to stand from his place, look northward, southward, eastward, and westward, and that He would give that land to Abraham and his descendants.

I wish he could have had a helicopter, for then he could have gone up high and seen all the Middle East, and thus avoided the many past and present problems there. But since he had no binoculars and no helicopter, his vision was limited.

Seeing is possession. Abraham saw the land; he then went back to his tent, and to his bed, to dream of the lands which were going to become his. In his fourth dimension the Holy Spirit began to use that language. The Holy Spirit began to carry out dominion.

It is interesting that Abraham got his child Isaac when he was one hundred years old, and when Sarah was ninety. When Abraham was almost one hundred years old, and Sarah almost ninety, God came and told him that he was going to have a child. When God came to him and said, "You are going to have a son," Abraham laughed and laughed. This means that Abraham was totally unbelieving.

We also see that Sarah laughed behind the tent. God asked, "Sarah, why are you laughing?" She replied, "No, I didn't laugh." But God said, "No, you laughed."

Both Abraham and Sarah laughed. They were both unbelieving. But God had a way to make them believe, for God used the fourth dimension, the language of the Holy Spirit. One night God said to Abraham, "Come out." In the Middle East the humidity is very low, so in the night you can see the many stars sparkling. Abraham came out, and God said, "Abraham, count the number of the stars." So he started counting the stars.

Scientists say that with the human eye we can count 6,000 stars. So we can imagine Abraham kept on counting and counting, eventually forgetting the number. He finally said, "Father, I can't count them all." Then the Father said, "Your children are going to become as numerous as those stars."

I imagine that Abraham was struck with emotion. Soon tears began to well up in his eyes, and his vision became completely blurred. When he looked up at the stars, all he could see were the faces of his children, and suddenly he felt that he was hearing them call to him, "Father Abraham!" He was all shaken up, and when he returned to his tent he was shaking all over. He could not sleep when he closed his eyes, for he saw all the stars changing into the faces of his descendants, and once again shouting, "Father Abraham!"

Those pictures came to his mind again and again, and became his own dreams and pictures. Those pictures immediately became part of his fourth dimension, in the language of spiritual visions and dreams. These visions and dreams carried dominion over his one-hundred-year old body, and it was soon transformed as if it were like a young body. From that time on he believed the word of God, and he praised the Lord.

Who could change Abraham so much? The Holy Spirit, because God had applied the law of the fourth dimension, the language of the Holy Spirit. A vision and dream changed Abraham, not only his mind, but his physical body as well—not only he, but his wife, too, were wonderfully rejuvenated. Later on in the Bible you can read how King Abimelech tried to make Sarah his concubine:

ninety-year-old Sarah, who had been rejuvenated through the law and language of the fourth dimension.

We are not common animals. When God created us He created in us the fourth dimension, the spiritual world. Then God said, "You carry out dominion over all the third dimension."

I cannot carry out my ministry of winning souls by simply knocking on doors, struggling and working myself to death. I use the way of faith, and the church is growing by leaps and bounds. And even though our church has more than 50,000 registered members, when I go to the office I do not have a great deal to do, for I follow a path of faith, and am not constantly striving in my flesh to bring to pass those things that the Holy Spirit can easily do.

I learned that even while I minister in foreign countries I can go into the fourth dimension of the Holy Spirit, and I tell Him what is needed in my church in Korea, and He carries out the work. I call my wife about every two days, and she is continually giving me information which has served sometimes as a blow to my ego. I used to think that the members of my church would be very anxious for my return from my trips abroad; they would all be waiting for me, and I was sure that Sunday service attendance would go down. She would say, "Don't brag about it. The church is doing all the better, even without having you."

APPLYING THE LAW OF THE FOURTH DIMENSION

If God could use Abraham to possess the land through the miraculous fourth dimension, and if God could rejuvenate Abraham and Sarah through the Holy Spirit's language of visions and dreams, then you can also work in the fourth dimension.

There is a magnificent story about Jacob in Genesis 30:31-43. I had always disliked the portion of scripture in verses 37 through 39, where Jacob made an arrangement to ensure that solid colored sheep would give birth to spotted and speckled sheep.

I asked, "Lord, why do you permit this superstition in the Bible? This is the reason the Modernists are criticizing the Bible, and calling it a fairy story."

So whenever I came to this part of Scripture, I would skip it, fearing and worrying that there was a portion of the Bible I could not trust. One day while reading the Bible under the anointing of the Holy Spirit, I again came to these verses and said, "I'm going to skip this part. This is all superstition."

But the Holy Spirit said, "Wait a minute. Nothing in the Bible is superstition. The matter is that you don't understand. You are blind, but I am applying the special law of creation here. You watch."

Then a tremendous unveiling of truth came to me, and this added a new dimension to my ministry. If you do not use the miraculous laws of faith you cannot hope to see a thousand new members added to your church each month; your personal struggle apart from the working of the fourth dimension cannot bring this goal about.

In this part of his life, Jacob, whose name meant "the swindler," had gone to his Uncle Laban. He stayed for about twenty years, working as hard as a common laborer for his uncle. But his uncle changed the salary so many times that Jacob was being deceived; Jacob was in turn also deceiving his uncle. They were deceiving each other, and when Jacob became about forty years old, he had nothing in the way of material gain, but did have a lot of wives and children, and a desire to return home.

God felt sorry for Jacob, and showed him a portion of the secret of the fourth dimension. After receiving this revelation from the Lord, Jacob went to his uncle. He said, "Uncle, I'll work for you on this condition: you take away all the spotted and speckled animals from me, and I'll tend only the animals with coats of solid colors. And if someway these solid colored animals give birth to spotted and speckled offspring, then those would become my salary."

Jacob's uncle almost jumped. He thought to himself, "Oh, now this guy is cheating himself. Those solid colored animals have a very slim chance of giving birth to many of the spotted and speckled offspring. Now I can use him without paying much salary."

So Jacob's uncle said to him, "Yes, yes. That's wonderful. I'll make that contract with you."

Then Laban took all the spotted and speckled animals and removed them three days distance away, and Jacob was left with only the animals of solid color. Jacob went out to the mountain, cut down poplar, hazel and chestnut trees, and with his penknife made them all spotted and speckled. He made a wall out of those now spotted and speckled tree rods, and put that wall right in front of the cattle's drinking trough, where the cattle would drink and come to conceive offspring.

There Jacob would stand, day in and day out, watching the animals in front of those spotted and speckled tree rods. The Bible says that soon afterward all those animals gave birth to spotted and speckled offspring.

God created a vision and dream in the mind of Jacob. His subconscious before had been full of poverty, failure, and cheating; so his struggle was hard, and his rewards few. But God changed

Jacob's imagination, his subconscious, by using this wall of spotted and speckled tree rods as material to help him visualize and dream.

Jacob looked at that wall so much that his mind became filled with the sight; he slept and dreamed dreams of the sheep giving birth to spotted and speckled offspring. In the next chapter we read that the sheep did give birth to spotted and speckled offspring. Man's imagination plays a great role in the fourth dimension. Animals can never have an imagination in the way we do, because imagination is the work of the spirit.

When in Jacob's heart and imagination he began to grasp this vision and dream of spotted and speckled sheep, he began to learn the language of the Holy Spirit. You can converse with another person only through a known language, and you can never converse with an unknown language.

When Jacob began to learn the language of the Holy Spirit, immediately he began to converse with the Holy Spirit, and the Holy Spirit began to work. The Holy Spirit punched the proper keys for the necessary genes, and Jacob's sheep began to give birth to spotted and speckled offspring. Jacob soon began to have a vast multitude of spotted and speckled animals, and he became one of the richest men in the Orient.

There are over 8,000 promises in the Bible, and each of those promises is like a spotted and speckled tree for you. You do not need to go to the mountain to cut down a hazel, or a chestnut, or a poplar tree. You can rather take the promises from the Bible, all spotted and speckled, waiting for you. These promises, however, are a bit different, for these promises are all spotted and speckled by the blood of Jesus Christ.

Long after Jacob, God put up another spotted and speckled tree; this time that tree was on Calvary. And this tree was not spotted and speckled by a penknife, but by the real blood of the Son of God. Anybody and everybody can come gaze upon this spotted and speckled tree, and receive a new image, a new dream, and a new vision, by the power of the Holy Spirit, and be changed.

Now let me share something from my personal experience with you. One Christmas Eve I was busy preparing a sermon. Later an urgent telephone call came in the early morning hours of Christmas day. A man calling from Seoul National Hospital asked, "Are you Pastor Cho?"

"Yes, I am."

"One of your members is dying. He was in a car accident. A taxi hit him, then rode around all through the morning with him in the back seat."

In Korea at that time, if someone was hit and killed by a taxi, the taxi-driver would only have to pay the sum of $2500, and then would be cleared of all financial obligation. However, if the victim were only injured, then the driver would have to pay for all of the medical and hospital bills. So if a driver hit someone and no one saw the accident, he would then drive that person around until he or she died; it would be cheaper for him.

This member had bought a beautiful hat, with some other articles, for his wife. He was so carried away with the joy of giving these presents, that he jaywalked across the street without watching the light, and was hit by a taxi. Since it was late evening and no one saw, this taxi-driver had carried that man in his car throughout the evening. The man did not die, and eventually a policeman

THE FOURTH DIMENSION

caught the taxi, and carried the man to a hospital. The impact of
the accident had badly impaired his intestines, and his stomach was
full of dirt and blood; blood poisoning had already set in.

His doctor knew me and called, saying, "Dr. Cho, should we
operate on him? Medically speaking, it's hopeless. He was without
medical attention for such a long time that blood poisoning has set
in. There will be no way for us to cure him!"

But I said, "You go ahead and operate on him, and as soon as I finish
the Christmas sermon, I'll run to the hospital."

After the Christmas service I rushed to the emergency room of
Seoul National University Hospital, and there he was, totally
unconscious. The doctor again said there would be no hope,
"Reverend, don't expect anything. He is dying. We could do
nothing. When we opened his stomach, there were three places
where the intestines were completely cut off, and these areas were
filled with his excrement and dirt. There is no hope."

I replied, "Well, I'll try to do my best."

When I went in he was in a deep coma. I knelt beside him and said,
"Lord God, give me only five minutes, then I will try. Let him come
out of the coma for five minutes, then I will try."

As I was praying I felt something moving. I opened my eyes, and
the man opened his eyes.

"Oh pastor, I'm dying," he cried.

I knew then that I had five minutes. I replied, "You can't say that.
As long as you keep saying that you will die, then I can't help you.
You must change your imagination and thinking. Change your

vision and dream, for the only way to carry out dominion over this third dimension material world is through your imagination, your visions and dreams.

"So listen to me. Picture a young man. He says good- bye to his wife. He's full of beauty and health. He goes to his office, and completes his business successfully.

"All the people respect and admire him. Evening arrives and he buys nice gifts for his wife, who is waiting for him to come home and eat supper. When he arrives she rushes out to the gate and welcomes him with a big hug and kiss. They go into the house, share a delicious meal together, and a quiet evening at home.

"The man I am talking about is no stranger. That man is you! Think of that man! Draw that picture in your mind. Look at that man and say in your heart, that man is me!

"Don't draw a picture of death. Don't draw a picture of a dead corpse. Keep on dreaming about that man, and I'll do the praying. You just draw a mental picture, and leave the praying to me. Will you do that?"

"Yes, pastor, I'll change my dream. I'll change my thinking. I'll say that I'm that man. I'll try to make that vision and dream a reality… I see it!" he cried.

While we were talking this surgeon had come in with his nurses. They started giggling and laughing at me, and thought that I had lost my mind. But I was serious, for I knew the law of the Spirit's fourth dimension, and that man had begun to speak the language of the Holy Spirit. Like a missionary on a foreign field who gains a deeper level of communication with the local people of that country by learning to speak their language directly, instead of using an interpreter, so that dying man had learned the deeper language of the Holy Spirit.

As I knelt down and grabbed hold of his bed, I prayed, "Dear Holy Spirit, now he speaks your language. He has a vision and a dream. Rush into his physical body, and carry out your dominion. I command this man to be whole and to be filled with healing power!"

Suddenly the group of unbelieving nurses said, "This room is too hot. The heat is too high."

But the weather was very cold. There was no heat; it was the power of the Holy Spirit giving off all the heat. The surgeon and those nurses began to feel fire. Their ears turned red, and the power of God became so strong that we even felt the bed trembling.

Amazingly, in one week that man rose up and walked out of the hospital. He is now in the chemical business, doing wonderfully. Whenever I see him on Sunday morning, sitting in the balcony, I say to myself, "Praise God! We spoke the Holy Spirit's language. We created. Hallelujah!"

Let me tell you about another incident. One day I was in my office, and a lady about 50 years old came in crying: "Pastor, my home is completely destroyed and broken."

"Stop crying," I responded, "and tell me about it."

"You know we have several sons, but only one daughter. She has become a hippie, and she sleeps with friends of my husband and with friends of my sons, going from this hotel to that hotel, and from this dance hall to that dance hall.

"She's become a shame to our family," she cried. "My husband cannot go to his office. My boys are dying of embarrassment, and now they are all going to leave home. I've tried everything. I've even cried to the Lord to strike her dead! Oh, Pastor Cho, what can I do?"

"Stop whining and crying," I told her. "I now can see very clearly why God would not answer your prayer. You were presenting the wrong kind of mental blueprint to Him. In your mind you were always submitting just the picture of a prostitute, weren't you?"

She retorted, "Yes, well, that's what she is. She is a prostitute!"

"But if you want to see her changed, then you must submit another mental blueprint," I told her. "You must clean the canvas of your imagination, and you must start drawing a new picture."

But she rejected the idea, saying, "I can't. She's dirty, ugly and wretched."

"Stop talking like that. Let's draw a new picture. Let's bring to mind another kind of spotted and speckled tree. You kneel down here, and I will kneel down before you. Let's go to the foot of Calvary. Let's lift up our hands. Let's look at Jesus Christ dying on a cross, bleeding and beaten up.

"Why is He hanging there? Because of your daughter. Let's put your daughter right behind Jesus Christ. Let's see your daughter through His spotted and speckled cross. Can't you see your daughter forgiven, cleansed, born again, and filled with the Holy Spirit—completely changed? Can you draw that picture through the blood of Jesus Christ?"

"Oh, pastor, yes." replied the mother. "Now I see differently. Through Jesus, through the cross, I can change my image about my daughter."

"Wonderful, wonderful!" I exclaimed. "I will draw a new picture of your daughter. Keep that clear-cut, vivid and graphic picture in your mind day in and day out. Then the Holy Spirit can use you, for His language is carried with a vision and a dream. We know we are drawing the right kind of picture since we are coming to the foot of the cross."

So we knelt down and prayed, "O Lord, now you see this picture. Dear Holy Spirit, flow into this new image, this new vision and dream. Change. Perform miracles."

Then I sent this mother out, and as she was leaving she was all smiles. There was no more crying, for her image of her daughter had changed.

One Sunday, a few months later, she suddenly walked into my office, bringing a beautiful young lady with her.

"Who is this young lady?" I asked.

"This is my daughter!" she smiled.

"Did God answer you?"

She replied, "Oh yes, He did."

Then she told me the story. One night her daughter had been sleeping in a motel with a man. In the morning when she woke up she felt dirty and wretched. She felt a great unhappiness in her spirit, and had a deep desire to return home, but she was frightened and scared of her parents and brothers. Nevertheless, she decided to risk it, saying to herself, "I'll try one more time, and if they kick me out, then that will be my last attempt."

So she went to her parents' home and rang the bell. Her mother came out, and when she saw her daughter, her countenance lit up as if the sun was rising on her face. She greeted her daughter, "Welcome, my daughter," and rushed out to hug her.

The daughter was absolutely overwhelmed by the love of her mother, and she crumbled, crying. Her mother had prayed, and her image of her daughter was entirely changed. She had welcomed her daughter on the spot, and opened wide her arms of love.

Her mother brought her to the church for a period of two or three months. She listened to the sermons, confessed all sins, gave her heart to Jesus Christ, and received the baptism of the Holy Spirit. She became an absolutely new creation in Christ, and she eventually found a wonderful husband.

This daughter now has three children of her own, and is one of the foremost home cell unit leaders in my church. She is a burning evangelist; and all this happened because her mother changed her vision and dream, applying the law of the fourth dimension.

Throughout Scripture God always made use of this law of the fourth dimension. Look at Joseph. Before he was sold as a slave God had already imprinted in his heart pictures in the fourth dimension. Through several dreams God gave a clear-cut vision to the heart of Joseph. Even though Joseph was taken as a slave to Egypt, he was already carrying dominion over his faith. Joseph later became a prime minister.

Look at Moses. Before he built the tabernacle he was called to Mount Sinai. He stayed there for forty days and nights, and was given a mental picture of the tabernacle; exactly as he saw it in his vision and dream he went and built it.

God gave visions to Isaiah, to Jeremiah, to Ezekiel and to Daniel, all major servants of the Lord. God called them into the fourth dimension, and taught them the language of the Holy Spirit. They then made the prayer of faith.

This was true even of the Apostle Peter. His original name was Simon, meaning "a reed." When Peter came, led by Andrew, Jesus looked into his eyes and laughed. "Yes, you are the Simon. You are the reed. Your personality is so bendable, changeable. In one moment you are angry; in another you laugh. Sometimes you get drunk, and at other times you show how intelligent you can be.

"You really are like a reed, but I am going to call you a rock. Simon, a reed, is dead to the world, and Peter, the rock, is alive."

Peter was a fisherman and knew the strong and stable qualities of a rock. In his imagination he immediately began to see himself portrayed as a rock. He would watch as the wind-tossed waves of the Sea of Galilee would hit a rock, engulfing it with white foam; and the rock looked conquered. But in the next moment he would see all the water breaking against the rock, and sliding off, and the rock still stood. Peter again and again said, "Am I like the rock? Am I? Yes, I am like a rock."

Peter became a strong rock of the Early Church. But before he was changed into this rock, Christ saw a vision of Peter as a rock in His heart, and then he became that rock.

God changed the name of Jacob to Israel, meaning "the prince of God." He was a cheater and swindler, but he was named a prince. It was after then that he changed.

Non-Christians from all over the world are involved in transcendental meditation and Buddhistic meditation. In meditation one is asked to have a clear-cut goal and vision. In Sokagakkai they draw a picture of prosperity, repeating phrases over and over, trying to develop the human spiritual fourth dimension; and these people are creating something. While Christianity has been in Japan for more than 100 years, with only 0.5 percent of the population claiming to be Christians, Sokagakkai has millions of followers. Sokagakkai has applied the law of the fourth dimension and has performed miracles; but in Christianity there is only talk about theology and faith.

People are created in the image of God. God is a God of miracles, His children, therefore, are born with the desire to see miracles performed. Without seeing miracles people cannot be satisfied that God is powerful.

YOUR RESPONSIBILITY

It is you who are responsible to supply miracles for these people. The Bible is not of the third dimension, but of the fourth, for in it we can read of God, and the life He has for us, and can learn the language of the Holy Spirit. By reading Scripture you can enlarge your visions and your dreams. Make your dreams and your visions, and create. Let the Holy Spirit come and quicken the scriptures you read, and implant visions in the young and dreams in the old.

If you lack the mobility and opportunity of a missionary, then at least you can sit in your chair and dream. That is powerful. Let the

Holy Spirit come and teach you the language of the Holy Spirit, the language of visions and dreams. Then keep those visions, keep those dreams, and let the Holy Spirit flow through that language, and create.

God wants to give you the desires of your heart. God is ready to fulfill those desires, because the Bible says, "Delight thyself in the Lord, and He shall give thee the desires of thine heart." Also in Proverbs 10:24, "The desire of the righteous shall be granted." First make a clear-cut goal, then draw a mental picture, vivid and graphic, and become enthusiastic, praying throughout the process. Do not be deceived by the talk of mind expansion, yoga, transcendental meditation, or Sokagakkai. They are only developing the human fourth dimension, and in these cases are not in the good, but rather the evil, fourth dimension.

Let us rise up and do more than an Egyptian magician. There are plenty of magicians in the Egypts of this world, but let us use all our visions and our dreams for our Holy God. Let us become Moses, and go out and perform the most wonderful of miracles.

Miracles are a usual and expected occurrence in our church, so by experience I can say that man is not just another animal. You are not a common creature, for you have the fourth dimension in your heart, and it is the fourth dimension that has dominion over the three material dimensions—the cubical world, the world of the plane, and the world of the line.

Through dominion in the fourth dimension—the realm of faith— you can give order to your circumstances and situations, give beauty to the ugly and chaotic, and healing to the hurt and suffering.

CHAPTER 3

The Creative Power of the Spoken Word

There are certain steps we must follow for faith to be properly incubated, and a central truth we must learn about the realm that faith operates in; there is also a basic principle about the spoken word that we need to understand. So I want to speak to you about the creative power of the spoken word, and the reasons why the usage of it is of such importance.

One morning I was eating breakfast with one of Korea's leading neurosurgeons, who was telling me about various medical findings on the operation of the brain. He asked, "Dr. Cho, did you know that the speech center in the brain rules over all the nerves? You ministers really have power, because according to our recent findings in neurology, the speech center in the brain has total dominion over all the other nerves."

Then I laughed, saying, "I've known that for a long time."

"How did you know that?" he asked. "In the world of neurology these are new findings."

I replied that I had learned it from Dr. James.

"Who is this Dr. James?" he asked.

"He was one of the famous doctors in biblical times, nearly two thousand years ago," I replied. "And in his book, chapter three, the first few verses, Dr. James clearly defines the activity and importance of the tongue and the speech center."

The neurosurgeon was completely amazed. "Does the Bible really teach about this?"

"Yes," I answered. "The tongue is the least member of our body, but can bridle the whole body."

Then this neurosurgeon began to expound their findings. He said that the speech nerve center had such power over all of the body that simply speaking can give one control over his body, to manipulate it in the way he wishes. He said, "If someone keeps on saying, 'I'm going to become weak,' then right away all the nerves receive that message, and they say, 'Oh, let's prepare to become weak, for we've received instructions from our central communication that we should become weak.' They then in natural sequence adjust their physical attitudes to weakness.

"If someone says, 'Well, I have no ability. I can't do this job,' then right away all the nerves begin to declare the same thing. 'Yes,' they respond, 'we received instruction from the central nervous system saying that we have no abilities, to give up striving to develop any capacity for capability. We must prepare ourselves to be part of an incapable person.'

"If someone keeps saying, 'I'm very old. I'm so very old, and am tired and can't do anything,' then right away, the speech central control responds, giving out orders to that effect. The nerves respond, 'Yes, we are old. We are ready for the grave. Let's be ready to disintegrate.' If someone keeps saying that he is old, then that person is soon going to die."

That neurosurgeon continued saying, "That man should never retire. Once a man retires, he keeps repeating to himself, 'I am retired,' and all the nerves start responding and become less active, and ready for a quick death."

FOR A SUCCESSFUL PERSONAL LIFE

That conversation carried much meaning for me, and made an impact on my life, for I could see that one important usage of the spoken word is the creation of a successful personal life.

People easily adapt to speaking in a negative way. "Boy, am I poor. I've even no money to give the Lord." When an opportunity does come for a job with a good salary, the nervous system responds, "I am not able to be rich because I haven't received that reverse instruction from my nerve center yet. I am supposed to be poor, so I can't accept this job. I can't afford to have the money." Like attracts like, and since you act as if you were a poor person, you attract poverty; this attraction, if it remains consistent, will allow you to permanently dwell in poverty.

Exactly as the Bible said nearly 2,000 years ago, it is so today. Medical science has just recently discovered this principle. This one neurosurgeon said that people should keep saying to themselves, "I am young. I am able. I can do the work of a young person no matter what my chronological age is." The nerves of that person will then come alive and thus receive power and strength from the nerve center.

The Bible says clearly that whosoever controls the tongue, controls the whole body. What you speak, you are going to get. If you keep on saying that you are poor, then all of your system conditions itself to attract poverty, and you will feel at home in poverty; you would rather be poor. But if you keep on saying that you are able, that you can achieve success, then all of your body would be bridled to success. You would be ready to meet any challenge, ready to conquer it. This is the reason you should never speak in a negative way.

In Korea we have a habit of making frequent use of words having to do with dying. Common expressions are: "Oh, it's so warm I could die;" "Oh, I've eaten so much I could suffocate to death;" "Oh, I'm so happy I could die;" and "Oh, I'm scared to death." Koreans repeatedly use these negative words. That is the reason that throughout Korea's five thousand year history we have been constantly dying, constantly at war. My generation has never seen total peace in our country. I was born during World War II, grew up during the Korean War, and now still live in a country on the brink of war.

Before you can be changed, you must change your language. If you do not change your language, you cannot change yourself. If you want to see your children changed, you must first teach them to use the proper language. If you want to see rebellious and irresponsible youth changed into responsible adults you must teach them this new language.

Where can we learn this new language? From the best language book of all, the Bible. Read the Bible from Genesis to Revelation. Acquire the Bible's language, speak the word of faith, and feed your nervous system with a vocabulary of constructive, progressive, productive and victorious words. Speak those words; keep repeating them, so that they will have control of your whole body. Then you will become victorious, for you will be completely conditioned to meet your environment and circumstances, and achieve success. This is the first important reason to use the spoken word: to create the power to have a successful personal life.

FOR GOD'S PURPOSES

There is a second reason we need to use the creative power of the spoken word: not only can it help us to be successful in our own lives, but the Holy Spirit also needs us to use it to bring about God's purposes.

When I first entered the ministry I could feel myself in a struggle, even while I delivered my sermons, and sensed hindrances in my spirit. Then the Spirit of the Lord would come down into my spirit, and it would be as if I were watching television. On my mind's screen I could see growths disappear, tuberculosis healed, cripples leaning heavily on crutches suddenly throw them aside and walk.

Korea is such a distance from America, that I heard very little about this type of deliverance and healing ministry. Even the few missionaries around me then were ignorant of this type of ministry, and talking to them resulted in my being even more confused.

I came to the conclusion that this was a hindrance created by Satan. Each time it would happen I would say, "You spirit of hindrance, get out of me. I command you to leave me. Get out of me."

But the more I commanded, the more clearly I could envision people being healed. I became so desperate I could hardly preach. The visions constantly appeared, so I made it a matter of fasting and prayer, waiting upon the Lord.

Then in my heart I heard the Lord say, "Son, that is not a hindrance of Satan. That is the visual desire of the Holy Spirit. It is the Word of wisdom and of knowledge. God wants to heal these people, but God can't heal them before you speak."

"No," I replied, "I don't believe that. God can do anything without my ever saying a word."

Later I saw in the Bible, the first chapter of Genesis, "The earth was without form and void," and the Holy Spirit brooded over the earth, incubating it; but nothing happened. God then revealed an important truth to me. He said, "There was the presence of the Holy Spirit, the mighty anointing of the Holy Ghost incubating and brooding over the waters. Did anything happen at that point?"

"No," I replied. "Nothing happened."

Then God spoke, "You can feel the presence of the Holy Spirit in your church—the pulsating, permeating presence of the Holy Spirit—but nothing will happen— no soul will be saved, no broken home rejoined, until you speak the word. Don't just beg and beg for what you need. Give the word. Let me have the material with which I can build miraculous happenings. As I did when creating the world, speak forth. Say 'Let there be light,' or say, 'let there be firmament.' "

The realization of that truth was a turning point in my life. I then apologized to God: "Lord, I'm sorry. I'll speak forth."

But still I was afraid, for no one had taught me anything along these lines. I was also scared that nothing would happen when I spoke forth; then what would people say about me? So I said to God, "Since I'm afraid, I'm not going to speak out about the cripples

I see healed, or the disappearing cancer tumors. Father, I'll start with headaches."

After this when I preached, visions of healings would spring up from my spirit; but when in my mind's eye I could see cripples healed, or tumors disappearing, I ignored them. I would speak forth, "Someone here is being healed of a headache." And instantly that person would be healed. I was amazed that just by my speaking these things they would come into being.

Little by little I gained more courage. I began to speak of sinuses that had been healed, then of the healing of the deaf, and finally spoke of all the healings I saw pictured in my mind. Now in my church on Sunday mornings hundreds of people receive healing through that channel. Because time is so limited, because of the multiple services, I must act quickly. So while I am standing, the Lord shows me the healings that are taking place, and I call them out. I simply close my eyes and speak forth. In recognition of the fact that they have been healed, people stand up. They stand when the particular disease or illness of which they have been healed is called out. During this portion of a service many people, all over the auditorium, rise to claim their healing.

Thus I learned one secret: before you give the word, the Holy Spirit does not have the proper material with which to create. If the Holy Spirit imparts faith into your heart to remove a mountain, do not pray and beg for the mountain to be moved; rather speak, "Be removed to yonder sea!" and it shall come to pass. If you learn this, and make it a habit to speak under the Holy Spirit's anointing, and in the faith God gives you, then you are going to see many miracles in your life.

Ministering to 50,000 regular attending members is not an easy task. We have set up a 24 hour telephone service in our church, and assistants stay round-the-clock to receive calls and instructions. I try to keep my home phone number unregistered, but that unregistered number soon becomes known, and I receive telephone calls from the early part of the evening till late the next morning.

Many nights I will be lying cozily in bed. Then at ten o'clock a telephone call will come: "Pastor, my grandson has a high fever, please pray for him." So I pray.

Eleven o'clock another telephone call comes: "My husband still isn't home from his business. Please pray," and I pray.

Then at twelve o'clock midnight, the phone rings and a crying wife says, "My husband came home and beat me up. Oh, this is terrible. I don't want to live." Then I will counsel her.

One o'clock I receive a call from a drunken man saying, "My wife attends your church: why do you teach her to behave in such a way?" Then I will give him a full explanation.

In mid-morning a telephone call comes from the hospital, "Pastor, such and such a person is dying now. Would you come quickly? His last desire before dying is to see you." So I make plans to rush to the hospital.

The telephone keeps ringing so much that at times I have just unplugged the cord. I exclaim, "I'm not going to live this way!" Then I go to bed.

But then the Holy Spirit speaks to my heart. "Are you being a good shepherd? A good shepherd never leaves his sheep stranded." So I rise up and push the cord back in. There is one advantage I have when traveling out of my country: I can finally get a good night's sleep.

On one particular evening during a very cold winter night, when I was feeling so good and cozy in my bed, just about to fall asleep, a telephone call came. This man I had met called saying, "Pastor, do you know me?"

"Of course I know you. I married you and your wife."

"I have tried for two years, with my entire might, but our marriage is not working out," he said. "Tonight we had a big argument and decided to separate. We've already divided our assets, but there's just one thing—a blessing from you. We were married with your blessing and we want to be divorced with your blessing."

What a position for a minister to be in, to bless them in joining, and then bless them in disjoining! I replied, "Can you wait till tomorrow? It's too cold, and I'm settled in bed. Must I come now?"

"Pastor," he returned, "tomorrow will be too late. We're leaving each other today. We don't want you to preach to us. It's too late for that, we're beyond reach now; just come and simply give us your blessing so we can be divorced."

I crawled out of my bed and went into the living room. In my heart I was angry against Satan. I thought, "This is not the work of the Holy Spirit. This is the work of the devil."

As I began to pray I immediately went into the fourth dimension. Since visions and dreams are the language of the Holy Spirit, through the fourth dimension I can incubate the third dimension, and correct it. I knelt down, closed my eyes, and through the cross of Jesus Christ, by the help of the Holy Spirit, I began to see this family rejoined together again. I envisioned a clear picture, and prayed, "O God, make it like that."

While praying I was touched by faith, and in the name of Jesus Christ changed this situation in the fourth dimension. The fourth dimension with its positive power was mine, so I went to this couple's apartment.

They were living in a fantastically luxurious apartment. There was every convenience in that apartment, but when I walked in, I felt an icy chill, the hatred that existed between that man and his wife. You can have all the material goods of this world, but if there is hatred in your family, those material things will be no blessing at all.

As I came in I found the man sitting in the living room and the wife in the bedroom. As soon as I walked into the living room the man began to speak derogatorily about his wife. His wife then rushed into the room saying, "Don't listen to him! Listen to me!" Then she also began to speak out against her husband.

I would listen to the husband, and everything that he said seemed to be right. Then I would listen to the wife, and everything that she said seemed to be right; each was right in his own opinion. Both were right, and I was sandwiched between.

Both said they were completely finished in their marriage. "Don't pray for us," they kept repeating. "Just pray for our divorce."

But I had already overruled this third dimension decision by using the fourth dimension in my heart. Being confident, I took the hand of the husband and the hand of the wife, and I said, "In the name of Jesus Christ, I command Satan to loose his hold of hatred on this couple. And in this moment, in the mighty name of Jesus Christ I command that these two be melted together. Let them be tender and rejoined."

Suddenly I felt a warm drop fall on my hand, and when I looked at the man he was crying, and his tears were falling down.

I thought to myself, "Oh, praise God! It worked!"

When I looked at the eyes of the wife I could see that her eyes were watering also. So I drew their hands together and said, "What the Lord has joined, let no man or circumstances divide."

I stood up and said, "I'm going."

Both of them followed me out to the gate, and as I left said, "Good-bye, Pastor."

"Praise God," I replied, "it works!"

The next Sunday both of them sat in the choir and sang beautifully. After the service I shook their hands and asked the wife, "What happened?"

"Well, we don't know," she answered. "But when you said those words and gave such strong commands, we felt something break down in our hearts. It was as if a wall had been destroyed, and we were shaken.

"Suddenly we began to be conscious that perhaps we should try once again, both at the same time. After you left, we spent the entire night unpacking all of our things. Now when we think of it, we can't understand why we argued so much, and why we were going to separate. Now we love each other even more than before."

The Holy Spirit needs both your word and mine. If I had pleaded with them or if I had silently prayed for them, I would have missed the target. I gave the word, and the word went out and created. The Holy Spirit needs your definite word, the spoken word of faith.

Jesus used the spoken word to change and create. The disciples of Christ Jesus used the spoken word to change and create. Unfortunately the Church of Jesus Christ seems to have become a perennial beggar: begging and begging, afraid to speak forth the words of command. We need to learn the lost art of speaking forth the word of command.

FOR THE RELEASE OF THE PRESENCE OF CHRIST

There is a third reason to use the power of the spoken word: through it you create and release the presence of Jesus Christ. When you open the Bible and read Romans 10:10 you find that "with the heart man believeth unto righteousness; and with the mouth confession is made unto salvation." It is through confession of faith that man can grasp the salvation that comes only by Jesus Christ.

Now nowhere in this passage is it necessary that someone send up to heaven and bring Jesus Christ down to earth to give salvation. What is said is that the words which can result in salvation are near, for they are the words in your heart and in your mouth.

Where is Jesus Christ in this process? What is His address? Not high up in the sky, or below the ground. Jesus is in His Word.

Where are the words that can result in your salvation? Those words are on your mouth and in your heart. Jesus is bound to what you speak forth. As well as you can release Jesus' power through your spoken word, you can also create the presence of Christ. If you do not speak the word of faith clearly, Christ can never be released. The Bible says that "whatsoever you bind on earth shall be bound in heaven, and whatsoever you release on earth shall be released in heaven." You have the responsibility of carrying the presence of Jesus Christ.

Whenever I have a session with my 100 assistant pastors of our church, I give them a strict command: "It's your responsibility to create the presence of Jesus Christ wherever you go. To release Jesus and to meet specific needs is what you must do." Let me give you some examples.

In our vicinity there are several churches belonging to various denominations. In one particular Presbyterian church the minister speaks only about the born again experience. He speaks strongly only about the salvation experience, so he is just releasing and creating the presence of the Jesus who can give this born again experience to people. People come to his church and they receive salvation, but no more than that.

The Holiness Church next door speaks day in and day out about sanctification. "Be sanctified, be sanctified," they repeatedly exhort. Many people come and receive the touch of sanctification. The minister there is only creating the presence of the sanctifying Christ.

But in my church I preach about the saving Jesus, the sanctifying Christ, the baptizing Savior, the blessing Son of God, and the healing Jesus; and we have all of these aspects manifested in my church. I try to create the whole presence, the rounded out presence, of Jesus Christ.

YOUR ROLE

You create the presence of Jesus with your mouth. If you speak about salvation, the saving Jesus appears. If you speak about divine healing, then you will have the healing Christ in your congregation. If you speak about the miracle performing Jesus, then the presence of the miracle performing Jesus is released. He is bound by your lips and by your words. He is depending on you, and if you do not speak clearly because of your fear of Satan, how will Jesus Christ manifest His power to this generation? So speak boldly.

Many people have great problems in their homes because they do not have family altars. If the father maintains a family altar and speaks clearly about the presence of Jesus Christ in the home and in the family, he can create the presence of Jesus Christ, and Jesus can take care of all that family's problems. But since many neglect the family altar, they neglect speaking the clear presence of Jesus Christ, and their children are left without the full blessings of God.

You do not need to wait until you receive any special spiritual gift. I have always said that spiritual gifts reside in the Holy Spirit. You, yourself, can never own a spiritual gift.

Suppose I had the gift of healing. Then indiscriminately I would heal everyone who sought me for healing. If I had the gift I would give to everyone; I would not be truly discerning. The Holy Spirit sees a need, and then allows the operation of a gift to flow through someone to meet that need.

It is important to remember that all the gifts reside in the Holy Spirit, for it is the Holy Spirit who dwells in your church, and dwells in you. Through Him you can have every type of ministry— the ministry of teaching, the ministry of evangelism, the ministry of missions, the ministry of pastoring, and the ministry of divine healing. Through you as His channel the Holy Spirit manifests Himself. So do not worry about your acquisition of any of the gifts.

Be bold. Receive the gift of boldness, then speak the word. Speak the word clearly, and create a specific presence of Jesus Christ. Release that specific presence of Jesus Christ to your congregation, and you are going to get specific results. A father can create the presence of Jesus Christ through his spoken word, and Jesus can take care of all his family's problems. So, in the same way, I come to my church to speak a message, and plant specific seeds to harvest specific results.

I see one great fault in American services. American pastors deliver fantastic messages to their congregations; but right afterward the people are dismissed and leave. They are not given time to bear the fruit those messages have brought to life. They receive all the spoken words of the message, but have no time to pray through, to get that word so implanted that it becomes a part of them.

In America, services are dismissed too soon. Give the congregation time; shorten the preliminaries and entertainment. Give the Word, and let the people have more time to pray together. Let those spoken words be digested. If this were done you would see more results in these pastors' ministries.

Ultimately your word molds your life, for your speech center controls all the nerves. That is why speaking in another tongue is the initial sign of the baptism of the Holy Spirit. When the Holy Spirit takes over the speech center, He takes over all the nerves all over the body, and controls the entire body. So when we speak in other tongues we are filled with the Holy Spirit.

Speak the word to control and to bridle your whole body and your whole life. Give the word to the Holy Spirit so that He can create something of it. Then create and release the presence of Jesus Christ through your spoken word.

Preach the word. The spoken word has power, and when you release that word, it is that word, and not you, who performs miracles.

God does not use you because you are completely sanctified, for as long as a Christian lives he will be struggling with the flesh. God uses you because you have faith. So brothers and sisters, let us make use of the spoken word—for success in our personal lives, for material with which the Holy Spirit can create, and for the purposes of creating and releasing the presence of Jesus Christ.

Remember that Christ is depending upon you and your spoken word to release His presence. What are you going to do with this Jesus who is riding on your tongue? Are you going to release Him for the blessing of others? Or are you going to lock Him up with a still tongue and a closed mouth? May God bless you as you make your decision.

CHAPTER 4

Rhema

The spoken word has powerful creativity, and its proper usage is vital to a victorious Christian life. This spoken word, however, must have a correct basis to be truly effective. The principle for discovering the correct basis for the spoken word is one of the most important portions of God's truth. It is concerning this topic that I want to share with you now.

FAITH IN GOD'S WORD: PROBLEMS AND PRODUCTIVITY

One day a lady on a stretcher was carried into my office. She was paralyzed from her neck down, and could not even move her fingers. As she was being carried into my office on a stretcher, I began to feel a strange sensation. It felt as if my heart was being troubled. Just as there was expectancy by the pool of Bethesda, I knew that something was going to happen.

I went beside her stretcher, and when I looked into her eyes I realized that she already had the faith to be healed: not a dead faith, but a living faith. I touched her forehead with my hand and said, "Sister, in the name of Jesus Christ, be healed."

Instantly the power of God came, and she was healed. She stood up from her stretcher, thrilled, frightened and amazed.

She later came to my house bringing gifts, and after entering my study she asked, "Could I please close the door?"

"Yes," I replied. "Close the door." Then she knelt down before me, still amazed that she had been healed, and said, "Sir, please reveal yourself to me. Are you the second incarnate Jesus?"

I laughed, "Dear sister, you know that I eat three meals a day, go to the bathroom, and sleep every night. I am as human as you are, and the only way I have salvation is through Jesus Christ."

This woman had received such a miraculous healing that word of it instantly spread. Soon afterward one rich woman came to the church, also being carried in by a stretcher. She had been a Christian for a long time, and a deaconess in the church. She had memorized scripture after scripture regarding divine healing: "I am the Lord that healeth thee" (Exodus 15:26); "With His stripes we are healed" (Isaiah 53:5); "He Himself took our infirmities, and bore our sicknesses" (Matthew 8:17); "And these signs shall follow them that believe ... they shall lay hands on the sick, and they shall recover" (Mark 16:17-18).

So I prayed for her with all my might, but nothing happened. Then I shouted, repeating the same prayers for healing. I used the Word of God, and I even jumped, but nothing happened. I asked her to stand up by faith. Many times she would stand, but the moment I took my hand away, she would fall down like a piece of dead wood. Then I would say, "Have more faith and stand up." Again she would stand up, and again she would fall down. She would then claim to me that she had all the faith in the world, but her faith never would work.

I became quite depressed, and eventually she began to cry. She claimed, "Pastor, you are prejudiced. You loved that other woman so much that you healed her. But you don't really love me. So I am still sick. You are prejudiced."

"Sister," I replied, "I have done everything. You saw me. I have prayed, I have cried, I have jumped, I have shouted. I did everything that a Pentecostal preacher can do, but nothing happened, and I can't understand it."

In my church this bothersome problem of one being healed while another remains ill has not limited itself to this one situation. World famous evangelists have come to my church and enthusiastically preached, "Everyone of you is going to be healed! Everyone of you!" They poured out words of faith, and many people would receive healing.

But then they would leave, receiving all the glory, and I would be left to contend with those not healed. These people would come to me, discouraged and cast down, and say, "We are not healed. God has given upon us; we are completely forgotten. Why should we continue to struggle to come to Jesus Christ and believe?"

I then travailed and cried, "Why Father? Why should it be like this? God, please give me the answer, a very clear-cut answer." And He did. So now I would like to share this answer with you, and some realizations that led me to this understanding.

People think that they can believe on the Word of God. They can. But they fail to differentiate between the Word of God which gives general knowledge about God, and the Word of God which God uses to impart faith about specific circumstances into a man's heart. It is this latter type of faith which brings miracles.

In the Greek language there are two different words for 'word,' *logos* and *rhema*. The world was created by the Word, *logos*, of God. *Logos* is the general Word of God, stretching from Genesis to Revelation, for all these books directly or indirectly tell about the Word, Jesus Christ. By reading the *logos* from Genesis to Revelation you can receive all the knowledge you need about God and His promises; but just by reading you do not receive faith. You have received knowledge and understanding about God, but you do not receive faith.

Romans 10:17 shows us that the material used to build faith is more than just reading God's Word: "Faith comes by hearing, and hearing by the Word of God." In this scripture 'word' is not *logos*, but *rhema*. Faith specifically comes by hearing the *rhema*.

In his Greek lexicon Dr. Ironside has defined *logos* as "the said word of God," and *rhema* as "the saying word of God." Many scholars define this action of *rhema* as being the Holy Spirit using a few verses of Scripture and quickening it personally to one individual person. Here is my definition of *rhema*: *rhema* is a specific word to a specific person in a specific situation.

Once in Korea a lady by the name of Yun Hae Kyung had a tremendous youth meeting on Samgak Mountain. She had a great ministry. When she stood up and people came forward, they would fall down, slain under the power of the Holy Spirit. Many young people would flock to her meetings, and when she held a youth campaign on Samgak Mountain, thousands of young people came to join in.

During the week of the youth campaign it rained heavily, and all the rivers overflowed. A group of young people wanted to go to the town on the opposite side of the river, where the meetings were being held. But when they came to the bank of the river, it was flooded. There was not a bridge or a boat to be seen, and most of them became discouraged.

But three girls got together and said, "Why can't we just wade through the water? Peter walked on the water, and Peter's God is our God, Peter's Jesus is our Jesus, and Peter's faith is our faith. Peter believed, and we should do all the more. We are going to go over this river!"

The river was completely flooded, but these three girls knelt down and held hands together, quoting the scriptures containing the story of Peter walking on the water, and they claimed they could believe in the same way. Then, in the sight of the rest of their group, they shouted and began to wade through the water.

Immediately they were swept away by an angry flood, and after three days their dead bodies were found in the open sea.

This incident caused repercussions throughout Korea. Non-Christian newspapers carried the story, making headlines of it: "Their God Could Not Save Them;" "Why Did God Not Answer Their Prayer of Faith?" So unbelievers had a real heyday as a result of this occurrence, and the Christian church experienced a slump, feeling depressed and discouraged, having no adequate answer.

This became a topic of discussion all over Korea, and many previously good Christians lost their faith. They would say, "These girls believed exactly as our ministers have taught; they exercised their faith. From the platform our pastors constantly urge the people to boldly exercise their faith in the Word of God. These girls did just that, so why didn't God answer? Jehovah God must not be a living God. This must just be a formalistic religion we have been involved in."

What kind of answer would you give to these people? Those girls had believed. They had exercised faith based on the Word of God.

But God had no reason to support their faith. Peter never walked on the water because of *logos*, which gives general knowledge about God. Peter required that Christ give a specific word to him: Peter asked, "Lord, if you are Jesus, command me to come."

Jesus replied, "Come."

The word Christ gave to Peter was not *logos*, but *rhema*. He gave a specific word, "Come," to a specific person, Peter, in a specific situation, a storm.

Rhema brings faith. Faith comes by hearing, and hearing by *rhema*. Peter never walked on the water by knowledge of God alone. Peter had *rhema*.

But these girls had only *logos*, a general knowledge of God, and in this case, the working of God through Peter. They exercised their human faith on *logos*: that was their mistake. God, therefore, had no responsibility to support their faith, and the difference between the way these girls exercised faith and the way Peter exercised faith is as the difference between night and day.

Two years ago two Bible school graduates failed completely in their first venture into the ministry. These two fellows had been disciples of mine. They listened to my lectures, they came to my church and learned in concept the principles of faith.

They began their first venture into the ministry with what seemed to be a great deal of faith, clinging to such scriptures as: "Open your mouth wide and I will fill it" (Psalm 81:10); "If ye ask anything in my name, I will do it" (John 14:14).

They went to a bank and made a large loan. Then they went to a rich man and made another large loan. With this money they bought land and built a beautiful sanctuary—without even having a congregation. They began preaching, expecting the people to flock in by the hundreds, and their debts to be paid; but nothing like that happened.

One of these young ministers had borrowed approximately $30,000, the other about $50,000. Soon their creditors came to collect their payments, and these young men were cornered in a terrible situation, arriving at a point where they were near to losing their faith in God.

Then they both came to me. They cried, "Pastor Cho, why is your God and our God different? You started with $2,500, and now you have completed a five million dollar project. We went out and built things which cost only a total of $80,000. Why wouldn't God answer us? We believed in the same God, and we exercised the same faith. So why hasn't He answered?"

Then they started quoting scriptures containing promises from the Old Testament and New Testament, adding, "We did exactly as you taught and we failed."

Then I replied, "I am glad that you have failed after hearing my word. Surely you are my disciples, but you have not been the disciples of Jesus Christ. You misunderstood my teachings. I started my church because of *rhema*, not just *logos*. God clearly spoke to my heart, saying, "Rise up, go out and build a church which will seat 10,000 people. God imparted His faith to my heart, and I went out and a miracle occurred. But you went out just with *logos*, a general knowledge about God and His faith. God therefore has no responsibility to support you, even though your ministry was for the Lord Jesus Christ."

Brothers and sisters, through *logos* you can know God. You can gain understanding and knowledge about Him. But *logos* does not always become *rhema*.

Suppose a sick man were to have gone to the pool of Bethesda and said to those around it, "You foolish fellows, why are you waiting here? This is always the same pool in the same location with the same water. Why should you wait here day after day? I'm just going to jump in and wash myself."

Then he might have dived in and washed himself. But if he were to come out of the water, he would not have been healed. It was only after the angel of the Lord came and troubled the water that the people could jump in, wash, and be healed. Yet it was still the same pool of Bethesda, at the same location, with the same water. Only when the water was troubled by God's angel could a miracle occur.

Rhema is produced out of *logos*. *Logos* is like the pool of Bethesda. You may listen to the Word of God and you may study the Bible, but only when the Holy Spirit comes and quickens a scripture or scriptures to your heart, burning them in your soul and letting you know that they apply directly to your specific situation, does *logos* become *rhema*.

Logos is given to everybody. *Logos* is common to Koreans, Europeans, Africans and Americans. It is given to all so that they may gain knowledge about God; but *rhema* is not given to everyone. *Rhema* is given to that specific person who is waiting upon the Lord until the Holy Spirit quickens *logos* into *rhema*. If you never have time to wait upon the Lord, then the Lord can never come and quicken the needed scripture to your heart.

This is a busy age. People come to church and are entertained. They hear a short sermon and are dismissed, without having any time of waiting upon the Lord. They get the *logos*, but since they do not receive *rhema*, they miss out on seeing the miraculous workings of God, and begin to doubt His power.

People must come to the main sanctuary, listen attentively to the preacher, and wait upon the Lord. But they do not come and listen prayerfully to the preacher, waiting upon the Lord to receive *rhema*; therefore, they cannot receive the faith they need for the solutions to their problems. Their knowledge of the Bible increases as their problems increase, and though they come to church, nothing happens. So they begin to fall away and lose faith.

Another problem with many churches in this active age is that ministers are busy with too many matters. They spend hours and hours as a janitor, financier, constructor, and contractor, going in a hundred different directions.

By Saturday they are so tired that they fumble around trying to find some *logos* to preach on. They are so tired that they have no time to wait upon the Lord, no time to change the green grass into white milk. Their congregations are simply fed grass, and not even given the milk of the Word. This is a grave mistake.

Lay persons are not the pastor's enemies, but his friends. As did the apostles, so should the minister concentrate on prayer and the ministering of the Word of God, delegating any other type of work to his deacons, deaconesses and other lay leaders.

I follow this pattern in my church, and I dare not go up to the platform without first waiting upon the Lord and receiving the *rhema* God would have me give for that message. If I do not receive *rhema*, I will not go to the platform.

So I go up to Prayer Mountain on Saturday, crawl into a grotto, close the door, and wait there until the Holy Spirit comes and gives me the needed rhema. Sometimes I stay the whole night through, during that time praying, "Lord, tomorrow the people are coming with all kinds of problems—sickness, disease, family problems, problems in business—every type of problem that can be imagined.

"They are coming not only to hear general knowledge about You, but they are also coming to receive real solutions to their problems. If we don't give them a living faith, *rhema*, then they are going to go back home with out receiving their solutions. I need to have a specific message for a specific people at a specific time."

Then I wait until God gives me that message. When coming to the platform, I march in like a general, knowing that the message I preach is under the anointing of the Holy Spirit.

After I preach, people in the congregation come to me and say, "Pastor, you preached exactly the word I needed. I've got faith that my problem will be solved." This is because I helped supply to them the *rhema*.

Brothers and sisters, we are not building a holy country club in the church; we deal rather with matters of life and death. If the pastor does not supply *rhema* to his people, then you have just a religious social club. In the social world already one can see organizations such as Kiwanis Clubs and Rotary Clubs, and their members pay a type of tithe too.

The churches we build should be places where people get their solutions from the Lord, receive miracles for their lives, and can gain not just a knowledge about God, but get to know Him in a vital way. In order to do this, the pastor must first receive *rhema*.

Christians should be given time to wait upon the Lord, so that the Holy Spirit can have a full opportunity to deal with their lives and inspire them through the Scripture. The Holy Spirit can take Scripture, the "said word" of God, and apply it to a person's heart, making it the "saying word" of God. The *logos* then becomes the *rhema*.

Now I can tell you why so many people cannot receive healing. All the promises are potentially—not literally—yours. Never simply pick a promise out of God's Word and say, "Oh, this is mine; I will repeat it over and over again. This is mine, this is mine!" NO! It is potentially yours, yes, but make it yours in practical reality by waiting upon the Lord.

Before the Lord quickens a scripture to an individual, the Lord has many things to do. The Lord wants to cleanse your life and make you surrendered to Him. The Lord will never give promises rashly. As the Lord deals with you, take time to wait upon Him, confessing your sins, and surrendering your life to Him. When these conditions are met, then the power of God comes. Your heart—like the pool of Bethesda—is troubled by a particular scripture; and you know that its promise is yours, and you have the faith to bring about the needed miracle.

GOD'S UPPERMOST GOAL

The healing of the physical body is not the Spirit's ultimate goal. You must know where the priority lies. His ultimate goal is the healing of our souls. When God deals with you, He always deals with you through the healing of your soul. If your soul is not right with God, no amount of prayer, shouting or jumping will bring the *rhema* of healing to you.

You must first get right with the Lord. Confess your sins, apply the blood of Jesus Christ, be saved and receive eternal life; then the Holy Spirit is going to prick your heart with a scripture of divine healing, inspire you, and give you the *rhema* you need. But in order for this to happen, you must wait on the Lord.

Divine healing is all according to God's sovereign will. Sometimes a person receives healing instantly; another person must wait a longer time.

One of our church's finest deacons became ill; this deacon gave everything to the Lord, loving God, and working for the Lord in an amazing way. He was told that he had a growth inside his body and that the doctor wanted to operate. But everybody in my church knew that God was going to heal him, for he was a tremendous saint with great faith. This was their reasoning.

I prayed for his healing. All of our then 40,000 members prayed, storming the Throne of Grace. And that deacon claimed the healing.

But nothing happened. He became worse and worse. Eventually he bled so badly he was carried to the hospital and operated on. Many of my members were worried, and they complained, "Where is God? Why is God treating him like this?"

But I praised God, for I knew that He had some specific purpose in what was happening.

When he was hospitalized in the ward he began to preach the Gospel to all the people with whom he made contact. Soon the whole hospital knew that there was a living Jesus, His representative right in their hospital. The doctors, nurses, and all the patients daily became saved.

Then our members rejoiced, saying, "Praise God. It was far better for him to be in the hospital than to be divinely healed immediately."

God showed that His priority was the eternal healing of souls rather than the earthly healing of the physical.

When there is pain and suffering, we are apt to claim deliverance. But this we should not do. If your suffering should bring about redemptive grace, or if your suffering becomes the channel for the flowing of God's redeeming grace, then your suffering has been God-appointed. If, however, your suffering becomes invalid and starts to destroy you, then this is from Satan, and you should pray through and rid yourself of it.

I will relay to you one case in which God did not deliver people from their suffering.

It was during the Korean War when 500 ministers were captured and immediately shot to death, and two thousand churches were destroyed.

The Communists were vicious to the ministers. One minister's family was captured in Inchon, Korea, and the Communist leaders put them on what they called a "People's Trial." The accusers would say, "One man is guilty of causing this kind of sin, and for that kind of sin it is proper that he be punished."

The only response then given would be a chorus of voices agreeing, "Yah, Yah!"

This time they dug a large hole, putting the pastor, his wife, and several of his children in. The leader then spoke, "Mister, all these years you misled the people with the superstition of the Bible. Now if you will publicly disclaim it before these people, and repent of this misdemeanor, then you, your wife, and your children will be freed. But if you persist in your superstitions, all of your family is going to be buried alive. "Make a decision!"

All of his children then blurted, "Oh Daddy ! Daddy! Think of us! Daddy!"

Think of it. If you were in his place, what would you do? I am the father of three children, and would almost feel like going to hell rather than see my children killed.

This father was shaken. He lifted up his hand and said, "Yes, yes, I'll do it. I am going to denounce… my…"

But before he could finish his sentence his wife nudged him, saying, "Daddy! Say NO!"

"Hush children," she said. "Tonight we are going to have supper with the King of kings, the Lord of lords!"

She led them in singing 'In the Sweet By and By,' her husband and children following, while the Communists began to bury them. Soon the children were buried, but until the soil came up to their necks they sang, and all the people watched. God did not deliver them, but almost all of those people who watched this execution became Christians, many now members of my church.

Through their suffering the grace of redemption flowed. God gave His only begotten Son to be crucified on the cross so that this world could be saved and redeemed. That is God's uppermost goal—the redemption of souls. So when you desire divine healing, or an answer from above, always focus through the lenses of the uppermost goal, the redeeming of souls. If you see that your suffering brings about more redemption than your healing, then do not ask for deliverance, but ask God to give you strength to persevere.

To discern between suffering brought by satan that God would rather deliver, and suffering that God would use to bring about the flow of redemptive grace, is not always easy. To make this kind of decision you need to wait upon the Lord, and to know the will of the Lord. Do not become discouraged, and go around receiving prayer from one famous evangelist and then another. But through your prayer, fasting and faith, let God show you His will.

When the Holy Spirit quickens the *logos* of scripture to you, a miraculous faith is imparted to your heart. You know that the scripture no longer belongs to the "said word" of God, but is instantly the "saying word" of God for you. You must then stand upon that word, and go ahead and do it, even though you can see nothing. Even though you cannot touch anything and even though your whole life is pitch dark, once you receive the *rhema* do not be frightened. Just go ahead and walk on the water, and you will see a miracle. Be careful, however, not to move ahead of God.

Many people do move ahead of God, even as did Paul, in his eagerness to bring the Gospel of Jesus Christ. Jesus Christ had commanded that we go to the ends of the world and preach the Gospel; so Paul went out on the *logos*, and headed for Asia. But the Spirit of Jesus Christ did not permit him to go there.

Then Paul said, "I will go to Bithynia." But again the Spirit of the Lord said "NO."

Paul and his company then went down to Troas, an unknown city. We can imagine his wonderings there, that he was confused, thinking to himself, "I was just obeying the command of Jesus. Jesus said to go to the ends of the world and preach the Gospel. Why am I a failure?"

But as he was praying and waiting upon the Lord, he received the *rhema*, and a man from Macedonia appeared in a vision and said, "Come into Macedonia and help us!" So he took a boat and crossed over to Europe.

Through Paul's example we can again see the difference between *logos* and *rhema*.

RECEIVING RHEMA

People have come to me and commented, "Brother Cho, I can pray through about the various promises from the scriptures, and I can wait until the Holy Spirit quickens and applies them to me. But how can I get *rhema* about choosing a husband, or a wife? I read all the scriptures, but the Bible does not say whether I should go marry Elizabeth, Mary or Joan. How can I get the rhema about this?

"Also, the Bible does not say that you should go and live in Lakeland, Los Angeles, or in some northern area. How can I receive God's will about that?"

These are legitimate questions. Let me show you the five steps I use to get the rhema about these types of decisions.

NEUTRAL GEAR

The first step is to put myself in neutral gear— not forward or backward, but completely calm in my heart. Then I wait upon the Lord, saying, "Lord, I'm here. I will listen to your voice. If you say 'yes,' I will go; if you say 'no,' I'm not going. I don't wish to make decisions for my own benefit, but to decide according to Your desire. Whether it becomes good for me, or bad for me, I'm ready to accept your guidance."

With this attitude I wait upon the Lord. Many times the best action to take is to fast and pray, for if you eat too much you get so tired that you cannot pray. Then, if you know that you are really calmed down, you come to the second step.

DIVINE DESIRE

The second thing I do is to ask the Lord to reveal His will through my desire. God always comes to you through your sanctified desire. "Delight thyself also in the Lord; and He shall give thee the desires of thine heart" (Psalm 37:4). "The desire of the righteous shall be granted" (Proverbs 10:24). "What things soever ye desire, when ye pray, believe that ye receive them, and ye shall have them" (Mark 11:24).

Desire, then, is one of God's focusing points. Moreover, Philippians 2:13 reads, "For it is God which worketh in you, both to will and to do of His good pleasure."

Through the Holy Spirit God puts in your heart the desire, making you to will to do His will. So pray to the Lord, "Lord, now give me the desire according to your will."

Pray through and wait upon the Lord until God gives you divine desire. As you pray many desires, beautiful desires, will probably flow in. In your praying, then, also have the patience to wait for God's desire to settle in. Do not stand up and say, "Oh, I've got everything," and rush away. Wait upon the Lord a little longer. Desires can be given from Satan, from your own spirit, or from the Holy Spirit.

Time is always the test. If you wait patiently your own desire and desires from satan will become increasingly weaker, but the desire from the Holy Spirit becomes stronger and stronger. So wait, and receive the divine desire.

SCRIPTURAL SCREENING

After my desire becomes very clear-cut, then I proceed to step three: I compare this desire with biblical teaching.

One day a lady came to me. All excited, she said, "Oh, Pastor Cho, I am going to support your ministry with a large amount of money."

"Praise God," I exclaimed. "Have a seat and tell me about this."

She explained, "I have a fantastic desire to go into business. This business deal is going on, and if I join in I think I can make big money."

"What kind of business is it?" I asked.

She replied, "I have a burning desire to get a monopoly on the cigarette business. Tobacco, you know."

"Forget about it," I retorted.

"But I have the desire!" she said. "The burning desire, just like you've preached about."

"That desire is from your own flesh," I replied. "Have you ever gone through the Bible to see if what you would be doing is scriptural?"

"No."

"Your desire must be screened through the scripture," I instructed her. "The Bible says that you are the temple of the Holy Spirit (1 Corinthians 6:19). If God ever wanted His people to smoke, then He would have made our noses differently. Smoke stacks are supposed to be open upward to the sky, and not downward. Think about the nose; it is not pointing upward, but downward. God did not purpose that people smoke, because our smoke stacks are upside down. The Holy Spirit's dwelling is your body. If you pollute it with smoke, then you are polluting the temple of the Holy Spirit with smoke. Your desire is out of the will of God. It would be best if you just forget about this new business."

One man came to me and said, "Pastor, I've struck up a friendship with a beautiful woman, a widow. She is sweet, beautiful and wonderful, and when I pray, I have a burning desire to marry her. But I also have my wife and children."

"Look," I replied, "you forget about this, because it's from the devil."

"Oh, no, no. This is not from the devil," he disagreed. "When I prayed the Holy Spirit spoke in my heart and told me that my original wife was not exactly the right kind of rib to fit into my side. My present wife is always a thorn in my flesh. The Holy Spirit spoke and said that this widow is my lost rib, which will fit exactly into my side."

I told him, "That is not from the Holy Spirit. That's from the devil's spirit."

Many people make this kind of mistake. If they pray against the written Word of God, then the devil will speak. The Holy Spirit will never contradict God's written Word. That man did not listen to me, and he divorced his wife and he married that widow. He is now of all men the most miserable. He found out that his second rib was even worse than his first.

So all of our desires should be carefully screened with Scripture. If you do not have the self-confidence to do this yourself then go to your minister or pastor.

A BECKONING SIGNAL

After I screen my desire through the written Word, the teachings of God, then I am ready for step four: to ask God for a beckoning signal from my circumstances. If God truly has spoken to your heart, then He is bound to give you a signal from the outside external world.

When Elijah prayed seven times for rain, he received a signal from the eastern sky—a patch as large as a man's fist, a cloud, appeared.

Gideon also provides us with an example, for he, too, asked for a sign. And God would always show me a sign from my circumstances; sometimes this sign was very small, but it still was a sign.

DIVINE TIMING

After I have received a sign, then I take the final step: I pray until I know God's timing. God's timing is different from our timing.

You must pray—until you have a real peace, for peace is like the chief umpire. If after you pray you still feel a restlessness in your spirit, then the timing is not proper. That means there is still a red light; so keep praying and waiting. When the red light is switched off and you see the green light, peace will come into your heart.

Then you should jump up and go. Go then with full speed, with God's blessing and God's *rhema*. Miracle after miracle will follow you.

All through life I have carried out and conducted my business by using these five steps. So far God has always confirmed this way of walking with signs and miracles following. These results must show clearly the difference between *logos* and *rhema*.

In the future you need no longer be confused about the promises of God. No amount of claiming, travailing, jumping, or shrieking will convince Him. God is going to convince you Himself by imparting His faith into your heart.

The English translation of Mark 11:22-23 says that you should have faith in God and then you would be able to command a mountain to be removed and cast into the sea. The Greek, however, says that you should have the faith of God.

How can you have the faith of God? When you receive *rhema* the faith given is not your own; it is imparted faith that God has given you. After receiving this imparted faith, then you can command mountains to be removed. Without receiving God's faith you cannot do this.

If for no other reason, you should carefully study the Bible—Genesis to Revelation—in order to give the Holy Spirit the material with which He needs to work. Then when you wait upon the Lord, the Holy Spirit will impart His faith to you. Great miracles will follow you as you act on this faith, miracles in your ministry and in your home.

So wait upon the Lord; never consider it a waste of time. When God speaks to your heart He can in one second do far greater things than you could do in one entire year. Wait upon the Lord, and you will see great things accomplished.

The School of Andrew

When you receive Jesus Christ as your personal Savior your spirit is instantly reborn. Right away God's life is poured into you, and instantly your spiritual being receives eternal life. But your mind, your thoughts, must be renewed according to your born again spirit; that task of renewal is one that requires a lifelong process, taking time, energy and struggle. This renewal is necessary if one is to adequately receive and act on the *rhema* they are given from God, allowing the powerful creativity of the spoken word to remain vital.

A RENEWED THOUGHT LIFE

Many people experience a spiritual rebirth, but they do not renew their mind in order to truly grasp the thoughts of God. They do not align their personal lives according to the thoughts of God. For this reason God, who dwells in them, cannot freely move through the channel of their thinking life. Let me illustrate this more clearly.

One day my eldest son, who at the time was in fourth grade, came to me. I could tell he wanted to ask me something, but he was hesitant in speaking. Finally I spoke first: "Son, what are you trying to ask me?"

He smiled. "Daddy, if I ask you a strange question, will you get mad?"

"Of course I won't get mad," I assured him. "Go ahead. Speak."

"Well," he continued, "are you permitted to tell a lie before your own congregation?"

"When did I tell a lie?" I asked.

He laughed, "I've heard you telling a lie again and again to your congregation."

I was shocked. If my son distrusted me, then who could trust me? "Son," I said, "you sit down and tell me when I told a lie."

"Daddy, so many times you told your congregation that you had heard from the Lord, so I became curious. Every Saturday I would listen outside your study as you were preparing your sermons, and I would open the door a little to see if you were really meeting God there.

"But I never saw you really meeting God in your study. Yet on Sunday you come out to the platform and boldly declare to the people that you've met God. And that's a lie, isn't it? Don't be afraid of telling me the truth. I am your son. I won't tell the people."

Since he was so young I knew that he would not understand if I were to explain my feelings in theological terms. "Lord," I prayed, "you must give me wisdom. How can I explain to this young mind my relationship with you?"

Suddenly a tremendous thought flowed out of my heart, and I looked at my son and said, "Son, let me ask you a question. Have you ever seen your thoughts?"

He paused a moment. "No, I haven't seen my thoughts."

"Then you have an empty head, " I answered. "You have no thoughts at all."

"No, Daddy, I do have thoughts. Because I have thought I can talk."

"But," I pointed out, "I haven't seen your thoughts."

"How can you see my thoughts?" he asked. "They are somewhere in my brain, and you can't see them."

"Well, then," I said, "Even though you can't see them you really have thoughts, don't you?"

"Sure, Daddy," he answered.

"Well," I explained, "I met with God even though you can't see Him with your eyes. God is like your thoughts. The Bible says that God is the Word.

"Son, what is the Word? The Word is thoughts clothed with vocabulary. And if God is thought clothed with Chinese, the Chinese people understand God's thoughts; when God's thoughts are clothed with English, then American people understand. When God's thoughts come down to us clothed in the Korean language we Korean people understand.

"Son, I meet God by reading the Scripture, the Word of God; and God's thoughts touch my thoughts in an unseen realm, and I have conversation with the Heavenly Father through the Word of God. God is like thought."

Immediately my son caught the meaning, and he nodded. "I can't see my thoughts, but I still know that I have them. Yes, God is like thought. I can't see God, but God is there. I am satisfied. I am sorry, Father, because I misunderstood you."

When my son left I stood up and praised the Lord: "Father, I was afraid that he would not understand, but he did; yet I know it was not I, but the Holy Spirit who helped me to have the words to explain your wonderful presence."

Now let me ask you a question. What is God like? Does God have any form? Does He look like a human being? How can you explain the presence of God?

God is like thought. If you do not have any thoughts, then God has no channel through which to speak to you. You cannot touch God with your hands, you cannot breathe God as if breathing air into your lungs; for God does not belong to the sensual world. You can meet God only through the arena of your thinking life.

God's thoughts come through His Word, or through His Holy Spirit. His thoughts touch our thoughts, and it is there that you meet God. So if you do not renew your thinking life and if you do not renew your mind after conversion, then God cannot really manifest Himself to you.

Many people still live with their old minds after conversion. This old way of thinking is limiting; thus God becomes limited by the wrong kind of thinking life. To walk closely with God you must renew your mind and thinking life. If you do not renew your thinking life, God cannot come and commune with you. God will not dwell in a polluted mind, as fish and birds will not remain in a polluted lake.

You must renew you thinking in order that faith can rise up through your thinking life. Faith does not just well up from your inner spirit. Faith comes in cooperation with your thoughts, for faith comes by hearing, and hearing by the Word of God.

First you must hear; and through hearing, the Word of God comes to your thoughts; through your thinking life, the thoughts of God go into your spirit and produce faith. Therefore, if you do not renew your thinking, you cannot fully understand the Word of God; and without the renewal of mind and the hearing of the Word, you cannot have faith. Faith comes by hearing.

And what do you hear? You hear the thoughts of God. The arena of your thinking engrafts God's thoughts and produces faith, and through faith God can flow through you to others. Your thinking life is so important; you must renew your mind. There are three steps by which you can renew your mind, and these three steps must be followed before you can achieve a renewal of your thought life.

A CHANGED THINKING ATTITUDE

Your first step must be to change your thinking attitude from that of a negative attitude to that of a positive one. Let us look at Peter, Jesus Christ's disciple, as an example.

The disciples of Jesus Christ were in a boat on the Sea of Galilee. It was a dark and stormy night, and the waves were so high that the boat rolled heavily. They were fighting a losing battle to keep the boat afloat when suddenly they saw Jesus Christ walking on the water toward them. In those days there was a popular saying that if a seaman saw a ghost on the sea his boat would sink. So when these fishermen-disciples saw Christ they were frozen with fear, thinking that their boat was going to sink and that they were going to die.

But Jesus spoke, "I am Christ. Don't be frightened."

Peter cried out, "If you were Jesus, you would ask me to come to you."

Peter always spoke before he thought. He was a terribly emotional man; but he had the gift of boldness, so God used him.

Christ then told Peter to come. When Peter heard this command, he immediately accepted the command of Jesus in his mind, and his thinking was renewed.

Humanly speaking, Peter could never walk on the water, but when he accepted the word of Jesus Christ, he instantly renewed his mind. Peter changed his way of thinking from a negative to a positive attitude. Peter would never have believed that he could walk on water, but as he heard the command of Jesus and as he accepted the command, he changed his thoughts; he believed that he could walk on water. He changed his thinking, and man always acts according to his thoughts.

So as Peter renewed his thoughts, as he envisioned that he could walk on water, he acted accordingly, and he jumped out of the boat. It was a pitch-dark night, and the waves were high. But he risked his life boldly, launching out by faith, and began to walk on the water.

Miracles follow a renewed mind, and as Peter renewed his mind, he began to walk on water. He walked high on the crest of the waves; he was actually walking on water!

But suddenly he looked around. He saw the dark valleys the stormy waves created, and he began to regress into his old thinking. "Look at me," he thought. "Am I not a human being? I am walking on the water, and we are not supposed to be able to walk like this. We human beings are supposed to walk on land, not on water. I'm not a fish, but look at me. I'm walking on water. This is wrong; it's impossible for me to do this."

He changed his thinking pattern. He thought that he could not walk on the water, and instantly he sank.

God relates to each of us only through our thought life. When Peter received the *rhema* from Christ, renewed his thinking and therefore thought he could walk on the water, he walked. When he changed this thinking and thought it impossible to walk in the water, he instantly began to sink.

This is a very important concept, for as a man thinketh, so will he act. If you think you are a king or queen, you will act like a king or queen. If you think of yourself as being unworthy and of no account, then you will behave as if you are unworthy and of no account.

So it is vital that we renew our thoughts, and think positively. Let me illustrate this point with an actual example.

I once knew a doctor who claimed to be an atheist. I suffered much because of him; for a long time he was a great enemy to my ministry, challenging my faith, attacking my words and beliefs.

Then one day that doctor suffered a stroke and became paralyzed. As a result of his paralysis, he was slowly dying. The doctor then came to my church, asking that I pray for his healing.

Many people brag about their atheistic views; yet when these same people experience a pitch-dark night, and encounter the storm tossed waves, their atheism becomes very weak.

So this doctor came to church, and I prayed for him. He received the prayer of faith, and he stood up and walked from his wheelchair, his steps strong. All the people clapped their hands and shouted, praising God.

Next Sunday he came to church, walking by himself with no assistance. He again requested my personal prayer, but as I was busy I could not. When he saw that I could not personally pray for him, he changed his thinking; his thoughts regressed, and he returned into his old self. Because he could not receive the prayer of faith from me, he became unbelieving again, and as he walked out of my office to his car, he collapsed, and his wife had to call an ambulance to carry him to the hospital.

He collapsed because he changed his thoughts. The power of God left him, and just as Peter began to doubt and sink into the Sea of Galilee, so did the doctor lose himself to his fears, and again become paralyzed.

Thoughts are important, so do not neglect to renew your thinking life. Be absolutely positive in your thinking, do not think negatively. God is light, and in Him there is no darkness; there is nothing negative in God, for in God there is only the positive. Positive things are happenings; so to commune with God you must renew your mind to think positively. Feed your mind with Scripture, for the Word of God is full of positive life.

Also, be careful when you feed on the Word of God that you do not confine your thinking to traditional patterns of thought.

Be revolutionary. Many people are bound because they think only in the traditional, orthodox way, and therefore God is unable to accomplish the great works He desires to accomplish through them. But if you receive the Word of God and revolutionize your thinking, then you will achieve heights beyond your present limitations.

When I am in Korea I have a session with my one hundred associate pastors every morning. Each morning, from 9:00 to 9:30 a.m., I challenge them, asking them to revolutionize their thinking.

"Don't just think traditionally," I exhort them. "Don't go by the thinking and teaching of Cho. Go by the Word of God. Feed on the Word of God. Revolutionize your thinking life! Expand your thinking life according to Scripture; then God can have absolute freedom to express Himself through your thoughts."

After I speak these words those associates become increasingly motivated. They receive the Word, and if they hit a real revolutionary thought, they carry it out, and then I see results. I do not intervene with their work, except for those occasions when they experience difficulty.

Once I have delegated power, that power remains delegated, and I no longer worry about it. It is through this positive approach that I work with my associates, successful ministers, each responsible for meeting the needs of a certain portion of a 50,000 adult membership.

THINK IN TERMS OF MIRACLES

When you have changed your thinking attitude from that of a negative attitude to that of a positive one, your second step must be to constantly train yourself to think in terms of miracles. This can be seen in the lives of the disciples of Jesus Christ.

Once Jesus went out to the wilderness with 5,000 men following him. Besides 5,000 men there were probably 10,000 women, women who also had children; in actuality then, there was probably a total of 20,000 in this crowd. As evening approached the people became hungry. It was getting dark and cold, and the women and children began falling back along the side of the road.

Christ called Philip, "Philip, I can see all these folks are hungry. Feed them."

So Philip received the command from the Lord Jesus Christ to feed this large crowd. To transfer what happened in modern terms, can't you see Philip organizing what would be today a committee, in order to study how to feed this large number of people? Imagine him recruiting the members of his committee, calling together disciples with a high intelligence.

Philip opened the committee meeting as chairman, saying, "Gentlemen, our Lord Jesus Christ commanded me to feed these 20,000 people in the wilderness. So our committee has the responsibility to find the way to do so. Do you have any ideas?"

One fellow lifted his hand, and after Philip recognized him, said, "Don't you know that we are in the wilderness?

We aren't in downtown Jerusalem. It's absolutely impossible to even think of feeding these people."

I think so too," Philip might have answered. "Mister Scribe, write that down."

A second man lifted his hand, "Mr. Chairman, I want to ask you a question. Do we have enough money? We would need at least two hundred denarii to feed even a small portion of them. Do we have enough money?"

"No," Philip responded, "we haven't got a penny."

"Well, you are out of your mind trying to feed them then," the man retorted.

"Yes, I agree with you," Philip returned. "Mr. Scribe, write that down, also."

A third man spoke: "Mr. Chairman, do you know any bakery that could produce so much bread at one time?"

"No," said Philip, "I don't know any bakery around here."

"Well then, it'd take weeks to feed these people, and that's impossible!"

"Yes, I agree with you," said Philip. "Mr. Scribe, write that down, too."

Then another disciple spoke, "I want to express my opinion, too, Mr. Chairman. You know it's getting late. Why don't we just scatter them and tell them to each find a place to sleep and eat?"

The meeting was then concluded, and Philip gathered the information. But this information was only of a negative and impossibility nature, information that refuted the teachings of Jesus Christ, and directly opposed His command.

Philip then went to Jesus to inform Him, but as he began to speak, Andrew walked up with five loaves of bread and two fishes in his hand. "Andrew," Philip exclaimed, "are you trying to make fun of us? What are you doing? You have five loaves of bread and two fishes to feed 20,000 people! You are really out of your mind!"

But Andrew did not answer him. He just brought the five loaves and two fishes to Jesus.

"Jesus, this isn't enough to feed many people, but I brought it here anyway."

Andrew heard the command of Jesus; his mind accepted the command, and though he doubted, he brought the food he found to Christ. Andrew had possibility thinking, and through his thinking, caught the vision of Jesus Christ.

Then Jesus blessed that bread and fishes, multiplied them, and that great crowd was fed.

All Christians belong to Jesus Christ; but in Christ there are two schools of thought: Philip's school and Andrew's school. Unfortunately, many churches being to the school of Philip, only talking about the impossible. They cry that this is the wilderness and that it is too late, and that the people cannot be fed. They speak with little faith, and talk only of the impossible.

To what school do you belong? I know that many attend different schools and colleges, but what school do you belong to in your thinking life? Do you belong to Philip's school, or do you belong to the school of Andrew?

When God spoke to my heart in 1969, and told me to build a church that would seat 10,000 people, I was frightened. Every moment I felt like Philip. I talked with the board of elders, and all of them thought like the disciples of Philip. They would tell me it was impossible.

When I talked with my 600 deacons, again I found every one of them thinking the same way. So I, too, joined the school of Philip, and I came to Jesus and told Him I could not build that church. But in my heart Christ commanded me, "I did not ask you to confer with your deacons and elders. I told you to go and build."

"Lord," I replied, "you know that I don't have any thing to build with. It will take so much more money than I have now."

Then through the Holy Spirit Jesus spoke to my heart, "What do you have that you personally could give?"

In my heart I knew what He was asking, but I refused to recognize His request, saying, "Jesus, don't ask me to do that. I married when I was thirty years old, and throughout the years I've saved my money so that I could build a beautiful home and give it to my wife. I can't sell that house."

But the Lord replied, "Give what you have."

"Father, it's just $20,000," I cried. "That can't build the church and apartment complex. They cost $5 million. The amount my house would bring could not possibly be enough."

But God said, "Sell your home and bring that money to me with faith."

"Oh, God, this is terrible!" I responded. "How can I do that?"

"If you are ever to believe my Word," the Lord admonished me, "you must first be willing to give of what you have and what you own."

To a Korean wife the home is everything. It is the place she raises her children, it is the place she builds her life, it is a precious possession to her. So I was afraid to tell my wife, and I began to travail in prayer. I prayed that my wife would consent about the selling of our home.

That evening I bought gifts of flowers and scarves home to my wife. "Why are you bringing me these gifts?" she asked. "Are you worried that I don't love you any more?" But she was pleased, and she fixed the evening meal happily.

"Oh, praise God," I responded. "I'm so happy that I've chosen you. If God ever wanted me to choose another girl again, I'd still pick you. You are more beautiful to me each day." After a time, when I felt the moment to be right, I said, "Honey, I have a big problem."

Concerned, she looked at me, insisting, "Tell me."

"We are going to build this big church which will seat 10,000 people," I told her. "It will cost five million dollars and as I was praying about this matter, the Holy Spirit spoke to my heart and said that if I was to get the money for the church, I would have to start from my own household. God wants us to submit five loaves of bread and two fishes ... and those five loaves and two fishes are our house!"

My wife turned pale, and then looking straight into my eyes she said, "This home is mine, not yours. Don't you dare touch this house. It belongs to me and to my children. You cannot give this house up."

Her reaction was just as I had feared. Then I went to the Lord and prayed, "Lord, now I've done what I can. The rest is up to you. Send your Holy Spirit to prick her heart, so that she will surrender."

That night as I prayed, I could see my wife constantly turning and tossing in her sleep. I knew then that the Holy Spirit was working. I said to the Lord, "Oh, God, keep on nudging her."

And sure enough, the Lord nudged her; for almost a week she could not sleep, and her eyes became bloodshot. Finally she came to me, "I cannot stand it any longer. I cannot refuse what the Holy Spirit wants. I'll give up the house." So she brought the title deed for the house, and together we took that title deed and gave our home for the construction of the church. We were like Andrew, who though he had only five loaves and two fishes in his hand, had the faith that Jesus could take this small portion of food and feed an entire crowd. We, too, belonged to the school of Andrew.

One day, however, a problem about the land we planned to build on came up. The Korean government was developing a special piece of land called Yoido Island. This piece of property was going to be modeled after New York's Manhattan Island. They were building government buildings on the land and would allow only one church there. Church bids came from all over Korea: the Presbyterian, Methodist, Baptist, Catholic, Buddhist and Confucianists applied to the government. All were screened and passed through Congress for permission to build a church on this special land.

I also submitted an application. The man in charge looked at me and asked, "What denomination do you belong to?"

"The Assemblies of God," I replied.

"You mean that church where they shout praises to God in such a loud and noisy way? And pray for the sick and speak in strange tongues?"

"That's right," I responded.

He shook his head, "You know this church is going to be right in front of the new Congress Hall. This church has got to be dignified, and your church is not. We can't accept your application."

I was happy in my heart, however, because this would excuse me from building the church. I returned to the Lord in prayer, "Lord, you heard that, didn't you?" We are not dignified enough to build there."

You can bring every excuse you can think of to the Lord, but the Holy Spirit always has the answer. The Holy Spirit responded, saying, "When did I ask you to go and apply for a building permit?"

"Am I not supposed to?" I questioned.

"My child," He answered, "you should not follow the path you are now walking. You must walk the other way, the way of prayer and faith."

So I began to fast and pray. Then in my heart the wisdom of the Holy Spirit spoke, "Go and find who is in charge of developing that island."

I went and soon found that the city's vice mayor was in charge of developing the whole area. I began to ask about his personal home and life, and I found out that his mother was a member of a Presbyterian church. So I visited her, praying with her, and she became filled with the Holy Spirit. She then began to come to my church.

In Korea, the mother-in-law carries quite a bit of power and authority over the daughter-in-law. I told this woman to bring her daughter-in-law to church, telling her, "Your daughter-in-law has got to be saved."

So she prayed and I prayed, and she brought her son's wife to the church. After listening to the sermon she gave her heart to Christ and was filled with the Holy Spirit.

I then began to work through her, thinking to myself, "If I've got the wife, I know I can get to the husband." So I instructed her, "You've got to bring your husband to church."

"But he is so busy," she replied.

"You don't want him to go to hell, do you?" I sternly asked. "So bring him to church."

When eventually she brought him I preached a powerful message. Though I was not looking directly at his face, I was really preaching for him; and miraculously he gave his heart to the Lord.

The next Sunday he walked into my office. "Pastor, you know I'm in charge of the development of Yoido Island. We are permitting one Korean church to come and build there. I wish we could bring our church there."

I wanted to shout, but the Holy Spirit would not allow me to. Sometimes the Holy Spirit works in very mysterious ways; the Holy Spirit impressed my heart to say no, but I argued, "No. I've worked so hard for this." While my heart was crying to say yes, I replied, "No, Mr. Vice Mayor. To bring this church to Yoido would take an enormous amount of money, and we would have to buy at least three or four acres of land. That would cost more than five million dollars. I think it's impossible. To make matters worse, we are considered an undignified Pentecostal church, and they would not even accept my application."

He smiled and said, "I think I have a way. You pray for one week and then I'll come back. You can give me the answer then, because I can take care of it quickly."

For one week I prayed, and the next week he returned to my office. "Pastor, if you make the decision to move the church there, I'll make all the arrangements for you to have the choicest land. I'll also do all the paper work, with my own office paying the expenses. I'll send my man to Congress to get all the necessary agreements, and I'll do all the paper work for that, too. I'll do everything for you, and you will have the land. More than that, I'll make all the arrangements for you to buy the land by credit from the city government."

Then the Holy Spirit said in my heart, "SHOUT!"

"Mr. Vice Mayor," I said, "I accept."

God kept me from saying 'yes' for one week, and as a result we not only miraculously got the land, but were saved from doing all the paper work as well.

I then went and signed a contract with a construction company. Shortly afterwards they dug the foundation, and began the building of the church and apartment house complex. This Vice-Mayor is now one of the leading elders in my church.

In a similar way your faith is bound to be tested. If you have a small project, you will be tried in a small way; but if you have a big project, you will be tried in a big way. Never think that your faith will only travel through a field of roses. You will go through turbulence, by which God tests your faith.

So far in the building of the church I still belonged to the school of

Andrew, and with great faith prayed through each new problem.

But then the dollar devaluation came, and the contractor broke the contract. He said they wanted to renegotiate, and he increased the cost of building the church. Then the oil crisis came, and all the banks closed. My people began to lose their jobs, and even with my total income per month, I could hardly meet even the interest on the loans. Not only could I not pay my staff in the church, but I received no salary myself.

Then the company began to sue me because I could not pay the necessary increase. I would come to the church, and notice after notice came, filing suit: the electric company, the sewage company, the construction company. Papers were piled on my desk, yet I had no money to pay any of them. I didn't even have the money to hire my own lawyer. I would sit behind my desk, and one by one the workers in my church began to leave because I could not give them their salaries. Nobody wants to stay in a sinking boat, and I was sinking fast.

Since we had sold our home and had no place to go, I brought my family to an unfinished apartment on the seventh floor of the unfinished apartment complex. There was no running water and no heat, and it was very cold.

Each evening I would come home to the barren apartment, and all night we would shiver in the cold weather. We had no food, and everything seemed so dark. I was hitting rock bottom, and fast becoming a disciple of Philip. I said to myself, "Yes, I made a mistake. I should never have believed God in such a way. I should have thought in the traditional pattern. I should not have started to walk on the water. All this business about faith is a fake. All those voices that I heard in my prayer life must have been the voices of my own consciousness, and not from the Holy Spirit. Yes, I made a mistake." And I began to feel sorry for myself.

People were beginning to leave my church, and all reports were negative; my family even began to doubt me. Everything seemed impossible, and I was tired and hungry. "This is it," I said. "This is the end. This is the so-called life of faith. I am going to finish my life.

"I'm going to cast myself down," I continued. "I'm going to die. But I don't want to go to hell. I've been working for You all these years, and at least I should get something in return. If hell is worse than this place, why should I go there?

"But I can't live in the world like this. I am committing suicide, but please accept my soul and send me to heaven!"

The impact of prayer was more powerful than I realized, and as I prayed, I heard a voice saying, "You are a coward. You want to cast yourself down and become an object of ridicule for the people. Will you remain a coward? Or are you a man of faith?"

"Yes," I admitted, "I am a coward."

Again the voice spoke, "Not only will you go to hell, but you will also pull down many of your members who put their trust in you! You borrowed money from some of the elders and members. Remember the thousands of dollars you borrowed from the precious sisters in the church. They all put trust in you. And now you are throwing yourself down and committing suicide.

"You will cause a chain reaction. Because of your cowardice they will lose their faith. They will have broken homes, and some will also commit suicide. What a repercussion you will cause the Christian world to feel!"

These words poured into my heart. I slumped down crying, "Oh, God, then what can I do? Why won't you let me die?"

God replied, "You cannot die, for you must persevere. You must see all the debts paid; all the people's debts must be cleared."

I stood up, left the seventh floor and went to my office. I knelt down, travailing and crying. News of my desperate state began to spread among the people. Suddenly they experienced a reawakening of faith, including those who had already left the church. "Let's save our preacher!" they cried. "Let's save the man of God!"

In this way a Save Our Pastor movement began. It was a cold winter, and we had no heat, but by the thousands the people began to flock into the ground floor of the unfinished church, thousands also fasting and praying through many nights. They cried and prayed, "Save the man of God. Save our Pastor!"

Then God began to move. Ladies would cut their long hair, bringing it to the platform to make wigs that could be sold. One day, in an especially moving scene, an eighty year old woman who had no children, no support, barely living by the help of the government, came to the platform, crying and trembling. She brought an old banged-up rice bowl, a pair of chopsticks and a spoon. As she stood there crying she said, "Pastor, I want to see you delivered from this situation. I want to see you helped, for your ministry was such a great blessing to me for so many years. I want to do something, but I have no money. This is all I have— this old rice bowl, a pair of chopsticks and a spoon. But I want to give it all to the Lord's work. I can eat out of cardboard, and I can eat with my fingers."

My heart was broken. "Lady," I said, "I can't accept this. It's all you have! You need these to eat your everyday meals. I can't accept it."

She broke down in tears, saying, "Wouldn't God accept this gift from an old dying woman? Wouldn't He? I know that this can't be of much help to you, but I want to give something."

Suddenly one businessman stood up and spoke, "Pastor, I want to buy that." And he paid nearly $30,000 just for that old banged-up bowl, chopsticks and spoon.

This began to light a fire. People began selling their good houses and moving to small apartments. There were young couples who gave their whole year's salary to the church, deciding to live by faith.

This great movement brought results, for soon money began to flow in, and I could pay the interest on the loan. Banks began to open their doors to me, and amazingly, in less than a year everything began to work out. I paid all the debts, and was cleared until 1973. Not only was I able to pay the interest, but I also had the five million dollars to finish building the church and apartment complex.

And God again proved that the school of Andrew is best, and that to think in terms of miracles is to think as God would have us think.

Many people think that when you have faith, everything will flow easily, with few problems encountered. But it is important to remember that this is not so. Look at Abraham. He had faith, but he endured trials for 25 years; Jacob endured hardship for twenty years, Joseph for thirteen, Moses for forty, and the disciples of Christ passed through trials and temptations all their lives.

Do not be discouraged after going through a few weeks of difficulty or a few months of trial. Do not throw your hands up in defeat and cry, "Oh, where is God?"

God is always there, and He is testing you. Sometimes God wants to stiffen and strengthen your backbone; and sometimes while being strengthened you can almost hear the bones cracking. But if you stand on the Word of God and have faith, then God will never let you down. To illustrate this, I will relate another of my experiences.

I once wrote a $50,000 postdated check, payable December 31. I scraped money from every source available, but I was unable to gather even a small portion of the amount. If I could not put the money in the bank by the designated day, the newspapers would carry headlines saying that the pastor of the largest church in Korea wrote a hot check.

It was twelve noon of the day the money had to be in, and I was praying, "Oh, God, I've spent all my money, more than I had. I've borrowed money from many people. Father, where will I go? I've no place to go."

I continued praying. Then the clock struck one o'clock, then two o'clock, then three o'clock. My wife then called, "Honey, did you get the money yet?"

"No," I answered.

She said, "Don't you know that at four o'clock the last plane pulls out of Seoul? That's your chance to escape to America."

"I can't do that. I can't avoid my responsibilities," I told her, "I can't escape. And if I did, a smear would come to the name of Jesus Christ. I'd rather meet whatever happens here in Korea than to escape the country."

The bank was to close at six o'clock, and it was now five. I became desperate. I could not sit, and I could not stand; I just walked and walked, back and forth, like a lion in a cage. Again I prayed, "O God, please come and help me."

Suddenly the Holy Spirit let a thought flow through my mind. This thought was that I should go to the head of my bank and boldly ask him to write me a $50,000 check. "Father!" I responded. "I must be losing my mind. I've heated my mind's computer, and now it's become overloaded. I don't have anything to put up for mortgage. I have no paper work done. You want me to just go and ask him to write a $50,000 check? This is absolutely out of order!"

But the Holy Spirit insisted, "Yes, I do those things which are out of man's perceived natural order. You go and do it."

I called in my treasurer, "Mr. Park, would you go to the bank with me? I am going to ask the president of the bank to write me a $50,000 check."

He looked at me, then he began laughing, "You have really lost your mind, haven't you? This is December 31. It's five o'clock, you have no appointment, and people are lined up to see him.

"Moreover, we don't have any assets for collateral. No paper work has been done. It's foolish. I'm not going with you. If you want to go, go ahead; but I don't want to be a fool with you."

"Okay," I returned. "I am going with a renewed mind, whereas you are confined by a traditional mind."

I took the car and rushed to the bank. The parking lot was packed, but I managed to park, and I walked into the bank.

Humanly speaking, there was no way for me to meet the president. His secretary's office was filled with people. "Dear Holy Spirit," I said, "I've come this far. Please give me more instructions."

The Holy Spirit answered, "Walk courageously. Be very bold. Act like a big shot. Don't pay any attention to anyone else, but just walk straight through to the president's office."

So I straightened up, walking through. His secretary noticed me and asked, "Sir, where are you going?"

I looked right into her eyes, but said nothing. She again questioned, "Sir, who are you? Have you an appointment? Who are you?"

Suddenly an inspiration came to me. "I am from the highest authority," I responded. I meant I was sent from God, but she thought that I had been sent from the President of Korea, for in Korea the President is the highest authority. Thinking that I was a special emissary from the President, her attitude changed. She became polite, and ready to please. "You're from the highest authority?" she asked. "Yes, you may meet him." Then turning to the people waiting she said, "This man must go ahead."

She took me ahead of everyone else, straight through to the bank president's office. As I walked in I said, "Dear Holy Spirit, now I've gotten this far. What can I do now?" The Spirit of the Lord was upon me, and just as He had come upon other men of faith, I was made bold.

The Spirit kept repeating, "You are a child of the King, an important person. Keep acting like the big shot you are." So I boldly walked in, sat on the sofa and crossed my legs.

The president walked in, greeting me with a big smile, and extending his hand asked, "What kind of business do you have? For what purpose did you come? Do I know you?" I did not answer his questions, but instead said, "Sir, I've come here with a tremendous project, and I am going to do a great favor for you."

"A favor?" he queried.

"If you do a small favor for me, then I will give you 10,000 new banking accounts the beginning of this New Year," I told him.

"Ten thousand new bank accounts!" he exclaimed.

"Pick up the phone and call the police. Ask about the name Yonggi Cho, and you'll find that he is the pastor of the largest church in Seoul. He has more than 10,000 members, and also has great authority over his Christians. He can have all of them transfer their bank accounts to your bank for the New Year. I will do this tremendous favor for you if you do one for me."

He called his secretary right away to check what I said. All the facts cleared as true. He then asked, "What is this favor I could do for you?"

"You write me a $50,000 check," I told him. "I have no time to do all the legal paper work. But you are a businessman. I am the King's Businessman. Many times a businessman enters a huge undertaking with nothing but faith and confidence to show that he will succeed. Small business matters need to go through the law and paper work, but when we make a big deal, we bypass these things and trust that the deal will be successful. If you are a big businessman—and I think that you are—then you will do this for me."

The president called in his vice-president, and the vice-president said, "You can't do that. Your neck would really be on the line. It's not just $5,000. It's $50,000, and he has no collateral, no papers. You can't do it."

"If you won't do it," I interjected, "then I have other places I could go. I could do this favor for the Cho Heung Bank.

The man sat down and shook his head. Then he said, "Sir, I feel funny. I've never felt this kind of emotion before in my life. I trust you. If I didn't trust you so much I would never do this. But I kind of like you; you are a bold person, and I like your faith. I'll be putting my whole career and life in your hands by doing this, and after this I'll never do it again; but this time I'll stick my neck out. Bring me a $50,000 check," he instructed his vice-president. "I trust you to keep your promise," he told me as he wrote out a check for $50,000 from his own personal savings.

As I walked out of the office with the check, I felt ten feet tall. Once again I was in the school of Andrew. I turned in the money just as the bank was closing at six o'clock, and I was saved.

Many times God waits until the last moment. Once you renew your mind and once you learn how to walk with God, then you must persist to the last moment. Do not be frightened.

Renew your thinking life. Do not be confined by traditional thinking, but study the Word of God. This is the textbook with which you can renew your mind, and fill your mind with positive thinking, and learn to think in terms of miracles.

ORIENT YOUR MIND TO GOD'S SUCCESS

The third step to a renewed mind is a mind filled with an orientation to success. You must permeate your mind with a victory consciousness, and an abundance consciousness. God never fails. So if it is God's thoughts you are receiving, you will always be successful.

God never loses a war, for He is the eternal victor; you should have victory consciousness. God never lacks for anything; you should have abundance consciousness.

This consciousness is important. If you have inferiority consciousness, poverty consciousness, sickness consciousness, or failure consciousness, God can never work.

God is your help, God is your abundance, God is your success, and God is your victory. If two men do not agree, how can they work together? So to walk and work with God, you must engraft God's types of consciousness to your own.

Renew your mind. Constantly think in terms of success, in terms of victory, and in terms of abundance. When you have completely renewed your thinking process, then you will receive the *rhema* of God. Boldly assimilate the Word of God into your thinking life. Through prayer produce faith, and through faith you will be able to lift your chin up high.

Look only to the Lord. Even though you may not feel anything, even though you may not touch anything, and even though your future looks like a pitch-dark night, do not be afraid. You are living by revelation knowledge. You are living with new thoughts, the thoughts of God, and the thoughts of His Word, the Bible.

Jesus Christ is the same yesterday, today and forever. Jehovah God never changes, and the Word of God never falls on the ground without being fulfilled.

We cannot live by bread alone, but by the Word of God. We are the righteous children of God, and we must live by faith. In Jesus Christ there is no difference, whether one is black or white, yellow or red, for we all belong to one race, the race of Jesus Christ. And we live by His thinking. So renew your mind and retrain your thought life.

Think big. Have big objectives. You have only one life to live, so do not grovel around in the dust, living with a failure consciousness. Your life is precious to the Lord, and you must contribute something to this world. Jesus Christ dwells with glory in every Christian. You have therefore an endless resource in your life.

Christ is as powerful as He was two thousand years ago. You can renew your thinking by engrafting the thoughts of Jesus Christ into your heart, by thinking positively, by thinking in terms of miracles, and by developing a success orientation of victory and abundance consciousness. This provides a foundation from which you can see the Word of God in your mind, renewing it completely. You will then see great miracles occur.

THE LAW OF THINKING-ASKING

Ephesians 3:20 reads, "Now unto Him that is able to do exceeding abundantly above all that we ask or think, according to the power that worketh in us." I call this principle the law of thinking-asking. Many people think that they will receive just by asking. The Bible, however, says "ask or think." God gives answers through your thought life, "exceeding abundantly above all that we ask or think."

What do you think? Do you think poverty? Do you think sickness? Do you think impossibility? Do you think negatively? Do you think failure? If you pray this way God has no channel through which to flow.

What is your thinking life like? Have you renewed your thought life? God is going to do exceeding abundantly, according to the renewal of your thinking life.

You must read the Bible. But do not read the Bible for religious pretenses; do not read the Bible to seek out new legalistic rules for living; do not read the Bible for historical purposes. Rather, read the Bible to feed your mind and to renew your thinking life. Fill your thinking with the Word of God. Then God can have a free approach to your life and flow out to do mighty things for the glory of God through you.

CHAPTER 6

God's Address

When we become Christians not only do we need to retrain our thought life through thinking positively, thinking in terms of miracles and developing an orientation to success; we also need to be aware of our source of power and enablement.

THE CONFUSION

In 1958 I went on my first pioneering work in the worst slum area of our city. But I was not equipped or trained for that kind of ministry. In less than three months all my sermons ran out, and after three months I had nothing to preach.

You may easily say that you will go out and tell the story of salvation, but you cannot speak of salvation only, day in and day out. To make one sermon I spent one entire week going from Genesis to Revelation, and I had the summaries of all the books of the Bible, but I had not one sermon. I almost felt that I was not called into the ministry because I could not make any more sermons.

The poor people in my area were not too concerned about heaven or hell; they lived from hand to mouth each day, and their concern was with everyday survival. They had no time to think of their future. Wherever I went they asked me to help them with rice, or clothes, or some money to build a shack to live under. But I was no better off than they, as I, too, was living under a shack, going without food, and owning only one suit. So I had nothing to give to them.

I was in a discouraging situation, and though I knew that God had all resources, in those days I did not know how to touch the Lord and tap those resources. There were times I felt that I was near to the Lord, and I felt I was touching Him; but the next day it seemed I was completely out of touch.

So many times I was confused and wondered whether I was really living in the Holy Spirit. Many a time I would say, "O Lord, I know that I am in Jesus Christ." But after having a difficult day, in the evening when I tried to pray I would find that I was completely out of touch with Him. So I would say, "Father, I am confused. I am so much in and out of Thy Person that I do not know how to always keep You by my side." Then my struggle to find the permanent presence of God began.

Oriental people in particular require the address and location of the god they worship. Most Oriental people grow up under the influence of heathen worship, and they need the location or address of their god in order to go and worship it. When I needed my god in heathenism, I would go to a temple and kneel down before an idol, so I could address myself to him directly. In heathenism one has the address of his or her god or gods.

But when I came to Christianity I could not locate the address of our God. That was always great trouble to my heart. In the Lord's prayer we say, "Heavenly Father." I would reason, "Where is heaven?" Well, since the earth is round, for the people living on top, heaven is above them; but for those people who are living on the bottom, heaven is below."

So whenever "Heavenly Father" was mentioned, I was confused. "Father, where are you?" I would ask. "Are you there? Here? Where? Father, please give me your address!"

Therefore, when Orientals come to Christianity they have a real struggle, because they cannot find the address of God. Many would come to me and ask, "Pastor Cho, give us at least some picture, or even an image, to address to. You ask us to believe in God, but where is He?"

In the first portion of my ministry I would reply to them, "Just speak to the Heavenly Father. I don't know His address or location. Sometimes He comes to me, and other times He doesn't."

I would often cry to Him, for I could not keep on preaching like that. I needed to have a definite address. So I started seeking the address of our God.

In my imagination I went to Adam and I said, "Mr. Adam, I am sure that you are our forefather. I know that you know the address. Please tell me the address of our Heavenly Father."

Then he would very gladly tell me, saying, "Well, He dwelleth in the Garden of Eden. If you go there you will find the location of the Father."

"When you fell from grace," I asked, "you were removed from the Garden of Eden. What is the address of it?"

Adam replied, "Well, I guess I don't know."

I then decided in my imagination to visit Abraham. I was

discouraged but I came to Abraham and said, "Mr. Abraham, you are a father of faith, and you met God often. Will you please tell me the address of our Father?"

Abraham replied, "Well, whenever I needed God I put up an altar and I killed an animal, and I waited upon Him. Sometimes He would meet me, and other times He wouldn't. So I don't know His address."

Then I left Abraham and came to Moses and said, "Mr. Moses, surely you know the address of God the Father. You had His presence continually."

"Of course I know Him," Moses replied. "He was in the tabernacle built in the wilderness. During the day He was in the pillar of cloud, and in the night He was in the pillar of fire. You go there and you will meet God. God's address is there."

"But," I said, "when the Israelites came into the land of Canaan, the tabernacle of the wilderness disappeared. Where is the tabernacle of the wilderness?"

"I don't know now," Moses answered.

Again discouraged, I came to King Solomon. I said, "King Solomon, you built a magnificent temple with colorful granite stones. Do you know God's address now?"

"Of course. God dwells in the wonderful temple of Solomon," he told me. "When a curse or sickness spread in my country, the people would pray to the God who dwelled in the temple, and God would listen to them and answer their prayers."

"Where is the temple?" I. asked. "That temple was destroyed six hundred years before Christ by the Babylonians. We don't have the address of that temple now."

"Well, I'm sorry," Solomon returned. "That temple was destroyed, and now I don't know the address."

Then I went to John the Baptist. I said, "Mr. John the Baptist, surely you know the address of God."

"Yes," John replied. "Look at the Lamb of God who carried away the sins of the world, Jesus Christ. He is the address of our God."

So in my journey to find the address of God I came to Jesus. Surely in Jesus I would find God. Through Jesus God spoke, and through the one and only Son He performed miracles. Wherever Jesus dwelt, there God also dwelt.

I rejoiced in my heart to find the address of God. Yet still a great question came into my heart. Jesus died, was resurrected and ascended into heaven; so where is the address of Jesus Christ? Once again then, I came all the way back to the starting point. I asked, "Jesus, where are you? I don't know your address and I can't tell my people your location."

THE SOLUTION

Then the answer came. Jesus said, "I died and I am resurrected. I have sent the Holy Spirit to each and every one of my followers. I told you that I would never leave you as an orphan. I told you that I would pray to the Father and He would send the Holy Spirit to you, and in that day you would know that I am in the Father; the Father in me, I in you, and you in me."

Gradually I began to see that through the Holy Spirit, God the Father and God the Son dwelt right in me. I read in II Corinthians that God sealed us and sent His Holy Spirit right into our own hearts. I found the address of God. I found that His address is my address.

I then went out to my Christians and began to boldly preach to them, "We can find the location of God. I have now found His address. His address is my address and He dwelleth in me with all power and authority. Through the Holy Spirit God the Father and God the Son dwelleth in me, and He goes with me where I go.

"He also dwells within you, and His address is your address. If you stay in your home, He is there; if you go to your place of business, He is there; if you work in the kitchen, He is there. God dwelleth within you, and His resources are found in you.

"Brethren," I would continue on, "silver and gold have I none. Food, rice and clothes have I none, but I have something to give you. God dwells within you. Those of you who have not, come to Jesus Christ, receive Him as your personal Savior; and the Creator of heaven and earth, with all of His resources, is going to dwell within your heart. He is going to supply your every need." Hearing this message they began to develop their faith.

That was the starting point of my ministry, and the foundation stone of my preaching life. Up until that time I was trying to catch God from this place to that. When famous evangelists would come, I would rush to hear them in order to catch God. Sometimes I would go to a mountain to pray, sometimes to a valley. I searched everywhere to find God, but after finding this truth I wandered no more. I had found the address and the location of God.

I say to my people, "God is not a million miles away; He is not God of two thousand years ago; He is not just God of the future. Your

God dwelleth in you with all His resources, power and authority; His address is in you. So you can talk and pray to Him everyday, and at any time. You can touch Him and tap His resources through prayer and faith. When you cry aloud, God listens. When you speak softly, God listens. When you meditate, God still hears, for He dwells within you, and He can supply all your needs."

After the Korean war, when the missionaries came out to work for the Lord, I used to attend executive committee meetings. There, most of the Korean ministers would introduce all kinds of different projects, such as the construction of churches or the operation of the Bible colleges, and among themselves, discuss the various ways they could bring solutions. But when the problem of finance came up, immediately they would say, "Let a missionary come and take over." They used the missionary just as financier.

I became aggravated in my heart and would ask, "Why do you always turn to the missionaries?"

They would reply "God only supplies through the missionary, not through us."

However, from the time I graduated from Bible school I was determined to make God my absolute resource. I found that my God was dwelling in my heart, with all the needed resources. I discovered how to tap God's resources, and all through these twenty years of ministry I have never depended upon any other.

I have crossed over the Pacific Ocean more than forty times to minister in foreign countries, and I have never asked for a penny from a single church. I would express appreciation for the sending of missionaries to Korea, but I have never asked for financial help from foreign churches.

I depended upon God every time; through thick and thin He has supplied all my needs: building the church, sending out missionaries from my church to other countries, and building the Bible college.

Right now we are in the process of building our new Korean Assemblies of God Bible College, and we are giving half a million dollars from my church. God indeed supplies all our needs.

THE CHALLENGE

I want to impress upon your heart the fact that you have the resources you need within you right now—not tomorrow, not yesterday, but right now; you have all of God dwelling within you. God is not there sleeping. God never came just to put up a tent and enjoy a vacation. God is there to work out your salvation. And God never works without coming through your thinking, without coming through your vision, without coming through your faith. You are the channel.

You can say, "O God, please work mysteriously in the universe and do all things." God will reply, "No! I am dwelling within you. I will never come out to the world with power, without coming through your life."

You are the channel. You have all the responsibility. If you do not develop your way of believing to cooperate with God, God will be limited. God is as large as you allow Him to be; He is also as small as you confine Him to be.

When sinners come to the Lord, broken and unhappy, I teach them first that God is dwelling within them and that they have all resources in Jesus Christ. Then I reeducate them to develop their hearts for cooperation with God. One by one, without exception, they strike out with new faith and lead a miraculous, victorious life.

If these people were all poverty-stricken and filled with failure, how is it that they have given more than twenty million dollars to their church from 1969 to 1977? Every year we carry out projects costing from one and a half to two million dollars. These members can give because they have been enriched, and they are tremendous successes because they know how to tap the Resource. But first they must be cleansed of sins of the flesh.

Most people are at war with four sins of the flesh that should be conquered before the Christian can work actively with God. Without ridding themselves of these sins their channels will be so clogged that God would have no opportunity to flow through them. These are four things I have discovered as a result of twenty years of counseling people.

THE SIN OF HATRED

People suffer because of hatred, the first sin we will discuss. If you keep hatred in your heart you can never have God flowing through you. But that hatred, that unforgiving spirit, will be the number one enemy to your faith life. In Matthew 6:14-15, Christ Jesus pointed this out, "For if ye forgive men their trespasses, your heavenly Father will also forgive you: But if ye forgive not men their trespasses, neither will your Father forgive your trespasses."

Usually because I am so tired I do not meet anyone after preaching the fourth multiple Sunday morning service. But if someone does come to my door he must first come through my secretaries, who carefully screen people. If someone does successfully reach my door, then he must be in great need.

One day, after the fourth service a man knocked on the door of my office.

I opened the door and this man came into the room. I thought he might be drunk, for he walked with such a staggering step. He sat down and pulled something from his pocket. It was a sharp dagger, and I was frightened. I thought, "What are these girls doing letting him in here? Here he is with a dagger, and they let him in."

I was really frightened, and as he handled the dagger I prepared to defend myself. I then said, "Don't use that knife. Tell me why you came in here."

He replied, "Sir, I'm going to commit suicide. But first I'm going to kill my wife, my father-in-law, my mother-in-law and everybody around me. My friend advised me to come and attend one of your services before I do all these things, so I came and attended the fourth service. I listened intently but I couldn't understand one word, because you were speaking with such a strong Southern provincial accent. I couldn't understand your accent, and I couldn't catch any of your words. So after listening to you, I am going to go and carry out all of my plans.

"I am a dying man. I have tuberculosis, and I am constantly coughing. I am dying."

"Calm down," I urged him. "Sit here and tell me your story."

"Well," he replied, "during the last stage of the Vietnamese War I went out as a technician and bulldozer driver. I worked all through the front lines making bunkers and roads, risking my life in order to make more money. I sent all the money to my wife, and when the war was over I had scarcely enough to come out of Vietnam.

"I sent a telegram from Hong Kong to my wife, and when I arrived at Seoul Airport I was expecting to see her with our children; but when I got there I couldn't find even a shadow of them. I thought that perhaps they hadn't received my telegram, but when I rushed home I found strangers living there.

"I found out that my wife had run away with a young man. She had left me, taking all of my savings, and was running away with another man, and was living in another part of town. I went to her and begged her to come back to me; but she was adamant, determined not to return.

"I went to my wife's father and mother's home and protested. They gave me $40 and then chased me out of their house. In less than a week I had a burning hatred in my heart, and I began to vomit blood. Now tuberculosis is fast eating me away, and there is no hope for me. I am going to destroy them, every one of them, and then I am going to kill myself."

"Sir," I told him, "this is not the way to carry out your revenge. The best way to get yourself healed is to find a new job, make a better and more beautiful home, and show yourself off to them. In this way you can really carry out your revenge; but if you kill all of them and then kill yourself, it would not bring any satisfaction."

"I hate them," he cried.

"So long as you hate them you are going to destroy yourself," I said. "When you hate you destroy yourself more than you do others.

"Why don't you try Jesus?" I asked. "When Jesus comes into your heart all the power of God comes and dwells within you. The power of God will flow through you. God will touch you, heal you, and restore your life. You can reconstruct your life, and that would be real revenge against your enemies."

I sent him to Prayer Mountain, where he accepted Jesus Christ as his personal Savior. But still he could not totally forgive his wife. So I asked him to bless his wife, "The best way of forgiving your wife is to bless her: bless her spirit, soul, body and life. Pray to God that He will open the door of heaven with blessings for her."

"I can't bless her!" he exclaimed. "I will not curse her, but I cannot bless her."

I answered, "If you don't bless her, you are not going to be healed. When you bless, the blessings start from you and go out; you are going to be more blessed by your words of blessing than she is. In Korea there is an old saying, "If you want to smear the face of others with mire, you will have to smear your hand first.' So if you curse your wife, the curse will flow out of your mouth first, and you will be cursed first. But if you bless your wife, the word of blessing bubbles up from your heart, going through your mouth, and you become blessed first. So go ahead and bless her."

He sat down and began to bless her, at first while grinding his teeth. He prayed, "O God, I bless... my wife. Bless... her. And ... give her salvation. O God, give her ... a blessing."

He kept on blessing her, and in less than a month he was completely healed from tuberculosis and a changed person. The power of God began flowing out of him, and his face shone.

When I met him after a month he excitedly said, "Oh, Pastor Cho, I rejoice in the Lord! I praise God that now I really appreciate my wife, for it was because she left me that I found Jesus. I pray for her every day. I have renewed my license as a bulldozer driver. I have a new job, I'm making a new home, and I'm waiting for my wife to come back."

This man was praising the Lord. He was reconstructing his life through the power of God which had begun to flow out of him. He was healed in spirit and body.

Without getting rid of your hatred you cannot really get in touch with the Lord. When you go out in the ministry you must help people to realize this.

One day a schoolteacher came to see me. A principal of a school, she was suffering from arthritis. She had gone to every hospital but could not be cured. I laid hands on her, prayed, rebuked, shouted—I did everything I could, but God did not touch her.

Many people had been healed in the church, but in spite of everything, she was not healed. Eventually I began to feel like giving up. But one day the Holy Spirit said, "Don't shout, pray and rebuke. I can't flow out of her because she hates her former husband."

I knew that she had been divorced ten years ago, but as she was sitting there I said, "Sister, please divorce your husband."

She looked at me and said, "Pastor, what do you mean, divorce my husband? I divorced him more than ten years ago."

"No, you didn't," I replied.

"Oh yes, I did!" she insisted.

"Yes," I replied, "of course you did—legally. But mentally you have never divorced him. Every morning you curse him. Every day you curse and hate him; in your imagination you have never divorced your husband. In your mind you are still living with him, and that hatred is destroying you and drying up your bones. Because of this your arthritis is incurable. No doctor could cure you."

She retorted, "Oh, but he did such harm. When I married him he never got a job. He used all my income. He messed up my life, then he left me to go with another woman. How could I love him?"

I replied, "Whether you love him or not is your business; but if you don't love him you are going to die from arthritis. The arthritis is going to be healed only by the power of God. The power of God will never fall down from the sky like a meteor and touch and heal you.

"No!" I continued, "God is dwelling within you, and He is going to well up from within you and heal you. But you hinder the flow of God's power with your hatred. Please begin to bless your husband. Bless your enemy and do good to him. Then you will grow to love him and create a channel through which God's Holy Spirit is going to flow and touch you."

She had the same struggle as the man with tuberculosis. Crying she said, "I can't love him. Pastor, please forgive me. I will not hate him, but I will not love him."

"You can't stop hating him if you don't positively love him," I replied. "Look at your husband in your imagination; touch him and tell him that you love him, and bless him."

Once again she struggled, so I led a prayer for her. She cried, gritting her teeth. But eventually she began to feel love for him, and praying she asked God to bless and save him and give every good thing to him. God's power started flowing in her, and she was touched. In less than three months she was delivered from her arthritis.

Yes, God is dwelling within you. But if you do not rid yourself of that archenemy hate, then God's power cannot flow through you.

THE SIN OF FEAR

Many people live under fear. It is our responsibility as Christians to help people rid themselves of this fear, the second sin in this group of four.

Once I had tuberculosis. I had tuberculosis because I was constantly living under the fear of tuberculosis. When I was a student in junior high school, one of the classes I went to had bottles of alcohol filled with bones and intestines. The sight of these bottles filled with bones and intestines frightened me.

One morning the biology teacher was teaching on the subject of tuberculosis. In those days there were no miracle drugs, and the teacher said if you ever had tuberculosis you would be dissipated, your insides looking like these bottles, the rest of your life.

He told of the dangers of tuberculosis, and at the close said, "There are people who are born with a tendency to have tuberculosis. Men with narrow shoulders and long necks seem more apt to catch tuberculosis."

All the students began to stretch their necks out like cranes, and in looking around I saw that I had the longest neck in the classroom. Right away I knew that I would get tuberculosis. Fear struck me; when I got back to my room, I stood before the mirror, looking at my neck all afternoon. Fear came into my heart, and every moment I lived under the grinding fear of tuberculosis.

When I turned 18 years old I did have tuberculosis. Like attracts like, and like produces like. If you have fear, the devil has an open channel through which to come and strike you; fear is negative faith. So, as I feared tuberculosis, I contracted tuberculosis, and as I vomited blood I said to myself, "Yes, this is exactly as I expected."

I read in a Korean medical journal that some doctors claim that many Korean people die habitually. I thought to myself, "How can people die from habit?" Then I read the article.

These non-Christian doctors wrote how strong a role fear plays in our lives. For example, a man's grandfather died from high blood pressure in his fifties, His son, when in his fifties, also died of a stroke. Now the grandson lives in fear of dying of a stroke.

When he reaches his fifties the moment he feels a dizziness in his head he thinks, "Oh, a stroke is coming. I am ready." If he feels something in his chest he waits momentarily for a stroke, each day living with this fear and expectancy. The fear creates this situation in his body, and soon he does die of a stroke.

Many women die because of the fear of cancer. One woman might say, "Well, my aunt died of cancer, and my mother died of cancer, so I'll probably die of cancer, too."

When she reaches an age similar to that of her aunt and mother at their deaths, she will feel any type of pain and say, "Oh, this is cancer. It certainly is coming now." Everyday she will wait, saying to herself that she is going to have cancer, repeating this thought over and over. It is in this way that the doctors said people were dying from habit. If a person has a specific fear, then the power of destruction begins to flow.

In 1969 when God asked me to move from my second church, I had 10,000 members with 12,000 regularly attending. I was happy, feeling good and satisfied. I had a good home, a wonderful wife, children, a beautiful car and even a chauffeur. I responded, "God, I am going to stay at this church until my black hair turns white."

But one day while I was praying in my office, the Holy Spirit came, "Cho, your time is up here. You must be ready to move."

"O Lord," I said. "Move? I already pioneered one church, and this is my second pioneer work. Do you want me to pioneer again? Why should I pioneer constantly? You are choosing the wrong person. Go to someone else," and I started arguing with God.

No one, however, should argue with God, for He is always right. Eventually God persuaded me, saying, "You go out and build a church which will seat 10,000, a church that will send out at least 500 missionaries."

"Father," I replied, "I can't do that. I'm scared to death of building a church like that."

But God said, "No, I've told you to go. Now go."

I calculated roughly with a contractor about costs. He told me that we needed two-and-a-half million dollars to build that size of church, another half million to purchase the land, and an additional two-and-one-half million to build an adjacent apartment complex. So I would need five-and-one-half million dollars.

The contractor asked me how much money I had. I told him I had $2,500. He looked blankly at me, shook his head, and did not even comment.

Then I went to a meeting of our church's elders and told them the plan. One elder said, "Pastor, how much money are you going to raise in America?"

"Not a penny," I answered.

Another elder asked, "How much money can you borrow from the American Bank?"

"Not one penny," I replied.

They said, "You are a good, genuine minister, but you're no businessman. You can't build a church and apartment house like that."

Then I called the 600 deacons together. And I told them the plan, but they immediately began to act like scared rabbits, as if I were levying a high tax on their lives.

I became discouraged. Full of fear, I came to the Lord, "Lord, you heard every word the elders and deacons said. They were all in agreement, so you've got to think this over again."

Then the Spirit spoke strongly in my heart, "Son, when did I ask you to go and talk with the elders and deacons?"

"Am I not supposed to?" I asked.

The Spirit answered, "I commanded you to build the church, not to discuss it. That's my command."

I lifted myself up and said, "Yes, if it's your command, then I will do it."

I went to City Hall and on credit bought four acres of expensive land located near Congress Hall, one of the choicest pieces of land in Korea. Then I went to the contractor and made a contract to build that church and apartment house complex, also on credit. I thought to myself, "They will build the church easily. I will trust God and see."

After the ground breaking service I went out to look around. I thought they would just dig a few yards down and put up the building. But there they were, digging as if they had to develop a lake, with dozens of bulldozers digging the earth.

I became crazy with fear. I asked, "Father, do you see how they're digging? And I have to pay for all this? Oh, I can't," and I was frozen with fear. My knees trembled and in my imagination I saw myself carried away in a prison van. I knelt down and prayed, "O God, what can I do? Where can I stand? Where are you? I know that you are the total Resource, and I put my trust in You."

When I prayed I could envision God's workings and I no longer had any fear; but when I opened my eyes and looked at the situation, again I became fearful. So for the duration of the construction I lived with my eyes closed more than I lived with my eyes open.

The same principle holds true in many situations. If you look at your circumstances with your physical eyes and live by your senses, Satan will destroy you with fear. But if you close your eyes and look to God, then you can believe.

There are two different kinds of knowledge—sensual knowledge and revaluation knowledge. We should live by the revelation knowledge found in Genesis to Revelation, not by our sensual knowledge.

We should instruct people to give up their fear of the environment and of their circumstances. If they do not, they cannot develop their faith nor can God flow through them. Ask them to surrender their fears to the Lord, and teach them to put their faith only in the Word of God.

THE SIN OF INFERIORITY

Many people live with inferiority complexes, and are constantly frustrated; this feeling of inferiority is the third problem area I will discuss.

If people feel that they are inferior because they live in a slum area, you cannot pull them out. Perhaps they failed in their businesses and have resigned themselves to being a failure. But so long as they have this attitude, you cannot help them. You must ask each to surrender his inferiority complex, and let himself be reconstructed by the love of God.

One day an older brother of elementary school age killed his younger brother with a knife. This became a sensational news topic. It was found that the parents had loved the younger son very much, constantly praising him in the presence of his older brother; eventually the older brother began to feel inferior. One day when his parents were out, his younger brother came back from school, and the elder brother killed him. An inferiority complex is very destructive.

I once suffered with an inferiority complex. After two years in my first pioneer work, my church was progressively growing; but it was a loud church, a true Pentecostal church. People were filled with the Holy Spirit and many were healed. One day the Executive Committee of my denomination called me. At that time they stood somewhere between the expressive Pentecostal and the staid Presbyterian.

They questioned me, "Are you really praying for the sick and getting the people to shout and speak in other tongues in your services?"

"Yes," I replied.

"You are a fanatic," they asserted.

"I am not a fanatic. I am doing everything according to biblical teaching," I defended.

After discussing this, they took my ministerial license and sent me out. I was chased out of my own denomination. Afterwards missionary John Hurston came and took me back.

When I was cast out I was struck with feelings of inferiority. That inferiority complex brought about a feeling of destruction in me, and I had a difficult time struggling out of that situation.

At the time the members of the Executive Committee put me out, however, they did not realize I was one day to be General Superintendent of that same denomination. That is a post I held until recently. When I first came to that responsibility, we had only 2,000 members. By applying the laws of faith and teaching them to the pastors, we experienced rapid growth. By the time I resigned from that position our census revealed that the denomination had a total of 300 churches with more than 200,000 members.

We must deal with those who feel that they are unable to conquer life. We must pull them out of their depression and pessimism, build them up in the love of Jesus Christ and impart faith to them, telling them that nothing is impossible to the person who believes.

We must heal them and train them, and by and by they are going to pull out of their inferiority feelings.

One Sunday morning as I was preaching at the second worship service, I saw a man I knew was mentally sick, brought in with his hands and feet bound. That particular day we were making pledges for the fifth stage of our building plans. Many people were filling in pledge cards; when a pledge card came to this man, he wrote in $100 with his bound hand.

His wife laughed when the deacon came to take the pledge card. "Don't believe him," she said. "He's crazy."

But after the service when I met him, he was completely healed by the power of the Holy Spirit, having returned again to his right mind. He had been deeply suffering from an inferiority complex. He explained, "I had a fertilizer factory, and I failed and went heavily into debt. I worried so much I lost my mind. Then they took me to an institution and gave me all kinds of electric shock treatments; but I couldn't be cured.

"But as I was sitting there listening to your words, I suddenly came out of my state of sickness and recognized reality. I've lost my friends, my prestige, and my credit. I have a mountain of debts. I can do nothing. I am nothing."

"You are something," I told him. "You are not inferior. You came to Jesus, and now all of the power of Christ and all His resources dwell within you. You are going to be used by God. You are not inferior, for you are God's man. Stand victoriously. You have all power and resources dwelling within you, just waiting to be tapped."

"What kind of job am I going to have?" he questioned me.

"I don't know," I replied, "but keep on reading the Bible, and pray."

One day he returned, filled with excitement. "Pastor, I read the verse of Scripture that says we are the salt of the world. How about my going into the retail business of selling salt?"

"If you believe in it," I said, "go right ahead. Do it!"

So he went out, selling salt on a small scale. He paid tithes, paid his pledge and all the time was rejoicing in the Lord. God began to bless him, and his salt business grew and grew. Eventually he built a large storehouse right beside the river, where he placed $50,000 worth of salt.

But one summer night it rained heavily, and in the morning when I got up all the area had completely flooded. His storehouse also was flooded, and I was struck with fear. That afternoon when the rain stopped, I rushed out to his store.

Other articles and materials can still be found after a flood, but salt has a great friendship with water. When I entered the storehouse there was no salt left. The man, now an elder in the church, was sitting in the middle of his warehouse, singing and praising God. I walked in, trying to discern whether or not he was in his right mind. I went up to him and asked, "Are you okay, or are you crazy?"

"Pastor, I'm the real me," he smiled. "I'm not crazy. Don't worry. I've lost everything. God took it away; but as you always told me, I have all the resources here. Water could take away my salt, but water can't take away the total resources of the presence of God dwelling within me. I can tap those resources again and again by prayer and faith. You wait. Give me time. I'll rebuild my business again."

He was not suffering from an inferiority complex then. He was full of confidence. Now he is a multimillionaire through his salt business. He also went into watch production and has his own company. He has accompanied me to Los Angeles, Vancouver and New York; he recently went to Europe.

His is just one example of how we can help rid people of their feelings of inferiority by stressing that they have all God's resources at their disposal to tap.

THE SIN OF GUILT

Many people also suffer from feelings of guilt, the fourth problem that needs to be overcome before the Christian can work actively with God; for as long as someone suffers from guilt, God can never flow through him. We need to help people rid themselves of their guilt feelings; we need to stress to them that when you feel that you are unworthy and full of guilt, then you can simply come to the Lord, and He will cleanse you.

One day I was in my office and a beautiful couple walked in. The man was quite a handsome person, and his wife very lovely. But even though this lovely wife was in her early thirties, she was emaciated, so emaciated she could hardly open her eyes.

Her husband said, "Pastor, my wife is dying. I've tried everything—psychology, psychiatry, and all the internal and external medicine imaginable. I'm a rich man. I've spent thousands and thousands of dollars on her, but the doctors could do nothing. Now they've given up hope. I have heard that you have really helped many people, and they have been healed."

I told him that this was true, and I looked at her, searching for the discernment and wisdom she needed in this situation. Silently I prayed, "Lord, she has come here. Now what can I do?"

Right away God's still, small voice spoke, "She is suffering from a psychosomatic sickness. This is not an organic sickness; this is a mental sickness."

I asked her husband to leave the room and said, "Lady, do you want to live? You need to live for your husband's sake, at least. If you were going to die you should have done so before, because now you have three children. If you die now, leaving your children with your husband, you'll really mess up his life. So sink or swim, you've got to live for your husband and your children."

"I would like to live," she told me.

"Then I can help you only on one condition. You must open up your past life," I answered.

She straightened up and with anger glaring in her eyes said, "Am I in a police station? Are you a dictator here? Why do you ask this? This is not an interrogation, and I don't have to open up my past."

"I can't help you, then," I replied. "If you persist like this, I am going to ask God to directly reveal the problem areas of your past."

She was frightened, and taking out a handkerchief from her purse she began to cry. After a long sigh she said, "Sir, I will open up my past life. But I don't think this is the trouble."

"Yes, it is," I said "This is the cause of your problem."

"My parents died when I was young, and I was practically raised in my elder sister's house. My sister was like a mother to me, and my brother-in-law like a father. They took care of me wonderfully, and I lived with them while attending junior high school, high school, and college.

"When I was in my third year of college my elder sister went into the hospital to give birth to her last child. During that time I took care of the home and children. Without recognizing what was happening, my brother-in-law and I fell in love with each other.

"I don't know what happened to me, but we fell into an immoral relationship; then guilt really struck into my heart. From that moment on I was dying from guilt. But my brother-in-law would keep calling me from his office, and we would constantly meet at motels, hotels and resort areas.

"I went to the hospital and had several abortions, and even then I could not refuse the requests of my brother- in-law. I was scared to death of letting my sister know, so my brother-in-law continually intimidated me; I was slowly being destroyed.

"When I graduated from college I determined that I would marry the first man who proposed to me. I found a job, and the young man who is now my husband asked me to marry him, with no questions asked about my past; I accepted, just so I could get away from my brother-in-law. I married him, and in time he became quite prosperous. He resigned from his former work and began his own business. Now he is well off. We have a good home, money—everything.

"But since that time with my brother-in-law, I have been suffering from these strong feelings of guilt. Whenever my husband makes love to me I feel like a prostitute, for I have no right to receive his love; inside I am torn and crying. My children are like angels, and they come and hug me, saying, 'Mama!' And I hate myself. I know that I am a prostitute. I am not worthy to receive this kind of love from my children. I don't like to look at my face in the mirror. That is the reason I can't attire myself in the proper way. I've lost my taste for food and have no happiness or joy in my heart."

"You must forgive yourself," I told her. "I have good news for you. Jesus Christ came and died for you and your sins on the cross."

"Not even Jesus can forgive my sins," she cried. "My sins are too great and too deep to be forgiven. I've done everything. Everyone else can be forgiven, but not me! I deceived my sister, and I can't confess what I've done to her. That would mean breaking up her whole life."

Silently I wondered, "O Lord, how can I help her now? You've got to help me." Then I listened for a still, small voice within my heart and suddenly got an idea.

"Sister, close your eyes," I instructed her, also doing the same thing myself. "Let's go to a very silent and beautiful lake. Now you and I are sitting beside the lake, and there are many pebbles. In my hand I hold a very small pebble. You please pick up a big rock. Let's throw this pebble and this rock into the lake.

"First it's my turn. I take hold of the pebble and cast it in. Did you hear the sound it made? A ripple. Where is my pebble now?"

She answered, "Well, it went down to the bottom of the lake."

"Right," I replied. "Now it's your turn. Cast your rock in. Yes, you cast it in … okay, now that you've cast it in, did it make a light noise?"

"No," she asserted, "it made a big sound, and a large ripple."

"But where is your rock?" I asked.

"Down at the bottom," she replied.

"Well, it seems that both my small pebble and your big rock went to the bottom when they were thrown. The only difference was the sound and ripple. Mine made a plop, yours made a boom. Mine made a small ripple, yours a large ripple. People go to hell with small sins just as well as big sins, for they are without Jesus Christ. And what is the difference? Sound and its influence on society. Everyone needs the forgiveness of Jesus Christ. The blood of Jesus cures all sins, big and little."

This touched her soul, and she woke to the truth. "Does that mean that my sins could be forgiven by God?"

"Of course," I replied.

She slumped in her chair and began to cry, shivering. I tried to encourage and cheer her, but she continued to cry and cry. Then I laid my hand on her and led her in the sinner's prayer.

Afterwards, when she lifted her face, I saw her eyes shining like the stars, and glory began to shine from her face. She stood up and exclaimed, "Pastor, I'm saved! All my burdens are lifted!"

I began to sing, and she began to dance. Before this time she had never danced for joy before the Lord, but this day she jumped and danced, making quite a bit of noise. Her husband heard the noise and rushed into the office. When she saw him she rushed to him and hugged his neck. She had never done that before, and her husband was unbelieving.

He asked, "What have you done to her?"

"God has performed a miracle!" I answered joyfully.

"You must give your whole heart to the Lord," I said, turning to his wife. "The Lord has done great things for you." She soon was rid entirely from her guilt; then the power of God welled up in her, and she was healed completely.

That couple now attend my church, and whenever I look at the face of that lady, I cannot help thinking of the love of Jesus Christ. Now she has no sickness and is completely healed; when she let go of her clogging sin of guilt, the power of God flowed forth.

Brothers and sisters in Christ, right now you have all God's power dwelling within you. You can tap that power for your tuition, your clothes, your books, your health, your business, everything! When you go out to preach the gospel you are not preaching a vague objective, a theory, philosophy, or human religion. You are actually teaching people how to tap endless resources. You are giving them Jesus, and through Jesus, God comes and dwells within our hearts.

Introduction

In 1978 I wrote the first volume of *The Fourth Dimension*. At that time, I knew the spiritual condition of North America, but I endeavored to soften the impact of the revolutionary principles which I stated. Since then, I have gone to America often and have developed a television ministry there. I also have become much more aware of the spiritual maturity of the Christian community in America. Therefore, I have written this second volume to share in more depth and with more updated examples the principles of success that have allowed me to lead the largest single congregation in the world which now comprises over 275,000 active members.

Some might not understand what I mean when speaking of the fourth dimension. Therefore, I will try to explain briefly my use of the term.

"Dimension" is a common word used in the disciplines of physics and mathematics. In mathematics, it is a term of measurement. For example, the term "one-dimensional" would be used to indicate the extension of a line. It also indicates that whatever has only one dimension has no thickness, only length. Two dimensions would indicate the properties or extension of a plane, having length and breadth. Three dimensions would indicate not only length and breadth but also depth or thickness. In physics there is another aspect to the measurement of physical phenomena. That is time.

Sir Isaac Newton is credited with the development of many great discoveries in the field of physics. He explained the movement of planets in their orbits by the law of gravity. However, he used only three dimensions in the development of his theories.

Einstein introduced the concept of time and space as another physical dimension. Some have called this the fourth dimension. Therefore, if I use the standard three-dimensional Newtonian cosmography, I would be correct in using the fourth dimension. If I used Einstein's view of the universe, I should call it the fifth dimension.

Feeling that the importance of the truths which I am about to share overshadow scientific technicalities and knowing that I have confidence in the reader to be aware of the differences in the systems previously stated, I will retain the title I originally used, *The Fourth Dimension*.

God originally created us as physical beings. Yet, having breathed the breath of life into Adam, He gave him the capacity to understand and communicate with God in another than the physical level. He could communicate in the dimension of spirit. "God is a Spirit. They that worship God, must worship Him in spirit and truth" (John 4:24).

In Genesis 2 we see that God took the lowest and mixed it with the highest to create man. He took earth and breathed into it the breath of divine life. Everything else God created by merely commanding it to be so. Yet, when it came to man, He physically formed man after His own likeness. Since the likeness of God is Christ (John 14:9), we were created after the image of Christ.

In Genesis 2:17, God told Adam that if he disobeyed His commands he would die. He disobeyed yet continued to live and beget children with his wife, Eve. Adam did not die physically; he only died spiritually. Nonetheless, that capacity for communicating with God and understanding spiritual dimensional reality continues to exist within man till this day. After a person is regenerated by the Holy Spirit, when he accepts Christ as his Savior, he is reactivated spiritually. He is born again.

As Christians we, therefore, must become aware of spiritual reality and familiarize ourselves with the fourth dimension so that we might be as comfortable in it as we are in the three dimensional plane in which we live.

Therefore, the fourth dimension is that plane of existence where God dwells, which exists in a greater reality than the three-dimensional plane that we are all familiar with. "The lesser is always contained in the greater." We must understand that the three dimensions of physical reality are contained in the greater plane of spirit. It is possible for us to know the length, breadth, and depth of the love of God as well as all other spiritual reality. The Holy Spirit has been given to us to guide us to this new reality we experience as Christians. It is with sincere trust and confidence in Him that we endeavor to share the truths and experiences which are outlined in this book.

Preface—My Story

I was born in the southern part of Korea during the Japanese occupation. I cannot express in this chapter the untold suffering that we experienced during that time in our history.

Korea is situated between Japan and China. This unfortunate geographical position has meant that we have been the battleground of many wars between these two nations. But these circumstances have developed an independent and proud people who are proud of their heritage and language, which have been in continual existence for more than five thousand years.

My father was a hard-working man and was also very religious. In fact, he was a leading Buddhist layman in our area. Buddhism is somewhat different in Korea and Japan than in Southern Asia. We practiced a more intellectually philosophical Buddhism.

Christianity received respect from the Korean people because of the way in which Christians suffered during World War II. Their patriotism and heroism was appreciated by all Korean people. Right after the war we began to start rebuilding our country. Many American missionaries came to help us and their assistance was never forgotten. But, not long after the war was over, the Russians encouraged the North Korean Communists to invade the South.

This was called the Korean Conflict by the United Nations and was even more devastating than World War II. After the war with the North, we were totally demoralized and impoverished.

It was during this time that I had to leave school and look for work so that I might be able to help my family financially. My only hope was for survival. Some say that this instinct is man's primary motivational force. This was true of me during this time. I took any job I could get just to be able to buy food. Sometimes I held several jobs in one single day. During a normal afternoon, while I was tutoring a junior high school student, I felt very sick. My chest was heaving convulsively, and I began to vomit blood. After bleeding profusely from my mouth and nostrils, I fainted and collapsed.

After an indeterminate period of time I regained consciousness and struggled to get home. My parents had to sell their precious possessions in order to take me to the hospital so that I could be diagnosed. It did not take the doctors long to diagnose the trouble. I bad advanced and terminal tuberculosis. I was now eighteen years old and dying. With no future or hope for cure, I was simply sent home to die. "You have three or four months to live," was the last thing the doctor told me as I was sent home.

"Why me?" I cried, as I lay on my straw mat in our tiny house. The calendar by my bed had only three months left on it. "Dear Buddha, won't you help me to get better and live?" I prayed daily. But nothing happened. Every day I felt weaker. I could only hope for a quick death as painless as possible. Then one day, I prayed a prayer that was to change my life. "O unknown God, if you exist, please help me. If you can give me my life back, I promise you that I will spend the rest of my days serving you and helping others."

Interestingly, there is a Korean word for the One God, *Hanna-neem.*
Hanna is our word for "one"; *neem* is a suffix used after any proper
noun which means, "honorable one." The Japanese don't have a
word like this in their vocabulary, so it is much more difficult for
them to conceive of a single, all-powerful God.

Paul states in the first chapter of Romans that God's truth is revealed
to all men. However, it is man's sinful nature that suppresses the
truth of God. Therefore, there is no excusing man's ignorance of
God and His laws. In preaching the gospel to those who are not
aware of the God of the Bible, we simply have to state the truth in
the power of the Holy Spirit. It is the Spirit's job to convince the
world of God's reality. There is no question in my mind that those
hours spent in silence and contemplation were not wasted. It did
not take me long to lose confidence in the Buddha and begin to
grope in the darkness of my knowledge for the true and living God
who has been revealed in Jesus Christ.

Not long after my prayer to the One, True and Living God, a
young lady came to visit me. The girl was in high school and she
came after school with a large book under her arm. "I want to speak
to you about Jesus Christ, Yonggi," she said. "Now you must listen
to me." "Thank you for coming, but as you know, I am a good
Buddhist. Since I am about to die, I would not consider changing
religions," I responded to her as kindly as I could. She did not know
how upset I really was.

"That's all right," she continued. "I am going to speak to you about
Jesus anyway." She then told me the life of Christ, His virgin birth,
His life, His death on the cross and His resurrection. Then she told
me how I could be saved by believing on Christ and accepting His
forgiveness for my sins.

151

I listened patiently to her strange story, but when she left I was relieved. The next day, after school, there she was again. Again she told me about the love of God for sinners like me and His ability to deliver me from all my sins and torments. Well, the only torment I was concerned about was the torment of tuberculosis. But I did not say much. I just listened patiently and hoped that she would leave and leave me alone with my misery.

The rest of the week I knew that, at about three o'clock in the afternoon, I would be receiving a visit from my high school missionary telling me the same story which I did not want to hear.

Finally, after I had heard her story over and over again, I lost my patience and told her to get lost. "Please, don't tell me any more. I'm sick and tired of your persistence and foolish stories; allow me to die in peace," I screamed in desperation.

I thought that my rudeness would drive her away. But she did not leave. Instead, she simply lowered her head by my bed and began to pray for me. Then she began to cry: "Please, Jesus, forgive him. He is sick, he does not mean what he is saying," she prayed, unable to hold back the tears. The sight of her kneeling and praying before me touched me very deeply. I could not understand why she would concern herself so much for me. Why should she love me enough to cry? Who is this God that she talks about so much that would send someone to spend every afternoon talking to me and sharing the concern that she shared? Could this girl's God be the God that I prayed to when I was begging for my life?

Suddenly, I felt a strange, tingling sensation. Goose bumps were all over my body. I was scared, confused, but also challenged. "Please stop crying," I begged as I touched her head. "I'm sorry I got so angry with you. I will become a Christian for your sake." With that, she looked up at me and began to smile. Although the tears were still flowing down her cheeks, they were no longer tears of sorrow but now they were tears of joy and happiness.

"I want you to take my most prized possession," she said softly as she handed me her Bible.

I bowed politely and thanked her, the pain now rushing again through my chest. Still in pain and now coughing convulsively, I turned to Genesis 1. "Oh no, I'm afraid with the severity of your sickness, you won't be able to get past the Old Testament," she said with great concern. "You better start at Matthew."

This was the first time I had ever held a Bible in my hand. I found it rather large and cumbersome. Yet, with her assistance, I found the Gospel of Matthew, the beginning of the New Testament.

As I began to read, I became quite disappointed.

"'Abraham begat Isaac,'" I thought to myself." What kind of religion is this?" Buddhism is quite systematic and logical. Its rituals are not hard to understand. This new religion was full of genealogy. I could not accept this kind of a boring religion. "I'm sorry, but I think this book reads too much like a telephone directory," I said politely as I handed her Bible back to her.

"Oh no. You can't do that," she said firmly. "Don't worry about all these Hebrew names right now. Later they will be a great blessing to you, but now read on." After she left, I began to read again through the Gospels. Although I was not challenged intellectually by the simple stories, I found myself drawn to the person of Jesus Christ.

In my terrible physical and emotional condition, I needed someone to guide me through to victory. I didn't need a new philosophy that would stimulate my mind. I needed someone who could touch my heart and my body. That someone has become the most important person in my life.

The more I read about Jesus, the more I loved Him. His compassion and love caused me to weep. How could this man suffer all of the pain of the cross for my sake?

Still struggling with pain, I knelt down as my young friend had done when she had cried over me. Then I uttered the words that would revolutionize my whole life and would affect my country: "Dear Jesus, please forgive me my sins. I am not worthy to belong to you. But if you can, accept me. I give myself to you. Please save me and heal me. Amen!" As I prayed I was unable to hold back the tears.

Suddenly, I felt clean. It was as if someone had given me a bath on the inside. I stood up and shouted, "Hallelujah! Thank you, God!"

After that experience, every morning I would pick up my Bible for breakfast and I would feast till dinner. I felt that I had to learn as much as possible, because this was God speaking directly to me. As a young man falls in love for the first time with a young lady, so I fell in love with Jesus Christ.

This love affair has intensified over the pasty twenty-nine years. Without anyone telling me, I knew I was going to live. After the pages of my calendar were gone, I was still alive. In six months, I was able to get out of my bed and I have not had trouble with tuberculosis since.

I then attended the Full Gospel Mission in Bilsan pastored

by Reverend L.P. Richard and enjoyed fellowship with other Christians. My parents were understanding and soon followed their son into a relationship with Jesus Christ.

After attending Bible school, I pioneered my first church in a very poor town outside Seoul. Building a strong congregation of about six hundred people, I felt that I could settle down and enjoy my ministry. But then God told me to resign my church, go into downtown Seoul and build another church. My second church grew to a congregation of eighteen thousand and became the largest church in Korea. In 1969, God spoke to me again to resign and move to Yoido Island. Yoido was a marshy island that was being developed as the new seat of government by a young and successful vice-mayor, Il-Suk Cha. At that time he was a deacon in my church. His mother, one of my best members, had brought this man to my church. He took a real interest in my ministry. We then developed a four-acre section of land near where the new congress building was planned. Through much suffering we built a church which seats ten thousand people and is now being expanded to seat twenty-five thousand. This auditorium and numerous chapels throughout the complex allow us to seat thirty thousand per service for seven services. Soon, with the addition and closed circuit television, we will be able to seat sixty-thousand people per service for seven services. However, by next year even this will be too small. At our present growth rate, we will still need seating capacity for another eighty thousand people per Sunday by 1984.

The past twenty-five years of ministry has taught me many things. In this book I will share the key to success in building the largest single congregation in the history of Christianity.

CHAPTER 7

The Holy Spirit and You

We are now living in the age of the Holy Spirit. We will never be able to accomplish our mission successfully in this world if we don't recognize His work.

The Old Testament described the time during which God the Father was in the foreground in the divine formative and creative work. The Father worked through the Holy Spirit, who used the prophets, priests and kings of Israel to accomplish His will. However, in the Old Testament, the prophets spoke about the coming of Jesus Christ, the Messiah, more than three hundred times. At His coming, our Lord Jesus Christ, the Son of God, became the central divine figure through which God spoke and accomplished His will. Although Jesus Christ always glorified the Father, He was still in the forefront, as was the divine plan. Yet the Holy Spirit was quietly working. For the miraculous ministry of Christ began after Christ was baptized and filled with the Holy Spirit. John the Baptist said of Christ, "I did not know Him, but He who sent me to baptize with water said to me, 'upon whom you see the Spirit descending and remaining on Him, this is He who baptizes with the Holy Spirit.' And I have seen and testified that this is the Son of God" (John 1:33, 34 NKJV).

After Christ's ministry was completed, by living an exemplary life, dying on the cross, and redeeming humanity from sin, He was resurrected and He ascended to the Father. Christ then gave the Holy Spirit His mission which is to both the world and the church.

Since the day of Pentecost, the Holy Spirit has been with us for nearly two thousand years. His presence is in the world, the church and inside every Christian. In this age of the Church, God the Father and God the Son has chosen to work through the Holy Spirit. This does not mean that I am trying to define the Trinity in too sharp a fashion-the Father, Son and the Holy Spirit are One God. Yet God is manifested in three Persons. The point that I am making is that this age is the age in which the Holy Spirit is in the forefront in His work in the earth.

If we as Christians desire to do the work of God, then this desire has been placed within us by the Holy Spirit. Yet, as a divine person, we must learn to come into a personal relationship with Him. We just cannot depend upon our theological knowledge of God. We must learn to know Him. As we grow in our consciousness of the Holy Spirit, we develop a fellowship (koinonia) with Him.

In order to better understand the person with whom we desire to have a relationship, we must know something about Him. Without learning about the Holy Spirit, we shall never be able to learn about the fourth dimension. For it is the Holy Spirit that brings us into fourth-dimensional living.

WHAT IS THE HOLY SPIRIT LIKE?

Since we have a clear record of God the Father sharing His thoughts with the prophets, priests and kings in the Old Testament, and because we can relate to what a father is, we can have a general idea of what the Father is like. Jesus also revealed the Father in His life and teaching. The Holy Spirit has come to reveal Christ: "He will glorify Me, for He will take of what is Mine and declare it to you" (John 16:14). Therefore, the Holy Spirit takes the record in the Scriptures concerning Christ and enlightens not only His teaching but also the Son's personality. Yet the Holy Spirit's personality is not clearly and consistently referred to in the Old and New Testaments. We mainly see His work, but because of His function as a glorifier of the Son, He does not point to himself.

Since the Holy Spirit never takes physical form in the scriptural record, we cannot describe His appearance. We can only know Him in terms of His characteristics in our souls and spirits. The only clue to a physical characteristic is found in Scripture when the Holy Spirit descended upon Jesus like a dove. The reason He chose the dove as a symbol of His presence is due to the dove's gentle nature. The Holy Spirit's gentleness is also understood when we realize that the only unpardonable sin is that of sinning against the Holy Spirit.

Paul alludes to the Holy Spirit's nature when he tells the Ephesians, "And do not grieve the Holy Spirit of God, by whom you were sealed for the day of redemption" (Eph. 4:30, NKJV). Since the Spirit is living the life of Christ within the Christian, He has been associated not only with our faith but also with our actions. Then Paul goes on to describe the actions that will grieve the Holy Spirit: "Let all bitterness, wrath, anger, clamor, and evil speaking be put away from you, with all malice" (Eph. 4:31, NKJV). In verse 32, Paul then describes the actions which are characteristic of the Holy Spirit's nature and which thus please Him: "And be kind to one another, tenderhearted, forgiving one another, just as God in Christ also forgave you." Paul also reveals how we are to live in such obedience that we do not quench the Holy Spirit. Interestingly, the source of God's dynamic power, who has the ability to form the earth and move mountains, can be limited by the Christian's disobedience.

The Lord Jesus calls the Holy Spirit the Spirit of Truth. We know, therefore, that the Holy Spirit is full of truth and that His function within us includes to lead and guide us into all truth. This is a part of His nature. He is also called the Spirit of Wisdom, the Spirit of Understanding, the Spirit of Knowledge, and the Spirit of Judgment. Therefore, the way we are enlightened is to have a relationship with the Holy Spirit, who will impart His nature to us. For it is true that we will become like the one we fellowship with.

THREE LEVELS OF RELATIONSHIP

Jesus told us that He would be with us, in us and upon us. Therefore there are three distinctive levels of relationship with the Holy Spirit.

1. The Holy Spirit is with us.

Since the Holy Spirit is the wind of God, we must understand how the Holy Spirit functions as God's wind (pneuma).

The metaphor of wind is used to describe the Holy Spirit because wind is felt and not seen. Wind can also be either powerful or gentle. The wind is also experienced everywhere in the world at the same time. Therefore the Holy Spirit is at work in accord with God's desires everywhere in the world. By sending the Holy Spirit, Jesus could break the limitations of having to be in one place at one time. Now, through the work of the Holy Spirit, He is able to effect His will and presence everywhere. We never need to look for the Holy Spirit; in fact, the Holy Spirit seeks us everywhere.

Since the Holy Spirit was sent to the world and not only to the Christian, we must understand the Holy Spirit's role in dealing with the world. Jesus said, "And when He has come, He will convict the world of sin, and of righteousness and of judgment; of sin, because they do not believe in Me; of righteousness, because I go to My Father and you see Me no more; of judgment, because the ruler of this world is judged" (John 16:8-11, NKJV). Therefore, the reason why we were convicted of our sins and desired to have Jesus Christ come into our lives as our personal savior is because the Holy Spirit was working with us. Jesus told His disciples that the Holy Spirit was with them, but in the new birth, He would be in them (John 14:17). Yet once we receive Jesus Christ as our personal Savior, we are washed by His blood and then we become ready for the Holy Spirit to move inside us.

2. The Holy Spirit is inside us.

The way we can accomplish the will of God is because the power to perform His will is within us, the Holy Spirit. "Then I will sprinkle clean water on you, and you shall be clean; I will cleanse you from all your filthiness and from all your idols. I will give you a new heart and put a new spirit within you; I will take the heart of stone out of your flesh and give you a heart of flesh. I will put My Spirit within you and cause you to walk in My statutes, and you will keep My judgments and do them. Then you shall dwell in the land that I gave to your fathers; you shall be My people, and I will be your God' (Ezek. NKJV). In this passage of Scripture, the prophet reveals the new covenant to His people. In the past, Israel had been given commandments and had been told to live according to them. But now the Lord would do a new thing. He would wash them clean and then place within His people a new heart, one that would desire to do His will. This would be accomplished by placing His Holy

Spirit within them so that He would live out His life through them. Of course, we realize that this was accomplished when Christ sent the Holy Spirit to His disciples and they experienced the new birth.

3. The Holy Spirit is upon us.

"But you shall receive power when the Holy Spirit is come upon you; and you shall be witnesses to Me in Jerusalem, and in all Judea and Samaria, and to the end of the earth" (Acts 1:8).

Luke tells us that Christ responded to the disciples' desire to have political power by telling them of a more important power they would receive after Pentecost. They would have the power to be witnesses. Their witness would not be limited to just the area they had grown familiar with, but would be unto the ends of the earth. This new power would be known after they had experienced the Holy Spirit coming upon them. This promise of divine power (*dunamos*) is also called experiencing the fullness of the Holy Spirit.

We therefore understand that the Holy Spirit comes to us on three different levels. He is with us (conviction of sin); He is in us (new birth) and He is upon us (in fullness).

By experiencing the Holy Spirit on these three levels, we can have not only a personal friendship with the Holy Spirit, but we can also learn to work together with Him. Can we be satisfied with just a judicial experience? No! Since the Holy Spirit is a person, He must be experienced in a personal way.

Jesus said that the Holy Spirit would not be a temporary comforter, but He would be with us forever; we can therefore spend the rest of our Christian lives with the third member of the Trinity, being changed into the image of Christ. *The Living Bible* states: "But we Christians have no veil over our faces; we can be mirrors that brightly reflect the glory of the Lord. As the Spirit of the Lord works within us, we become more and more like Him" (2 Cor. 3:18).

In a day full of theory and theology concerning God and His love, people are left cold in the pew because what they are taught has no experiential element. This experiential level only comes through fellowshiping with the Holy Spirit. How do we learn to fellowship and have intimate communion with the Holy Spirit? There are four steps I have followed in developing this relationship which has revolutionized my life and ministry:

1. The Development of *Koinonia* (Fellowship) with the Holy Spirit.

To have communion with a person we must have fellowship. To have fellowship we must share our feelings, knowledge or will together through expression in words. We cannot just keep our feelings of love in our minds, they must be shared. When we want to have a relationship with the Holy Spirit, we must learn how to adore Him and thank Him! We should learn how to pray in the Holy Spirit; we should welcome His presence and show our appreciation for Him. Without doing this we can never develop fellowship. As long as He is not recognized, He will not push himself on us because of His gentle nature. Yes, the Holy Spirit is a gentleman.

The New Testament church experienced the Holy Spirit in a dynamic way. "As they ministered to the Lord, and fasted, the Holy Ghost said, 'Separate me Barnabas and Saul for the work whereunto I have called them'" (Acts 13:2, KJV). It is obvious that the Holy Spirit was given the credit for speaking and calling men to labor in the new harvest fields.

Yes, the Holy Spirit, who is the Lord of the Harvest, chooses His laborers. That is the reason we should take the Holy Spirit as our supreme Lord of the Harvest in our churches and give Him the recognition He rightly deserves. He is the administrator of the love of God and the grace of the Lord Jesus Christ.

I have learned how to develop this fellowship in my life. In 1964, by God's direct intervention, I found out that I should develop a deep fellowship with the Holy Spirit. Up until that time I recognized the Holy Spirit only as an experience, but God sharply rebuked me because I had neglected fellowship with the Holy Spirit. Since then, I determined to have intimate fellowship with the Holy Spirit. Before going into a service, I began to say, "Dear Holy Spirit, let's go and preach." After getting to the meeting, I would dwell in His presence and, having been announced, I would say, "Now, Holy Spirit, this is the time to preach, so let us give forth the Word of God together." After my message, I would say, "Holy Spirit, you did a great job today. I was blessed by your word."

In my office, as I prepared my messages, I would say quietly, "Dear Holy Spirit, let's read this word you wrote together. Now please, open my eyes to see Thy truth so I may teach your people how to live." Before retiring, I would say, "Good night, Holy Spirit, we have had a great day together." The first thing that I would do when I woke up the next morning was to say, "Good morning, Holy Spirit, together we are going to bring the message of Jesus Christ to this lost and dying world. You cannot fail. Therefore, I cannot fail."

I did not just turn to the Holy Spirit in time of trouble, I learned how to walk in the Holy Spirit as a natural way of life.

2. The Development of Partnership with the Holy Spirit.

We must realize that we are to be in partnership with the Holy Spirit. We understand the concept of partnership in a business. When two or more people get together to form a business, they must have very close contact with each other. Not only must they have communion, but they must also be in business to make a profit. No one goes into business to lose money. If a business does not show a profit after a reasonable period of time, then it will go bankrupt.

We are in God's business. We are in business to make a profit, not in money, but in souls. There are many churches throughout the world that are not making a profit in God's business. Many churches are sitting nearly vacant, year after year.

On a recent trip through Europe I was amazed at some beautiful cathedrals that were sitting absolutely vacant. Some were being used as factories and warehouses. My heart was broken when I saw all these unused buildings that were once dedicated to God. I only wished I had some of those buildings in Korea. We would have them full of Christians.

The reason so much of God's work shows little or no profit is because of the partnership arrangement. I am convinced that there is no vineyard too hard, no field too barren, no area too difficult for the Holy Spirit to be successful.

When you are in partnership with the Holy Spirit, He brings all of the finances, all of the grace and all of the love into the partnership. After all, the Holy Spirit is the senior partner; we are only junior partners. The junior partner's responsibility is to listen to the senior partner. The senior partner makes the strategy and the junior partner carries it out.

The Apostle Paul is a prime example. Paul had been fervent in his desire to persecute the Christians, believing that they were a false sect of the Jewish faith. While on his way to imprison followers of Jesus Christ, he was arrested by the Lord. He then wanted to work for God. Luke reports: "And straightway he preached Christ in the synagogues, that he is the Son of God" (Acts 9:20, KJV).

The Jews, however, tried to kill him. So Paul disputed with the Gentiles, but they also tried to destroy him. So the church decided to send him back to Tarsus, his hometown.

After Paul had left the area, Luke says, "Then had the churches rest throughout all Judaea and Galilee and Samaria . . ." (Acts 9:31, KJV). Paul had desire and ability. He was also trained in religion and logic, yet more was needed for success than just ability and training. Paul had to learn to go into partnership with the Holy Spirit.

In Acts 16, we read of an experience Paul had which would completely revolutionize his life and ministry. After having a successful ministry throughout Asia Minor there arose a series of problems that could have caused Paul to give up. Yet out of the trial of his faith, God developed a new strategy for His ministry that has literally changed history.

Barnabas was not only his close friend and partner in the ministry, but he was also the man that caused Paul to be accepted by the other apostles in Jerusalem. He was a formerly wealthy man that had given all to the church and was willing to sacrifice everything for the work of God. Barnabas' nephew, John Mark, who would later write one of the four Gospels, was repentant regarding his past failure, when he had given up the ministry and left the apostolic team. Paul did not want to take John Mark on the new journey which would cover the same ground as before, but Barnabas was more forgiving. He wanted to give the young man another chance. The argument between Barnabas and Paul was so strong that they decided to part company and go their separate ways.

Paul then chose Timothy, who was half Greek, and went on what he thought was a regular trip to re-establish the same churches that had already been built. Paul had used prayer and logic in planning his itinerary, but the Holy Spirit had something much larger for Paul than he could ever imagine. Without Paul realizing it, Timothy was the perfect man for his future ministry to the Gentiles. Paul tried to return home by going the route through Asia, but the Holy Spirit forbade him. Then he decided that he should go to Bithynia, but the Holy Spirit said, "No!" So Paul went down to the coastal town of Troas, not knowing what to do next. Then the Holy Spirit showed Paul a vision of a European calling to him for help. Did the Holy Spirit want them to preach the gospel to heathen Europe? If the answer was yes, then it would be a great change in the apostolic strategy, yet part of the plan of God.

Through Europe, the gospel has come to America and the rest of the world.

Paul learned that he had to surrender his strategy to the Holy Spirit in a partnership arrangement in order for him to be successful in the King's business. We also must be trained to wait on the Holy Spirit and hear His voice. As the early apostles learned the secret of partnership with the Holy Spirit, they built the church successfully in the first two centuries. How can you see your life flourish successfully? By taking the Holy Spirit as your senior partner.

3. Transportation in the Holy Spirit.

It has been said that the progress of a civilization can be measured by the volume of its transportation system. This is the age of quick and massive transportation. Seemingly, the world has become smaller because we are now able to travel completely around the world at phenomenal speeds using the latest means of transportation.

I have discovered that in order for us to have a successful Christian life, we must learn how to have a transportation or "moving together" with the Holy Spirit. What is the Holy Spirit's transportation system? The Holy Spirit transports the love and grace of God to us and then takes our prayers and supplications and transports them back to God.

"Then another angel, having a golden censer, came and stood at the altar. And he was given much incense that he should offer it with the prayers of all the saints, and upon the golden altar which was before the throne. And the smoke of the incense, with the prayers of the saints, ascended before God from the angel's hand" (Rev. 8:3, 4, NKJV).

There are great obstacles to having prayers answered. Daniel discovered that prayers can be hindered by spiritual forces opposed to God. Yet the way to have prayers rise to God quickly without any hindrance is to have them anointed by the Holy Spirit. Without this anointing, prayers can be hindered, but nothing can stop the transportational system of the Holy Spirit.

"And hope maketh not ashamed because the love of God is shed abroad in our hearts by the Holy Ghost which is given unto us" (Rom. 5:5, KJV). Why are we not disappointed when our hope is in God? Because of the transportational system of the Holy Spirit which takes the love of God and fills our heart with it.

4. The Unity of the Holy Spirit.

We are joined with the Holy Spirit when we receive Jesus Christ as our personal Savior; therefore, we can no longer consider ourselves as individuals apart from the Holy Spirit. We should be aware of the Holy Spirit being an intimate part of us, and that we are one with Him . I like to think of our relationship with the Holy Spirit in very practical human terms: we are actually living with the Holy Spirit, sleeping together, awakening together, eating together, doing our work together, and praying together.

If we don't maintain this consciousness of being together with the Holy Spirit, then our work is empty and unfulfilled. We must remember that whatever we do, God is measuring the work we do for Him in a qualitative, not quantitative way. The fruit of our human flesh cannot be accepted in heavenly places. Only the work which is done by the power of the Holy Spirit can be acceptable in the Kingdom of God. Therefore, we must have a divine union with the Holy Spirit. If we desire that our fruit remain, or be lasting, we cannot forget that that fruit is the fruit of the Holy Spirit.

Now that we have studied the essential fact of learning how to live with the Holy Spirit, we can learn to use the principle of incubation.

INCUBATION

When we read Genesis, we find out a very interesting Scripture. Genesis 1:2 says, "And the earth was without form, and void; and darkness was upon the face of the deep. And the Spirit of God moved upon the face of the waters."

When the whole earth was in a state of chaos, the Spirit of the Lord was upon the water. The words "upon the waters" literally mean the Holy Spirit was "fluttering" over the water, or the Holy Spirit was "incubating" over the water. Another word with the same thought is the word "brooding." The whole world, previously in a state of chaos, was incubated by the Holy Spirit. Then the word of creation was given and a new world came into being.

To have a creatively victorious life, we must learn the principle of incubation. In order to understand this principle, we can look at a very simple example of the chicken and the egg. I am not interested in the proverbial question of which came first. No. I just want to point out the obvious fact that in order to have more chickens, one must have eggs. When a mother hen lays her eggs, she has to sit on them, or incubate them, so that the eggs will hatch and become baby chicks.

In Hebrews 11:1, we see how the Holy Spirit uses our cooperation for faith to be produced. "Faith is the substance of things hoped for, the evidence of things not seen."

There are four major points that we can learn that will help us in following the Holy Spirit's example in incubation. As we learn these points, our lives will be revolutionized. We will become more creative and imaginative.

1. In order for us to incubate, we must have a clear goal.

"Faith is the substance of *things* . . . ." In this verse, "things" is comparable to the egg which we previously mentioned. You cannot begin to incubate without having something you desire to see come to pass. You must have a clear-cut idea in your mind as your goal is before you. This idea must be one which the Holy Spirit has placed in your mind. This "egg" (thing) must fill your heart and imagination. Your heart has to be filled with the desire; the Holy Spirit will answer us based upon the desires of our hearts.

Just as we were in Christ, before the worlds were founded, God had a clear goal of why He wanted the Holy Spirit to incubate this world. He wanted us to inhabit this planet and fill it. He wanted the human race to glorify Him. He wanted this earth as a place where He could send His Son to redeem not only humanity, but all creation. This earth then becomes the central stage upon which the mighty power of God will work and will bring forth His glory to all creation.

May I ask you, the reader, a personal question at this time? What is the desire of your heart right now? Is your desire for someone in your family to come to Christ?

Then I need to ask you further how great that desire is. Are you moved to tears thinking about your son or daughter accepting Christ as Savior? Have you ever dreamed about your son having such fervency in God's love that he is actually winning others to Christ?

If your answer to this question is yes, then that desire has been placed there by the Holy Spirit. That desire is like an egg, ready to be incubated. Of course the example can work for any other desire placed within us by the Holy Spirit.

Jesus said, "Verily I say unto you, whosoever shall say to *this mountain* [a clearly defined objective-not any mountain, but *this* mountain] be thou removed and be thou cast into the sea, and shall not doubt in his heart but shall believe that those things which he says shall come to pass, he shall have *whatsoever* he *says*.'" Therefore, we should have a clear-cut goal when we pray, or when we incubate. Without this goal our prayers are aimless and the meditation in our heart will go nowhere.

I have learned this principle since the beginning of my life and ministry. I was in one of the poorest areas of Korea. I fasted and prayed, not because of my great spirituality but because I had nothing to eat. Being single at that time, I was living in a small room. The room was so cold during the winter that I had to wrap myself with blankets in order to stay alive. Yet people were getting saved in our little tent church.

In my small room, all I had was a bare floor. I had no desk, nor did I have a chair or means of transportation. So I began to pray for a desk and a chair and a bicycle. When I first started asking God for these items, I thought that immediately someone would open my door and give me the three items which I had ordered. Months went by and still nothing happened. During that time, I got very discouraged and told the Lord, "Dear Lord, you know how poor we are here. Yet I have told these people that they can have confidence in you to provide for their needs. Now, all I have been asking for is for you to give me three things that I really need. I have been asking and asking, but you have not given me anything. Perhaps you are going to take a long time to answer me; after all, time means nothing to you. But if you wait until I die, then I won't need a chair, desk and bicycle."

In my discouragement, I began to cry. Then the peace of God settled on me. (Whenever I sense His divine presence I know God is trying to speak to my heart.) I got very quiet and began to listen. As I settled my emotions and opened my spiritual ears, I heard the still, small voice of God: "My son, I heard your prayer when you first prayed four months ago."

"So where," I yelled out, "is my answer?"

"Your trouble, my son, is that you do what so many of my children do. When you give me your requests, they are so vague that I cannot answer them. Don't you realize that there are dozens of chairs, many kinds of desks with differing woods, bicycles many makes of bicycles? Why aren't you more specific?"

This was the turning point of my life. Now I had the key to getting my prayers answered. I then started asking myself, "Why didn't the professors in Bible College teach me how to pray effectively?" Then I thought, "Perhaps they did not realize this principle themselves."

"Now, what should I ask for specifically?" I asked myself. I then prayed, "Heavenly Father, I would like to have a desk made out of Philippine mahogany. My desk is going to be large enough for me to be able to lay out all of my study books along with my Bible. As far as my chair is concerned, I would like to have one with a steel frame so that it is sturdy and one with the little wheels on the bottom so I can roll around like a big shot executive." I smiled as I thought of myself rolling around on a chair in a room like the one I was living in.

When it came time to ask about my bicycle, I gave it some more thought then asked, "Father, the bicycle is to be one made in the U.S.A." At that time there were German bicycles, Japanese bicycles and Korean ones. However, I knew that the United States made the strongest ones. Yet this would take extra faith, because American products were very expensive and rare in Korea at that time.

When I woke up the next morning, I did not feel any great anointing in my heart. It wasn't the same as the night before when God had spoken to me. In fact, I was still struggling with discouragement. How easy it is to believe God when His presence is so obvious.

But, when we return to normal, our faith level goes down and it is hard to stand upon the promise we received when our faith level was very high. This is the time to know that we do not stand on promises made to us in prayer, but we must stand on the Word of God in the Scriptures. I then opened my Bible and my eyes fell on Romans 4:17: "God raises the dead and calls those things which be not as if they were."

My confession was very important. If God calls those things which are not as if they were, why couldn't I do the same thing? God calls us complete in Christ, yet as we look at ourselves and one another, we appear anything but complete. Why can God call me complete if I don't feel complete, look complete or act in a complete way? Because God sees us in Christ. He does not look at us as we are, but He judges us as we shall be. God practices a principle which we must learn to follow. He does not look at the present circumstances, but He sees the end from the beginning and speaks as if all He is working on is already finished.

I learned that once I had prayed specifically and had received the assurance that my prayers had been heard, I had to then visualize the answer and begin to speak as if it had already taken place.

During the meeting, I shared my experience and began to tell the people about my new chair, desk and bicycle. Knowing how poor we were, many people in the congregation were amazed that I had come into such great possessions. Three of the young men asked if they could come to my room and see the three things that God had given me. Then my heart stopped.

"What am I going to do, Lord?" I thought. "When they come to my room and see it is vacant as it was yesterday they are going to lose faith in my word and I might as well pack up and leave town. Nobody will ever trust me again."

When the young men came, they noticed that all I had in the room was the small mattress on the floor where I slept. So they asked me, "Pastor, where is the desk, chair and especially the American bicycle?" However, I found myself speaking prophetically to them:

"When you were in the womb, did you exist?" I asked them now with complete confidence.

"Yes," they answered.

"Could anyone see you?" I continued. "Obviously not," they retorted.

"Then you were not visible," I stated confidently, knowing that they were finally getting my point. "Last night while I was in communion with the Holy Spirit, I conceived the chair, desk and bicycle. They are not visible yet, but they do exist. Just like you were not obvious until you were born. You see, I am now pregnant with these three items. I am calling those things which God has revealed to me that I have received (although they are not obvious) as if they were obvious," I stated, not expecting their response.

With that, they began to laugh and said, "Pastor, you are the first man in history who ever became pregnant." Even worse, the news spread around town. People would come to my church just to see the first pregnant man in history. They would come and just stare at my stomach. I was tall and very skinny, so that made me even more the object of ridicule.

"Pastor, look how big you are getting. When do you think you will be giving birth?" teased a group of youngsters outside the church one Sunday afternoon. I did not like teasing, but I knew in my heart that I had discovered an important spiritual principle that was destined to be a great blessing in my ministry in months to come.

After several months had passed I received all three of those items, exactly as I had requested them. I was given a Philippine mahogany desk, and a Mitsubishi chair with the little wheels on the bottom. And an American missionary gave me his son's slightly used American bicycle. From that time until this, I have never again prayed in vague terms. I have prayed specifically and expected God to answer me in the same way. And He has!

2. We should know how to visualize the end result of our goal.

Just as a hen dreams the chick out of the egg, so we should clearly see the end result of our goal, in our vision and dream.

"Faith is the substance of things *hoped* for." When you hope for certain things then you can only have a strong vision or dream for that which you have hoped for. If you have not visualized clearly in your heart exactly what you hope for, it cannot become a reality to you. This is because you don't know yourself what you really desire the Lord to do for you. The things you really hope for can only be possessed as you visualize them clearly in your heart and mind. When they are clear in your mind the deep desire for God to grant that request now becomes a vision in your heart as well as a prayer. You will dream about it day in and day out as you are in prayer and as you go about your daily work. Without visualizing them you cannot have those things in the realm of the "hoped for."

Romans 1:17 says, "God raised the dead and called those things which be not as if they were." Because God's promises are true, all of the "hoped for" things are a reality in His plan for His children. The next step is for His children to incubate those "hoped for" things in visions and dreams. How? Dare to place that "hoped for" desire in your heart, which the Holy Spirit placed there, in a completed stage as if it has already taken place and the answer were finished. Dream it as "completed." Thank God for the total victory as "completed." As you visualize this in prayer and apply Romans 1:17, your faith will grow to believe God all the way to the final reality of that dream or vision! God is a good God! Hath He not promised and shall He not make it good? Have faith in God, Dare to believe!

What if we don't visualize the answer to our prayer? If we do not, we may not know the fullness of joy when God does answer, because we may not know if it was a direct answer to our prayer or not. We've got to learn how to use our visions and dreams. We can begin to learn by using our faith to visualize and dream the answer as being completed, as we go to the Lord in prayer. We should always try to visualize the end result as we pray. In that way, with the power of the Holy Spirit, we can incubate that which we want God to do for us.

We see a lot of these experiences in the Old Testament. God used this process of visualizing the situation to help Abraham. Abraham was ninety-nine, and Sarah his wife was ninety years old. God wanted to give them a son but they, because of their great age, greatly doubted that it could happen. In the middle of the night, God called Abraham out from his tent and asked him to count the stars. While he was counting the stars they became innumerable to him. Then God said, "Your children shall be as innumerable as those stars." By that associated thought (seeing the stars as faces), Abraham could see the faces of his children in that night sky! By that visualization through the associated thought Abraham could see his children in visions and dreams and possess those children as a present happening in his own heart. And through that visualization he could incubate his children and dispel the doubts from his heart.

We can see that same thing happening in many places in the Old Testament and also in the New Testament, but the main thing is that we should know the importance of visualization.

In my own personal ministry in 1958, when I came out to the slum area in Seoul to start a church it was not easy. I put up an old American marine tent with a few rice mats strewn around on the floor as our sitting area for the congregation, I began to preach the gospel. Very, very few people came to hear my preaching and I was very discouraged. But when I prayed at that time suddenly my spirit would be lifted up and I could see in visions and dreams what God would do for our small church. I could see three thousand people. I could see those faces clearly in my heart. I could see the goal of three thousand in my spiritual vision and dream. I could clearly visualize them. I was finally completely possessed with that vision and dream and I was living and acting as if I had already received that many converts to minister to. Every week I was preaching like that and acting like that! By 1964 my church had three thousand members!

When you have visions and dreams like that they will bring a tremendously strong desire to see those visions and dreams all the way into reality! You know, to have a successful ministry you need this kind of powerful desire. You can only have this kind of desire aroused in you through your clear-cut vision and dream. God responds to those dreams too. Psalm 37:4 says, "Delight yourself also in the Lord and He shall give you the desires of your heart!"

3. After having a vision you must pray fervently to have the substance.

Faith is the "substance." To make faith substantial you must have the assurance in your heart. "Substance" in the Greek is *nupostasis* or "the title deed." Just as if you own a piece of property you have its title deed, you should have such an assurance in your heart that excludes all doubts about the fulfillment of that goal and vision which you have already incubated. So, when you have a clear-cut goal and have those things in the visions and dreams, then you have to pray until your faith rises up to become the "substance". Sometimes it will take a short time for the assurance to come; sometimes it will take a long time to pray through. When God gives you the assurance suddenly in your spirit you will know that you know that you have your desire, and that it is only a matter of time until you see it in reality! That is a tremendous thing!

God wants us to be specific in our prayers. Jesus passed by Jericho on His way to Jerusalem, we are told in the Gospel according to Mark. On the side of the road was a beggar, Bartimaeus, who was totally blind. He cried out to Jesus, "Jesus, son of David, have mercy on me." Others told him to be quiet, but he cried out the louder. Jesus called him out of the crowd and asked, "What do you want me to do for you?" Jesus saw that he was blind, but He wanted him to make a specific request. When Bartimaeus asked specifically for his sight, the Lord healed him.

I was preaching in a foreign country. The pastor of the church asked me if I would agree to pray for a woman in his church. She was a lovely lady, over thirty and had never been married.

"What do you want me to pray for?" I asked.

"I want to have a husband," she responded very shyly.

"What kind of a husband do you want? There are many kinds of men," I said to her.

"Well, I'll take any man that the Lord wants to give me," she answered. I told her that God does not answer vague prayers. She had prayed for many years for a husband and her prayers had not been answered because God wanted to give her a husband that would be according to her desire, not just any man.

I asked her to sit down. Giving her a piece of paper and a pen, I asked her to write down the numbers one through ten. She did.

"I'm going to ask you ten questions about the man you want and I want you to write each answer down by each number," I continued. "Number one: Is he European, Asian or African?" I asked.

"European," she said.

"Number two: How tall should he be?" "Six feet."

"Number three: What is his profession?" "School teacher."

"Number four: What is his main hobby?"

"Music," she continued.

On we went until she had written down ten traits describing this man that God was going to give her to marry. I then told her to take the paper home, hang it up by her mirror and look at it every day. She did.

Every day, as she prayed, she prayed specifically for this one man. She visualized him and became strong in her faith. She knew that

God would provide him for her. One year later as I passed by the town I called the same pastor.

"Dr. Cho, you must come to my house for lunch today," the pastor said. When I arrived the first thing he said to me was, "She is married! She is married!"

"Who is married?" I asked.

"The old maid you prayed for," he continued. He then went on to tell me the story.

An American high school teacher had come by the church and had sung in the services during a special series of meetings. He was tall, slender and very handsome. All the young girls were interested in him, but he did not seem to pay them much attention. However, when the single lady came that I had prayed for, he immediately took an interest. They went out to dinner and by the end of that week he had proposed. No one had said anything about the ten-point list on her wall by the mirror. But, when she saw him and learned more about him she knew that this was God's answer to her prayers.

Interestingly, I received word from an unmarried Japanese girl who had read this story and began to practice praying specifically for her husband. She put up her ten-point list by her wall and within a few months she was married, too. She wrote me and told me that God had answered her prayer when she prayed specifically, having visualized her answer.

This is not a guarantee to all single ladies in the world. However, these stories of people that I have mentioned signify the results of praying to God with a clear goal and then visualizing the answer from God, even before it comes.

4. To have a successful incubation you must release your faith power through your mouth confession.

In Genesis, when the Holy Spirit had been incubating on the chaotic world, then the Word of God was released. It was exactly like that. When you have the substance, when your faith becomes substantial, you've got to release that substance through your mouth. You've got to confess that it is going to be just as your faith reassured you! By confessing you can have a tremendous thing happen. Concerning salvation the Bible clearly says, in Romans 10:9-10, *"That if thou shalt confess with thy mouth* the Lord Jesus, and shalt believe in thine heart that God hath raised him from the dead, thou shalt be saved. For with the heart man believeth unto righteousness; and *with the mouth confession is made unto salvation."*

Also in Mark 11:23-24, "For verily I say unto you, That whosoever shall *say* to this mountain, Be thou removed, and be thou cast into the sea; and shall not doubt in his heart, but shall believe that those things which he *saith* shall come to pass; *he shall have whatsoever he saith."*

Only by mouth confession can faith power be released allowing tremendous things to happen. As you see, you have to have a definite incubation period with the Holy Spirit. Without having this incubation it is impossible to have great things happen in our life. Many people are neglecting this part of the technique of their prayer life, and many others do not know ". . . those things which he saith shall come to pass; he shall have whatsoever he saith" (Mark 11:24, KJV).

God has taught me this valuable truth in my own experience. Nowadays, without having this period of incubation I do not dare to *speak* or to *say* what I would like to have created in my life because now I know that greater things cannot be created in my life unless I have that period of incubation.

Since 1980, I've been incubating for half a million members in our church. By the help of the Holy Spirit and prayer I've set a goal of arriving at half a million membership by 1984. That goal became my "egg," but in my vision and dreams I began to incubate that goal. I placed that goal in my vision and I began to dream and visualize that many members as if I already had them in our church. I have been incubating those goals day in and day out. I've been incubating those numbers for the glory of God twenty-four hours a day! Of course I have been praying fervently, and now I have this assurance. My faith has become substantial, and that is the reason why I am boldly declaring that we already have half a million members, and we will "see" them by 1984. In my heart, in the realm of visions and dreams I already have half a million members. Just as the time flows, the incubated goal is going to be hatched successfully.

CHAPTER 8

The Fourth Dimension

My present understanding of the fourth dimension came through an experience I had in Korea. An old woman moved into downtown Seoul and claimed that she had been given the power to heal the sick. Many people went to her for prayer with some successful results. Even some genuine Christians were fooled by her and allowed themselves to be prayed for.

Realizing that she did not give credit to God for her power, discerning that her spirit did not confess Jesus Christ as Lord, I knew that the woman was not from God. Therefore, I told my church members to stay away from her. The Bible teaches us to test the spirits: "Beloved, do not believe every spirit, but test the spirits, whether they are of God; because many false prophets have gone out into the world. By this you know the Spirit of God: Every Spirit that confesses that Jesus Christ has come in the flesh is of God, and every spirit that does not confess that Jesus Christ has come in the flesh is not of God. And this is the spirit of the Antichrist, which you have heard was coming, and is now already in the world" (1 John 4:1-3, NKJV).

Although John was specifically referring to the heretical Docetic and Corinthian Gnostics, this Scripture is applicable today.

Many false prophets are rampant throughout the whole world in increasing numbers. Christians are admonished in the first verse to test the spirits and not believe someone is from God by merely accepting their claim to divine inspiration.

"But pastor, why is this woman able to heal people?" asked a bewildered man in our church. This question caused me to go to prayer. I began to pray with my Bible by my side and began to ask God to give me the correct answer.

The question of miracles performed by people who do not represent Jesus Christ may not be as relevant to the West as it is here in Korea, but I have been faced with this same dilemma for many years. We have seen Buddhist monks performing miracles. Practitioners of Yoga have been healed of several diseases through the practice of meditation. Japanese Sokagakkai are reputed to heal the sick in their meetings. I was confused, but I approached God with the question in full confidence that He would give me the understanding.

I have discovered that prayer is the answer to dilemmas that Christians face. It takes several hours to clear your mind from all the hindrances of the world around you. However, once your mind has been cleared, you will then be able to hear the "still, small voice" of God speaking.

After several days, the answer came. The Holy Spirit revealed to me the nature of the new dimension of reality I had been born into when I became a Christian. The first three dimensions are the boundaries which govern the material world. However, there is a greater dimension which governs and includes the lesser. That dimension is the realm of spirit, the fourth dimension. The superior nature of the fourth dimension was made clear to me when I read Genesis 1:2.

Genesis is not a history book, but its history or recorded events are accurate. It is not a science book; however, its science is perfect. Genesis shows God revealing to Moses, and through Moses to us, the beginnings of this earth, its living creatures and, most importantly, man, with whom He will be forever linked in Christ.

Concerning the universe, He simply states that He created it. That's all. No detailed explanations are necessary because God is interested in developing the main theme of the book. He begins in verse 2 with a chaotic, uninhabitable world. Yet, as stated in the first chapter, the Holy Spirit brings order out of chaos. The three-dimensional plane of present existence was brought into order by a divine act moving in a greater dimension. The Holy Spirit was the creator of the material dimensions we are all familiar with.

There are three spiritual forces in the earth. The Spirit of God, the spirit of man (as is noted in Genesis 2:7), and the spirit of Satan, who is in opposition to God, also alluded to in Genesis 3.

The first three chapters of Genesis describe the three moving forces that dominate the rest of history. All three spirits are in the realm of the fourth dimension, so naturally spirit can hover over the material third dimension and exercise creative powers. Of course, the human spirit and the spirit of the devil have definite limitations in exercising their fourth dimensional creative influence on the physical world. But God's spirit has no limitations.

As I continued to ponder these things, the Holy Spirit continued to give me the answer to my question. The Holy Spirit said, "My son, man still does not realize the spiritual power that I have given to him. Did I not want him to rule his environment?"

"Yes," I said, realizing what God was referring to. Man was

originally told to name the other creatures that God had created. He was given the ability to cultivate the earth and grow his own food. He was to have dominion. When man fell, he still had a spirit, but his ability to communicate with God was lost. False prophets had power in the realm of the spirit because they had come to realize their potential. Christians had the greater power if they would only realize the power of the Holy Spirit that had been given to them.

Now the picture became very clear. Instead of fearing those who exercise spiritual powers motivated by Satan, we were to use the power of God, which is greater, to bring glory and honor to the Living God.

What about those who use their human powers? Human power is manifested when man realizes his natural ability (as a descendant of Adam). Man's power is limited, but the individual eventually will be drawn into the camp of Satan unless he yields to God.

The important thing I had to teach my church members was that the power in us is greater than any power that is in the world (1 John 4:4). As I shared these things with my people, the confusion vanished and a new era of understanding dawned upon us. Although this understanding came to me many years ago, I have continued to learn how to become more comfortable living in the fourth dimension. This does not mean that I have stopped living in the material world, but it does mean that I am becoming more aware of the greater sphere of spiritual existence we have as Christians.

WHAT IS MAN?

What is man? This important question is asked by David in a poetic way in Psalm 8. This psalm was sung by David during the festival of Israel commemorating the grape harvest. Gittith, in its Hebrew root, means winepress. There are two other psalms sung near the winepress and they are also joyous and commemorative of the glory and excellency of God (Psalm 81, 84). Psalm 8 was written at night when all the stars were shining and David could appreciate the magnitude of God's creation. When David looked up at the greatness of God's creation, he realized the smallness of man and the futility of his pride.

Man is insignificant if you only consider his physical size. In comparison to the vastness of the earth, he is only a speck. Then, when you become aware of the solar system in which our earth is located, man becomes even less significant. Finally, being cognizant of the fact that one visible star can be millions of times larger than our own solar system, man becomes by comparison totally insignificant. Yet David's question must be completed: "What is man that thou art mindful of him?"

What gives man dignity is the fact that the Creator of our vast universe has chosen to center His attention on him, to the degree that God became man in Jesus Christ in order to save him. Man is not only dignified by God's attention and visitation, but he is also dignified by his high calling: "You have made him to have dominion over the works of Your hands; You have put all things under his feet" (Ps. 8, NKJV).

Man's blessed calling becomes through sin his curse in that his potentiality for dominion causes his aggression. Instead of desiring to rule God's creation, which was originally placed under his dominion, he has historically endeavored to rule other men. This is only one aspect of man's enigmatic nature. He has the ability both to ascend to the heights and descend to the depths. He is capable of the best and worst. He was created for so much, but settles for so little.

Yet, whether a saint or sinner, man was still created in the image of God. According to Genesis 1:26, man did not evolve from a lower form of life; he was created by God as man. He was also made in the image of God in that He placed His breath into him, causing him to be more than a material being. This is in sharp contrast to modern thought concerning man.

Our young people are taught in our schools that man evolved from a lower form of life. This could be one of the causes of man's present decline in morality and lifestyle. However, this notion is not new.

J.B. deMonet Lamarck, a well-known French naturalist of the nineteenth century, adopted a theory that all living things developed from simple germs that were placed on this earth by God, the one who created the universe. All living creatures became alive by developing cells capable of being stimulated by a force such as heat or electricity. Lamarck also stated that living things adopted new organs as the need arose through the process of selectivity. Lamarck published his work in 1809, the very year that Charles Darwin was born.

How could an unintelligent cell develop by itself and adapt to circumstances beyond its control? To someone studying these theories with the same critical standards men have studied the Bible's account of man's creation, he would have to exercise more faith in believing the former than the latter.

Although present theories have disputed Darwin, they have simply added another dimension to man's attempt to rid himself from a dependence upon a divine being in order to explain his origin. Modern man seemingly solves the dilemma of natural selection simply by adding time. If this is not possible in a comparatively short period of time, then it might be possible in a much longer period of time. Natural selection might even be possible in a period of time such as millions or billions of years.

THE BIBLICAL VIEW

God elevates man from mere matter. This is why cultures that have accepted the biblical view of man have a respect for life and the individual. Biblical Christianity shows that man is more than what he seems to be. He is made in the image of God.

Man is made in the image of God in that he is a trinity: body, soul and spirit.

1. Body

Man was first created a physical being. God created him physically before He breathed into him the breath of life (Gen. 2:7). After his sin, man was told by God, ". . . Dust thou art, and unto dust shalt thou return" (Gen. 3:19, KJV). Therefore, man has a temporary body which dies and decays. Strangely, that part of man which is only temporary receives his most attention.

There are eight aspects of the Body, according to Scripture:

a. The body houses the soul and spirit (Dan. 7:15).
b. It is affected by the soul based upon what it sees (Matt. 6:22, 23).
c. It can be made alive by the Holy Spirit (divine health) (Romans 8:10).
d. It becomes the temple of the Holy Spirit at conversion (1 Cor. 6:19).
e. It is to be taken care of and not neglected (Col. 2:23).

f. It is strongly affected by our spoken words (James 3).

g. It is the chief symbol of the church (Eph. 4:12, 16).

h. It shall be transformed at the resurrection (1 Cor. 15:14).

2. Soul

The Old Testament makes a clear distinction between the soul and the body. In Eccles. 12:7, it is said, "Then shall the dust return to the earth as it was, and the spirit shall return unto God who gave it." In the New Testament, Jesus makes a clear distinction: "Fear not them which kill the body, but are not able to kill the soul: but rather fear him which is able to destroy both soul and body in hell" (Matt. 10:28, KJV). The soul and the body are so closely linked in our vital functions that often it is difficult to differentiate between the two.

The soul controls our will and desires and has a strong influence over the body. I have heard doctors tell me that often it is the person with the will to live that will survive a difficult operation. Since the soul also has what is referred to as the mind, there are many effects which the mind produces upon the physical body. For example, the mind sees, using the physical organs of the eyes. The mind hears, using the physical organs of the ears. The mind senses, using the body's ability to feel.

The soul also comprises that which we call emotions. Joy, shame and happiness are all emotions which also have an effect on the body. For example, if a person is embarrassed, he might blush, a physical manifestation of an emotional reaction. If a person becomes angry, it might cause him to have unusual strength in his muscles or cause his heart to beat much more quickly.

The soul also contains what we call desires. What a person desires often motivates his activities and physical nature. We have all heard of people that have trained their bodies to perform unusual athletic feats. This was done because of an unusual desire which drove the body to excellence.

The soul also comprises what a man calls his intellect and his taste. The soul is man's self; it is his conscious being. When we refer to someone, we are referring to more than his body, we are referring to the person. When we marry, we begin to develop a greater attraction for the person with whom we have a relationship than for the person's body. Although the body might cause initial interest, the person will shine through their physical appearance. It is that person which is the soul of man.

3. Spirit

In understanding man's spirit nature, we come into a sphere of much controversy among theologians. Charles Hodge, in his *Systematic Theology*, states, "This doctrine of a threefold constitution of man being adopted by Plato, was introduced partially into the early Church, but soon came to be regarded as dangerous, if not heretical. Its being held by the Gnostics that the 'Pneuma' in man was a part of the divine essence, and incapable of sin; and by Apollinarians that Christ had only a human 'soma' and 'psucha,' but not a human 'pneuma.' The Church rejected the doctrine that the 'psucha' and the 'pneuma' were distinct substances, since upon it those heresies were founded. In later times the SemiPelagians taught that the soul and body, but not the spirit in man, were the subjects of original sin. All Protestants, Lutheran and Reformed, were, therefore, the more zealous in maintaining that the soul and spirit, 'psucha' and 'pneuma,'are one and the same substance and essence. And this, as before remarked, has been the common doctrine of the church."

Hodge holds to the dichotomy of man and rejects the trichotomy of man. In other words, man is made up of only soul and body; not body, soul and spirit. Berkhof, in his *Systematic Theology*, agrees with Hodge.

"The Teaching of Scripture as to the Constituent Elements of Human Nature. The prevailing representation of the nature of man in Scripture is clearly dichotomic. On the one hand the Bible teaches us to view the nature of man as a unity, and not as a duality, consisting of two different elements, each of which move along parallel lines but do not really unite to form a single organism. The idea of a mere parallelism between the two elements of human nature, found in Greek philosophy and also in the works of later philosophers, is entirely foreign to Scripture."

These scholars point to Gen. 2:7 where there is no mention made of a spirit being created by God. However, we must remember that it is told in chapter 3 that man sinned and that the result of his sin would be death. If man died, then what died? Obviously he continued to live with a body and consciousness, so what died was his spirit. Also in 1 Thes. 5:23, we can see that Paul is making a distinction: "Now may the God of peace Himself sanctify you completely; and may your whole spirit, soul, and body be preserved blameless at the coming of our Lord Jesus Christ."

The writer of Hebrews also makes a distinction: "For the Word of God is living, and active and sharper than any two-edged sword, and piercing even to the dividing of soul and spirit, of both joints and marrow, and quick to discern the thoughts and intents of the heart" (Heb. 4:12, NKJV).

Paul places Adam and Christ in juxtaposition and shows the former bringing death to man and the latter bringing life (Rom. 5:17, 19; 1 Cor. 15:22). And especially in 1 Cor. 15:45, "And so it is written, The first man, Adam, was made a living soul; the last Adam was made a quickening spirit.". In the verse just quoted, Paul again divides soul and spirit. Adam was made a soul, through his sin, but through Christ's sinless nature, we are able to be made alive by His life-giving spirit.

Although it is not my desire to solve the theological disagreement which has lasted for the entire history of the church in this book, I believe the issue does not warrant a charge of heresy in either camp. Perhaps, what Paul refers to as spirit is a heightened aspect of the redeemed soul. Yet what remains certain is that man becomes different after the new birth. His spirit is made alive by the Holy Spirit and he is brought into a new dimension of spiritual experience with which he must become familiar. The spirit is that part of man that is made alive by Christ so that he might have vital union and communication with his Creator.

FIVE ASPECTS OF OUR SPIRIT

1. God wants to direct our lives, by His Spirit (Romans 8:14).
2. Man in his natural state is incapable of understanding spiritual reality. In fact, spiritual things seem foolish to him (1 Cor. 2:14).
3. Spiritual men are to differentiate between those things that are of God and those things which are of this world or of Satan, because he has developed his spiritual senses (1 Cor. 2:15).
4. Only those who have developed their spiritual senses are capable of understanding mature things (Heb. 5:14).
5. Spiritual people are ones that are not destroyers but ones who are restorers of those who have fallen (Gal. 6:1).

As I have previously indicated, the lesser is always contained in the greater. However, there should be no confusion. God desires that we keep in mind that we are not three people vying for power. We were not created to be divided too distinctly. We are one person; however, we have different functions within our one person that must be understood if we are to grow and develop as whole men.

Our bodies are important. We are commanded not to neglect them. The Christian should therefore be concerned about his health by eating properly, exercising and adopting the proper habits. What is often the case is that people have a tendency to overemphasize one aspect of their nature above the others. A man who is more intellectually oriented should not feel that his body is unimportant. A spiritual person should not neglect his intellectual or physical condition. In all things there must be a balance. The greater does not mean to detract from the lesser; the greater includes the lesser.

VISIONS AND DREAMS: THE INSTRUMENTS OF THE FOURTH DIMENSION

If a man understands what he is, he will desire to know how he can grow in his fourth-dimensional capabilities. If the Holy Spirit has come to lead us and guide us into all truth, how does He operate?

The age of the Holy Spirit began on the day of Pentecost. Peter preached his first message the day that the Holy Spirit came in clear manifestation. His text was from Joel 2: "And it shall come to pass in the last days, saith God, I will pour out of my Spirit upon all flesh; and your sons and your daughters shall prophesy, and your young men shall see visions, and your old men shall dream dreams" (Acts 2:17, KJV).

Dreams and visions are very similar in nature. Young men have a tendency to envision the future; old men naturally dream about the past. However, both dreams and visions work within the framework of the imagination.

Before we can understand how visions and dreams operate, we should understand something about the framework within which they operate: the imagination.

THE IMAGINATION: THE SOUL OF THE VISION AND DREAM

In 2 Cor. 10, Paul tells us that we are to walk in the Holy Spirit and not in the flesh. The King James Version uses the word "imagination" in the fifth verse. However, the word could be better translated "reasonings" or "logic." Paul does not mean that we should not reason, but he does tell us not to rely on our natural logic that has not been sanctified by the Holy Spirit. Our problems are greater than just natural ones and the solutions must be found by using our spiritual minds. "For the weapons of our warfare are not carnal but mighty in God for pulling down strongholds, casting down arguments and every high thing that exalts itself against the knowledge of God, bringing every thought into captivity to the obedience of Christ" (2 Cor. 10:4-5, NKJV).

Paul uses military language when referring to the realm of the imagination. The unregenerated mind uses natural reason which cannot understand spiritual things. Paul refers to these natural reasonings as strongholds or fortifications which the spiritual mind must bring down in order for the Christian to live victoriously.

When the Bible refers to the heart, it is referring to the area of our soul which comprises the imagination. Jesus said, "Let not your heart be troubled" (John 14:1, NKJV). There are seven areas which Jesus revealed were problems in the heart:

1. The heart can be hardened to spiritual reality (Mark 6:52).
2. The heart can be blind, incapable of seeing what would be obvious to the spiritual person (John 12:40).
3. The heart is where sin begins (Matt. 15:19).
4. Words spoken are first conceived in the heart (Matt. 12:34).
5. Satan operates his tempting powers in the heart (John 13:2).
6. Doubts begin in the heart (Mark 11:23).
7. Sorrow and trouble work within the heart (John 14:1, 16:6).

Therefore, Paul's teaching the Corinthian Christians to guard their hearts was based on the clear emphasis which Christ gave to this important part of the soul.

I liken the heart of man to a painter's canvas. What a man dreams and envisions is the paint. If the Christian takes the brush of faith and begins to paint on the canvas of his heart the pictures that God has revealed to him, those revelations become reality.

THE UNCONSCIOUS MIND

What is referred to as the subconscious is really the unconscious mind. The unconscious mind is the motivational force that causes men to act or to behave without conscious perception. I have noticed a number of books on this subject in recent years.

Carl Gustav Jung, the son of a clergyman and a student of Sigmund Freud, developed the field of psychology known as analytical psychology as a reaction to Freud's psychoanalysis. In his view, man was not only motivated by conscious thought and reasoning, but also by his unconscious mind. He broke down the unconscious into two categories:

1. The personal factor or one's individual unconscious.
2. The collective factor or one's collective unconscious that is inherited from one's ancestors.

There developed a sociological belief that man's collective unconscious was inherently good. Society's rules were thought to tend to inhibit man. Anthropologists, artists and philosophers began traveling to primitive cultures searching for the goodness and simplicity in man which had not been spoiled by the prohibitions of Western culture.

The belief in man's inherent goodness is in direct contradiction to Scripture. "The heart is deceitful above all things, and desperately wicked; Who can know it? I, the Lord, search the heart, I test the mind, even to give every man according to his ways, and according to the fruit of his doings" (Jer. 17:9-10, NKJV).

God reveals to man in Jer. 3 things about his heart:

1. The heart is not inherently good, but inherently evil. This is because of sin.
2. Man is not naturally capable of understanding his own heart. Only the Lord knows a man's heart and is capable of revealing it to him.
3. A man's actions will reveal his heart.

If our actions and accomplishments result from a motivating force that is beyond our conscious perception, then should not the Holy Spirit choose to work within this realm in order to sanctify it and cause it to motivate us to do God's will?

THE ABILITY TO SEE AND DREAM

The Holy Spirit is pictured by Peter on the day of Pentecost as a river. God had promised to pour this river into humanity irrespective of social standing, gender, or age. Joel prophesied that the moderate former rain and the stronger latter, or harvest, rain would both fall at once in "the day of the Lord." The torrents of God's Holy Spirit forming a spiritual river would fill every believer and bring forth spiritual fruit.

When the final day of the first fruits (first harvest) festival arrived, the Holy Spirit descended in a forceful manner. It must be remembered that the Pentecost feast (fifty days after the wave offering of the Passover festival) was a feast of anticipation. If there was a good grain harvest, then the fruit harvest, celebrated as the Feast of Tabernacles, would also be good.

The Church was born within the festival of anticipation. The anticipation will be culminated at the Second Coming of Jesus Christ. By that time, the Church will have accomplished her divine purpose of bringing the gospel of Jesus Christ to every creature. The success of the Church is assured because the Holy Spirit has empowered her with supernatural ability.

The Holy Spirit came on the day of Pentecost not only to cause men to be able to prophesy (speak forth the Word of God), but also to give the ability to have visions and dreams.

In the Old Testament we often see God giving visions and dreams concerning future events. In fact, Samuel was called a seer (1 Sam. 9:9). Daniel was able to see from Babylon the development of successive kingdoms and looked into the Church age and beyond. Ezekiel could see beyond his land into a foreign land.

This phenomenon was not limited to the Old Testament. In the New Testament, Ananias, Paul and even a Roman, Cornelius, had prophetic visions and dreamed dreams.

This does not necessarily mean that we should all remain in ecstatic states. However, it does mean that we are to participate in God fulfilling His will in our lives by first envisioning His purpose and then filling our imagination with it through dreaming.

Consequently, the believer should not be limited to the three-dimension plane, but should go beyond that into the fourth-dimensional plane of reality. We should live in the Spirit. We should guard our minds from all negative and foolish thinking. This keeps the canvas clean for the artwork of the Holy Spirit to be painted on our imaginations. Creativity, perception, intelligence, and spiritual motivation will be by-products of an imagination which has been activated by the Holy Spirit.

"For as he thinks in his heart, so is he" (Prov. 23:7, NKJV). There is no question in my mind that we become what we think, either for good or for evil. Television has had a great effect upon our present society.

Whenever I hear television people say that they don't affect society but they only mirror society, I then ask myself, "Why do corporations spend so much money on commercials?" The violence and amoral sexual activity depicted on television are responsible for much of the decay we see in society today.

Satan is out to destroy men's minds so that man will not be able to accomplish his purpose in this world. Pornographic movies and magazines cause minds to treat sex as an animalistic activity, thereby destroying man's dignity and self-image. Why? Because we eventually become what we dwell upon.

This is the reason God is so concerned with what we think. "Finally, brethren, whatever things are true, whatever things are noble, whatever things are just, . . . whatever things are of good report, if there is any virtue and if there is anything praiseworthy-meditate on these things" (Phil. 4:8, NKJV).

Becoming what we think is not only true for those who are motivated towards negative thinking, but also those who are desirous of doing the will of God. If you dwell on what God has destined for you to become, you will become just that. Therefore, I ask my people never to allow negative thoughts to dwell in their minds but to think positive things. A businessman will not succeed if he dwells on failure. If a person in my church fails, I tell him, "You are not a failure because you failed. You are only a failure if you don't try again. Fill your mind with success and you will become successful."

RESULTS OF FOURTH-DIMENSIONAL THINKING

Your success or failure depends upon your fourth-dimensional thinking: visions and dreams. We see this principle in operation from the very beginning of Scripture.

What caused Eve to eat the forbidden fruit? Her mind knew what God had said. She was aware of the consequences of her actions. But, Paul said, she was deceived. How was Eve deceived? The serpent asked Eve to look at the forbidden tree. When her eyes focused on the tree she began to admire it. Her imagination began to work; she wondered what it would be like to eat the fruit and be released from her innocence. She would never have been deceived if she had not allowed her imagination to begin to work upon an act of disobedience to God. Her failure came as a result of using her fourth-dimensional thinking in the wrong way.

Sodom was a place of extreme sin and perversion. God decided to destroy the city, but determined that Lot and his family would be spared. Living in the midst of Sodom's society must have had a powerfully adverse effect upon Lot's family. Therefore, God told them to leave and not look back. Although she had been warned not to do so, Lot's wife looked back at Sodom and became a pillar of salt. While this was happening, Abram was on a mountain top seeing the same thing. Why was Abram able to look and Lot's wife was not?

Her heart had been affected by Sodom's lifestyle. When she looked back at the wicked city, her imagination longed for what she had left behind. Abram had not contaminated himself with the sinful lifestyle God was destroying; therefore he was free from judgment.

We are not told in Gen. 19 how long she looked at Sodom before she became a pillar of salt; but she looked long enough to let her imaginative powers fill her heart with the remorse for what she was leaving behind, thereby becoming a partaker of the destroyed city's judgment. Lot's wife failed by misusing her fourth-dimensional thinking.

ABRAHAM THE DREAMER

God's testimony to Abraham's faith in Hebrews 11 is quite revealing. He was able to leave Ur of the Chaldees, the center of civilization, and travel to a place that had not been shown him. I can imagine that Abraham's first test was his conversation with Sarah. "We are leaving!" Abraham said to his wife.

"Where are we going, dear?" Sarah answered.

"I don't know, just pack," Abraham said.

"How are we to know when we get there if we don't know where we are going? What has gotten into you, Abe? Why are we leaving?" she asked, thinking that Abraham had succumbed to too much heat.

"God told me, so let's go!" Abraham responded, hoping that God would reveal the place he was going once he got there.

When Abraham came out of Egypt and Lot left him, he was commanded to look north and south, east and west of Canaan. All the real estate that he could see would be his. He could only possess what he could see. God only gave to Abraham what his eyes projected upon his imagination. His vision became his boundary line.

We never grow beyond our vision. Our experience will always be limited by what our vision sees. We learn this important spiritual lesson from Abraham.

All who are in Christ are heirs of the promise made to our spiritual father Abraham. Therefore, the innumerable number of God's children who have dwelled upon this earth from the time of Isaac till today are all the children of Abraham, whether they are of the natural or spiritual branch (Jew or Gentile). How did a one-hundred-year-old man become the father of so many? He used fourth-dimensional thinking. He was full of visions and dreams. He learned to incubate in faith.

It took twenty-five years for God's promise to come to pass, but it did come to pass. Abraham took several detours from the road of faith, but those detours are not mentioned in the letter to the Hebrews. Abraham's failures should cause all of us to believe that we are all capable of accomplishing the will of God to its fullest. His imperfection should encourage us to know that God doesn't use perfect people in accomplishing His perfect will.

God's commandment to Abraham was threefold:

1. He was to see the land (Gen. 13:14-16).
2. Abraham was told to look up to the stars. He was asked to number them. They represented his spiritual children (Gen. 15:53).
3. His name was changed from Abram to Abraham, which means "father of a great multitude."

1. By looking out in every direction, he filled his imagination in a concrete way with God's promise. He was not told to close his eyes when God spoke to him. He was told to look at something concrete and substantive. So often, when we are believing for something from God, we tend to neglect the role God expects us to play in the fulfillment of His promise. We are not to be idle or passive. God expects our faith to have form and substance. The Holy Spirit incubated the earth when it was without form and substance into a habitable planet. If the Holy Spirit had not incubated the earth into its present form, our earth would be like the rest of the planets in our solar system. So God expects us also to be active in the incubation of our faith by visualizing the final results of His promise.

My church has not grown to its present membership of 275,000 people because I am the most gifted pastor in the world. No. It has grown to its present size because I have followed Abraham's principle of visualization. In 1984, I see my church having half a million members. I can count them. I can see their faces in my heart. By 1985, I see our television program being aired throughout all of Korea, Japan and our English version in the United States and Canada. I see it. I have maps of these countries in my office and I have a clear vision of the transmitters beaming the programs.

2. When God focused Abraham's attention on his future seed, he was told to look at the stars. God wanted the sensitive film of his heart to capture not only the magnitude of the picture, but the lens of his eye was to capture each individual star in its individual beauty. Every one of his children were to be important to him, therefore, he was told to try to number each of them.

Each one of our children are different in their looks and personality. I have three boys. They are all different. I don't look out over the dinner table and see one picture depicting my children. I see each child individually.

I am sure that when Abraham went home at night, he could not get the stars out of his mind; his imagination was already filled with God's promise. His fourth-dimensional power began its work which resulted in a hundred-year-old man being able to naturally make his wife pregnant. This was because the fourth-dimensional vision dominated the third-dimensional physical circumstances.

3. God changed Abram's name to Abraham. His self-image had to be changed. He had to start calling himself "father of many." His family, friends and workers had to change their thinking. They could no longer refer to him in the way they had in the past. Every

time he heard his name, he was reminded of God's promise.

We cannot keep God's promise to us a secret from others. We must begin to speak as if the promise had already come to pass. "God calls those things which are not as if they were." We must follow His example. God has to deliver us from the fear of what others will think. We have to let our words agree with our vision.

But the miracle had to take place in Sarah as well. At first she laughed when she heard that God would make her a mother at the age of ninety. However, she began to visualize the return of her youth. She dwelt upon the promise of God and soon a physical change began to take place in her. Even king Abimelech found the old woman so attractive that he tried to take her as his concubine. If a woman begins to think of herself as attractive, she can be. Not only will physical changes take place, but her self-image will change and she will begin to take better care of herself and start to dress as an attractive person.

We must remember that the birth of Isaac was only a miracle in that two elderly people were physically able to conceive. God did not just hand them a baby from the sky. Both Abraham and Sarah participated in the fulfillment of God's promise. They allowed the canvas of their hearts to be painted with the artwork of faith in God's Word.

"For we are His workmanship, created in Christ Jesus for good works, which God prepared beforehand that we should walk in them" (Eph. 2:10, NKJV). The Greek word translated workmanship is the word *poema*, from which we get the English word poem. It literally means "a work of art." God created us as a work of art in Christ with the purpose of accomplishing His work in the earth.

Although we may have personality flaws, God sees us as complete in Christ." For in Him dwells all the fullness of the Godhead bodily; and you are complete in Him, who is the head of all principality and power" (Col. 2:9, 10, NKJV). If God has painted a picture of us in Christ as complete and has openly communicated it to us through the Apostle Paul, should we not follow His example?

ISAAC IS NOT A DREAMER

As we continue to follow the family of faith, we notice that the life of Isaac was unlike the life of Abraham. The "son of promise" was not a dreamer like his father. We don't see the example of faith in Isaac to the degree that was evident in his father. Therefore, we don't see the works of faith in action in his life. Isaac lived in his father's visions and dreams. He never allowed the Holy Spirit to create the same relationship with God that his father possessed.

JACOB THE DREAMER

Isaac had two sons, Jacob and Esau. Esau was a man's man; he was interested in hunting. Being strong and self-reliant, he was not too interested in the spiritual inheritance that belonged to him as the firstborn son. Jacob, which means "supplanter," was a man who was close to his mother and who enjoyed staying home. He was a natural deceiver. Most of us would have nothing to do with him, especially in business. Yet Jacob had one quality which distinguished him from his brother. He was a dreamer.

Having deceived his brother and later his father, Jacob had to leave home, fleeing for his life. He journeyed to a relative's farm. Jacob learned something from his experience with Laban: deceivers get deceived.

Jacob worked for seven years for the right to marry Rachel, Laban's younger daughter. However, Laban wanted his older daughter, Leah, married first. So, after the wedding party, Laban exchanged daughters. Jacob, who was guilty of misrepresentation, became victim of the same sin himself.

Jacob had to work another seven years for the wife he originally wanted. Therefore, Jacob ended up with two wives. However, God chose to bring forth Christ through the offspring of the first wife, Leah, whose fourth son was Judah, (a name which means "praise").

Laban had been greatly blessed because of Jacob's service. It was obvious to him that Jacob had something unusual, something which had to come from God. Yet Jacob desired to leave and build his own household. In order for him to leave, he needed means to provide for his wives and children. So he devised a scheme whereby he could become a rich man.

He told Laban that he would pass through his large flock and remove all of the speckled and spotted sheep, all of the brown lambs and all of the spotted and speckled goats. These were obviously of less value than the pure white ones. He then assured Laban that if ever there were found pure sheep, lambs and goats in his flocks, then they should be considered stolen.

Laban did not believe that Jacob could possibly be serious. He said to Jacob, "Oh, that it were according to your word!" So Laban took all of the spotted and speckled flocks and told his children to bring them about three-days journey away from where Jacob was living. This left Jacob with nothing. The prospects were dim that Jacob would ever have anything because it was unlikely that pure sheep and goats would ever conceive hybrid, colored flocks.

Laban thought that he could keep Jacob working for free forever. However, Jacob had learned how to have visions and dreams.

Jacob had begun to dream at Bethel, where he had built his first altar to the God of Abraham. Learning from his grandfather's experience, and discovering that his trickery would not accomplish his divine calling, he turned to God. God showed him how to create something from nothing; by taking impossibility and making it opportunity.

Jacob, being in charge of Laban's flock, began to dream spotted and speckled as he viewed the pure flock. He used spotted and speckled poles to concentrate his vision as the pure flocks were watering.

In time, the pure flocks began to conceive according to Jacob's dream. It was beyond Laban's comprehension how the miracle took place. But when explaining to his family why he had to leave, Jacob revealed his secret, "And it happened, at the time when the flocks conceived, that I lifted my eyes and saw in a dream,and behold, the rams which leaped upon the flocks were streaked, speckled, and grayspotted" (Gen. 31:10).

It was through using his fourth-dimensional ability (visions and dreams) that Jacob was able to leave Laban with almost his entire flock. Jacob heard the Word and filled his imagination with the promise. Laban's treachery only made the miracle even more spectacular. For Laban changed his wages ten times during the time Jacob had agreed to work. Yet when the blessing of God is upon you, no obstacle can stand in the way of success.

JOSEPH THE DREAMER

Jacob had twelve sons, but only one of them (Joseph) learned the secret to success. Having returned to the land of his fathers, Jacob (now called Israel) put Joseph in charge of his flocks. Joseph was his father's favorite son because he was the son of his old age. Seeing the open favoritism, the other brothers became extremely jealous. Their hostility became more acute when, at the age of seventeen, Joseph began to dream.

"Please hear this dream," Joseph told his brothers.

"There we were, binding sheaves in the field. Then behold, my sheaf arose and also stood upright; and indeed your sheaves stood all around and bowed down to my sheaf." The circumstances which could have brought about the fulfillment of the dream became even more impossible when Joseph was sold into slavery in Egypt. As the circumstances became more desperate, Joseph's dreams became more important in his life. Finally, the dream came to pass when Joseph became prime minister of Egypt. His famine-stricken family, which had come to Egypt for food, all bowed down to him.

God is called the God of Abraham, Isaac and Jacob. God is linked to those who follow His example of incubating results through visions and dreams.

NO BANKRUPTCIES

The past few years have been difficult for our business community in Korea. We have suffered a very severe recession. Interest rates have been high and inflation has cut deeply into our people's purchasing power. Yet, more than in times of prosperity, we see God's principles at work during hard times.

Through continually teaching my people the principles of success found in the Scriptures, we have seen no bankruptcies in our church. Our income has remained constant and we have embarked on the largest building program in our church's history. What has been the key to our practical success in business? We have taught our people how to use their fourth-dimensional powers. They visualize success. We do not dwell on negative thinking, but speak positive words motivated by positive thinking. Since we do not have the same tax structure in our country as is enjoyed by the church in other countries, our people have learned how to tithe and give sacrificially without tax breaks. What I am sharing in this book is practical and can be used by any believer anywhere in the world. It is part of the manifold wisdom of God that He has taken a man from a small country which is part of the developing world to build the largest church on this earth. No one could have predicted it, but through incubation we have seen God take our small gifts and use them to influence Korea and the world.

God can do the same thing through you!

INCUBATING YOUR HEALING

On Christmas Eve several years ago, I received an urgent phone call from a medical doctor whom I knew. "Pastor Cho, please come down to the hospital! One of your church members has been in a terrible accident and we don't expect him to last the night," the doctor said. Later I found out that this young man had just left work and was heading home to his family. Since it was Christmas Eve, he had bought his wife a special Christmas present and was preoccupied with the thought of how pleased with it she would be. He never saw the taxi that was speeding in his direction. Since it was late at night there were no witnesses. At that time, in Korea, if an automobile would strike a pedestrian, he was fined $2,500 and that was all. However, if the pedestrian lived, then the driver was responsible for all of the expenses the victim incurred until his recovery. So the driver of the cab dragged him into the back seat and began driving around the city, hoping that he would die.

After several hours, someone noticed the injured man in the back seat and called the police.

The man was rushed to the hospital, and found to be very close to death. His condition was aggravated by the fact that his intestinal tract was ripped open and dirt had caused an infection.

As I arrived at the hospital, I was told by the doctor that his condition was worsening and that he was unconscious. Yet I walked into the room knowing that circumstances don't dictate to God what He is not able to accomplish. There are no such things as easy or difficult miracles. To God, the parting of the Red Sea is no more difficult than healing someone's headache.

I went by the man's bed and prayed out loud: "Dear Lord, allow this brother to regain his consciousness for just five minutes." As I was praying, I opened my eyes and noticed that he was looking right at me. I could see the terror in his eyes as he pictured himself dying. What would happen to his wife? Who would take care of his children? These were the thoughts that must have been running through his mind.

Knowing that God had answered my prayer by giving him back his consciousness, and realizing that he would only have five minutes to hear what I had to say, I began to speak to him.

"I know what you are thinking," I said. "You are already envisioning death. But God wants you to participate in the miracle that is going to take place. The reason you have regained your consciousness is that God wants to use your fourth-dimensional power and begin to paint a new picture upon the canvas of your heart."

As I spoke these words, I could hear the nurse laughing quietly in the background. But this was no time to be self-conscious. This man was dying and I had to obey what the Holy Spirit was telling me to do. Therefore, ignoring the nurse, I continued. "I want you to start painting a new picture of yourself in your imagination. You are on your way home and no accident has taken place. You knock on the door and your lovely wife answers. She looks very pretty. On Christmas Day she opens up her present and you feel so proud you have such good taste. The next morning you wake up and have a good breakfast with your family. In other words, you are erasing death from your mind and you're painting a new picture of happiness.

"Do you have the picture? Is it clear?" I asked, hoping that he would be able to hear and understand the full implication of what I was saying. I could see his eyes light up for the first time.

I continued, "You leave the praying to me! I will pray in faith and you agree with me! Just use your ability to dream and see visions of your health and happiness!" When I prayed, I could feel the Holy Spirit very powerfully in the room. The nurse then said, "Pastor, I'm sorry to interrupt your prayer, but it has gotten very warm in this room. Don't you think so? Perhaps I'll open the window and let in some fresh air."

I knew that the room temperature had not changed and it was cold outside on this December night. Yet the nurse was sensing something that she could not understand. That something was God's power at work.

I continued praying, this time laying my hands on the bed. The bed began to shake. God was performing a miracle for His glory. Within a few days, the man returned to his wife and family, having been completely healed by the power of God.

He then shared with me how when I asked him to change his imagination from death to life, he began to sense a deep peace come over his body. He was no longer asking God to live, he began praising God because he was sure God was going to heal him.

The man is now in the chemical business and is very successful. Whenever I notice him in church, (he comes every Sunday but it's hard for me to see everyone), I remember the story and I praise God.

When the blind man approached Jesus, he knew that he was blind. However, Jesus asked him, "What do you want me to do for you?" Jesus wanted the man to be specific and as he confessed that he knew Christ could give him back his sight, he started to receive a new vision of himself. His faith began to rise and he could imagine himself able to see, able to work, and possibly able to have a regular life, instead of being a beggar. Jesus said to him, "Your faith has made you whole." The blind man was healed.

IT IS GOD'S DESIRE TO GIVE PROSPERITY AND HEALTH

"Beloved, I pray that you may prosper in all things and be in health, just as your soul prospers" (3 John 2, NKJV). Our soul's condition will affect the condition of our whole body. God desires for all Christians to prosper in body, soul and spirit. According to John, the key to prosperity is the soul.

A HEALTHY SOUL LIFE

It is not God's will for us to have an unhealthy soul. He wants our minds clear to accomplish His will. He wants our desires to be pure so that we will use our desires in the incubation process. He wants our emotions healthy so we don't become depressed and discouraged. As we guard our hearts, we will find a healthy soul capable of hearing what the Holy Spirit speaks to our spirits and able to put into action our fourth-dimensional capabilities.

GOD'S WORD IS NOT LIMITED

The great difference between people is the degree with which they are able to use their fourth-dimensional ability. The material world is governed by arguments and reason. We use reason, but we are able to go one step further. We have the Holy Spirit, who has invaded this three-dimensional plane of reality and is desirous of guiding us into a new plane.

The Word of God is not limited to the three-dimensional plane. Paul said he was not ashamed of the gospel of Jesus Christ because it was the power of God. He used reason in order to explain the great mysteries of the Kingdom of God. But Paul was not limited to reason. He told the Corinthians that he came to them in the demonstration of the spirit and power. Therefore, their faith would not be limited to natural wisdom but would transcend it.

The writer of the Letter to the Hebrews stated that the Word was sharp and powerful. It had the ability to not only reach the mind, but it could even penetrate the very intents of the heart.

Therefore, the Christian is equipped with the Word and the Holy Spirit. With these tools at his disposal, he can comfortably face any challenge and see the victory.

Satan's counterfeits are going to be increasingly manifested as the end draws near. There are going to be many claiming to be like Christ and will even manifest unusual power. But we should not be fooled by them nor fear them in any way. For as the Church draws to the end, she shall be equipped by the Holy Spirit with the grace to use the spiritual weapons at her disposal and see God's divine purpose accomplished in the earth.

THE DEVIL'S COUNTERFEIT

As we enter into the closing era of the Church age, the devil is unleashing his counterfeits as never before. It is no wonder we are seeing an increasing number of false religions springing up in the very seed-bed of modern Christianity, Europe and America. As God's people are entering a new understanding of fourth-dimensional Christianity and are seeing God performing miracles in their lives, so also spurious religions are performing their own brands of miracles.

Moses experienced the same thing when he was called to deliver Israel from the bondage of Egypt." The LORD spoke to Moses and Aaron, saying, "When Pharaoh speaks to you, saying, 'Show a miracle for yourselves,' then you shall say to Aaron, 'Take your rod and cast it before Pharaoh, and let it become a serpent.'" So Moses and Aaron went into Pharaoh and they did so, just as he LORD commanded. And Aaron cast down his rod before Pharaoh and before his servants, and it became a serpent. But Pharaoh also called the wise men and the sorcerers; so the magicians of Egypt, they also did like manner with their enchantments. For every man threw down his rod, and they became serpents. But Aaron's rod swallowed up their rods" (Exod. 7:8-12, NKJV).

One of the most deceitful false religions which is gaining popularity in the West is Zen Buddhism. In the past twenty years, many of the intellectual centers in Europe and America have increasingly turned to this religion which we in the East are increasingly discarding. Thomas Altizer has said, "Today, Buddhism is the religion that is most profoundly challenging Christianity (particularly in its Zen form). Contemplation is the highest of man's activity. For therein he can become God and therein can he become immortal . . . Genuine Christianity is the ultimate form of rebellion."1

While evangelical Christians are increasingly understanding how to use their imaginations by learning how to speak the language of the Holy Spirit (visions and dreams), the Zen Buddhists are increasing their activity in the West and are even affecting Christian centers of learning. As they teach people to look inside themselves and contemplate, they are producing counterfeit experiences, including miracles.

I have found it difficult to understand why Western intellectuals bypass Christianity and look to Oriental mysticism for spiritual fulfillment. As I travel throughout India and Japan, I see young European and American men and women in Oriental dress obviously searching for a spiritual experience to justify their existence. These people have abandoned their Christian heritage sociologically and psychologically and have turned to doctrines of devils that we have been delivered from in the East.

What has caused these sincere searchers for reality to look in Oriental temples for what is available in their local churches? Why has the Western church not been able to meet the need of its young intellectuals? These are questions that have caused me to concern myself with the Church in the West. As I have traveled throughout

Europe and the Americas, I have discovered the problem. So many traditional churches have forgotten the vitality of Christianity and have become dead and sterile. This is why attendance in churches in many Western countries has dropped continually in the past twenty years, while churches in former mission fields have grown dramatically.

THE WESTERN SPIRITUAL VOID

Arnold Toynbee said: "Man has been a dazzling success in the field of intellect and 'knowhow,' but a dismal failure in the things of spirit.[2]" Toynbee's *Civilization on Trial* traces the decline of Western thinking from its spiritual origins in biblical Christianity. Western culture extracted from its spiritual roots in the gospel took many years to disintegrate into what it has become today. Therefore, the spiritual void created in the heart of Western man has become a fertile soil for the seeds of Eastern false religion.

Albert Schweitzer stated that without a moral factor or foundation, all human endeavors, scientific inventions, cultures, and civilization itself would be doomed to decline and corruption.[3] Schweitzer's understanding of modern man's spiritual dilemma caused him to conclude that Western man needed to return to his spiritual roots in Christianity.

European culture as we know it today was founded on the spiritual philosophy of Augustine. His *City of God* became the cornerstone from which the building of honesty, hard work and positive self-image became an integral part of Western society. Before his teachings reached northern Europe, the Germanic and Scandinavian people were nothing like they are today. Philip Schaff said, "In his passion, the old Scandinavian was sometimes worse than a beast. Gluttony and drunkenness he considered as accomplishments. In his energy, he was sometimes fiercer than a demon. Revenge was the noblest sentiment and passion of man; forgiveness was a sin. The battlefield reeking with blood and fire was the highest beauty the earth could show; patient and peaceful labor was an abomination. They slew the missionaries and burnt their schools and churches. After a contest of more than a century, it became apparent that Christianity would be victorious; the pagan heroes left the country in great swarms as if they were fleeing from some awful plague."[4]

The Church conquered with the most powerful force known to man, the gospel of Jesus Christ. After many centuries of spiritual decline, during which churches lost their moral strength, Europe experienced the Reformation. John Calvin, Martin Luther, and John Knox not only had a religious influence upon their societies, but their influence permeated society as a whole. Although the Reformers were not overly concerned with mission, it has to be understood that they were fighting for the mere survival of biblical Christianity. It is upon the sacrifice of the Reformers that the late eighteenth-and nineteeth-century missionary movement rested. Once the Church was strong in what it believed and had influenced its own society, she was ready to reach out to the ends of the world.

However, beginning with Friedrich Schleiermacher (1768-1834), known as the father of modern theology, the church in Europe began to retreat into its present humanistic theology. Instead of depending on the Word of God as the Reformers had done, Schleiermacher began his concept of religion by calling it "feeling of absolute dependence." Although traditional Christians largely ignored Schleiermacher, his theology was to have a profound influence on all subsequent theology.

Ritschl, Von Harnack and Kierkegaard continued to motivate theology, and in turn their societies, resulting in the spiritual void many traditional churches have experienced to this day.

Carl Gustav Jung observed that modern man has lost all the metaphysical certainties of his medieval brother and set up in their place the ideals of material security. But it takes more than ordinary doses of optimism. Even material security has gone by the boards for modern man has begun to see that every step in material progress only adds so much force to the threat of a more stupendous catastrophe. Science has destroyed even the refuge of the inner life. What was once a sheltering haven has become a place of terror. The rapid and worldwide progressive growth of interest in psychology shows modern man has turned his attention from material things to his own subjective process. Jung observed that many people in our society consider Freud more important than the Gospels. It is this very aspect of man's thinking that has produced what Rousas Rushdoony calls "intellectual schizophrenia."

It is upon the cultural, spiritual, philosophical and religious bankruptcy of Western thinking that Zen has gained influence.

WHERE DID ZEN COME FROM?

Zen had its origins in India. The story is told that when Buddha was teaching his disciples upon a mountain, a Brahma-Raja (a royal priest) came to him with a Lotus flower and asked him to preach Dharma (law and truth). Instead of teaching, the story goes, Buddha simply gazed at the flower in complete silence. Confused by the continued silence of Lord Buddha, the disciples wondered what the Master was doing. The only one that understood was Mahakasyapa, a trusted disciple. He simply smiled and nodded his head. It is said that the wisdom received that day was transmitted in silence through the leadership of twenty-eight Patriarchs, Buddha being the first. It was the twenty-eighth Patriarch, Bodhi-Dharma (A.D. 480-528), who came to China during the Liang Dynasty who became the founder of Zen Buddhism in China.

During the seventh century, the Zen School of Buddhism split into two sects. The one which was mainly practiced in Northern China, known as the school of "gradual" enlightenment, only lasted one hundred years. The other sect, which believed in "instantaneous" enlightenment, continued to prosper and became the dominant Chinese religion.

Having reached Japan in the seventh century, the Japanese adopted Zen to its particular sociology. It became the religion of the military class, with its emphasis on rigor, self-discipline and contempt for death. However, by the thirteenth century, China began to lose interest in Zen, and turned to other forms of religion more in keeping with her own distinctive culture. My own country of Korea was influenced by Zen Buddhism which was brought to us by the Chinese.

WHAT IS ZEN?

Zen is not logical. In fact, as an iconoclastic mental process, Zen can be considered a non-religion. Zen seeks to draw man into himself to seek for nothingness or "the bottomless abyss." It seeks to "enlighten" man by causing him to bypass his natural reasoning and find an "ultimate essence of being."

If you ask a practitioner of Zen if it is a philosophy, he would say, "No. We teach ourselves; Zen only points the way."[6] Zen also claims not to be a religion, but a way to discover. It does not claim to be Buddhism, but the pinnacle of Buddhism. In essence, Zen tries to point man in the direction of himself. It rejects the concept of sin and salvation, and causes man to find reality through "self-hypnosis." To a Zen practitioner, "Form is Void and Void is Form." It leads man to seek for the nothingness in which he might find peace. The feeling of peace or "Enlightenment" is called *Wu*.

THE IMPACT OF ZEN IN THE WEST

Zen has had a considerable impact in Europe and America. With the traditional churches becoming further alienated from Western society, the spiritual void created has to a large measure been filled by spurious religions such as Zen.

Alan Watts, formerly an Episcopal clergyman, was one of the leading advocates of Zen in the West. His statements concerning Christianity clearly validate the writings of the apostle Paul: "For the wrath of God is revealed from heaven against all ungodliness and unrighteousness of men, who suppress the truth in unrighteousness, because what may be known of God is manifest in them, for God has shown it to them."

"Professing to be wise, they became fools" (Rom. 1:18, 19, 22, NKJV).

Alan Watts has stated: "Every Easter Sunday should be celebrated with a solemn and reverent burning of the Holy Scriptures, for the whole meaning of the resurrection and ascension of Christ into heaven (which is within you) is that Godmanhood is to be discovered here and now inwardly, not in the letter of the Bible."[7]

He continues: "In its early ages, the church was in constant expectation of the Parousia, the second coming of the Lord.

Obviously, the church has been looking for the Parousia in the wrong direction-in the outward skies not in the realm of heaven which is within. The true Parousia comes at the moment of crisis in consciousness."[8]

With the advocacy of man turning inwardly for understanding and then being told that the "Enlightenment" comes in the form of a void, his rational mind must be discarded and he then becomes the object of manipulation.

FOURTH-DIMENSIONAL CHRISTIANITY IN CONTRAST

The Holy Spirit desires to bring the Christian into a familiarity with a new dimension of spirit. He causes us to pray and meditate, not within ourselves, but on the Holy Scriptures. After all, Christianity was not born in a classroom. It was birthed through a dynamically impacting experience with the Holy Spirit on the day of Pentecost. Therefore, Christianity cannot be a sterile theological exercise. It must be a vitally impacting spiritual relationship with Jesus Christ.

Whereas Zen ignores or condemns the concept of sin, the Holy Spirit delivers us from it through the blood of Jesus Christ. While Zen asks its practitioners to meditate within themselves, the Holy Spirit delivers us from self-centeredness and causes us to be concerned with the needs of others. While Zen says that to attain spiritual perfection is to enter into a voidness of the mind, the Holy Spirit brings us into a personal relationship with Jesus Christ. God, therefore, can be known in an intimate relationship with His Son. While Zen tries to destroy our God-given natural capacity for reason, the Holy Spirit causes our minds to be renewed and rational powers to be sanctified so that we might understand His will for our lives and His glorious creation that He has meant for us to enjoy. While Zen gives man no hope for the future, the Holy Spirit causes us to experience Christ's divine kingdom here on earth with the expectation of experiencing much more for eternity in His divine presence.

While Zen Buddhism causes man to experience self-induced insanity through irrational meditation and abstinence, the Holy Spirit causes men to dream and see visions of God's divine will and become healthier in body, soul and spirit. Zen leads man to despair, but Christ gives us life and that more abundantly. Zen keeps man in ignorance; Christ causes man to know the truth.

Paul prophesied concerning these times: "Now the Spirit expressly says that in latter times some will depart from the faith, giving heed to deceiving spirits and doctrines of demons, speaking lies in hypocrisy, having their own conscience seared with a hot iron, forbidding to marry,and commanding to abstain from foods which God created to be received with thanksgiving by those who believe and know the truth" (1 Tim. 4:1-3, NKJV). Paul clearly saw what it would be like today. He saw Christianity being attacked by false religions. He saw that many of these doctrines would try to make man abstain from normal practices such as marriage and eating.

Yet, we are encouraged by the miracle of Aaron's rod. While Egyptian magicians were able to counterfeit God's miracle, their rods were swallowed up by Aaron's rod. As we approach the end of this age and as we see Satan's work within our society, we are encouraged by knowing that Christ has conquered. Our power is stronger than Satan's power. We are not subject to the devil's trickery, but we are more than conquerers through Jesus Christ our Lord.

CHAPTER 9

The Renewing of the Mind

"And do not be conformed to this world, but be transformed by the renewing of your mind, that you may prove what is that good and acceptable and perfect will of God" (Rom. 12:2, NKJV).

One of the greatest mysteries to mankind throughout the centuries has been his most prized and most complicated physical organ, his brain. A man's mind is more than just his physical brain. The mind is the brain at work in consciousness.

How is the mind different from our physical brain? How is the mind affected at conversion by the added influence of the Holy Spirit? Is the mind renewed by the Holy Spirit at once, or is there a process of renewal? How do the brain and the mind function under control of the Holy Spirit as the Christian learns to walk in the fourth dimension? These and other important questions will be addressed in this chapter.

Before we begin our study into the complicated yet rewarding questions we have stated above, we should analyze the passage which I quoted from the apostle Paul's Letter to the Romans. Paul wrote this letter to the church at Rome before his visit there. This makes the letter very useful in determining Paul's doctrine which was then unaffected by problems in churches which he had founded. After discussing the importance of natural Israel with this mostly Gentile church in chapters 9, 10 and 11, he then begins to tell the Roman Christians how to live.

According to Paul, Christians living in a Roman secular society were not to be conformed to that society. A.T. Robertson comments on this passage: "Do not take this age as your fashion plate."[1] Peer pressure, along with the social pressures brought to bear on the Roman Christian, would want to make him conform to Roman society, which had all the power in the world. However, Paul does not only give an injunction but he also gives the means by which Christians could avoid destructive conformity. He states that Christians are to be transformed by a renewal of the mind. As the mind is renewed, the Christian is able to rest in the will of God, which is good, acceptable and perfect.

The renewal of the mind brings a transformation. The word that Paul uses, which is translated "transformed," is the Greek word *metamorphousthe*, the same word which Matthew used to describe the transfiguration of Jesus Christ. Paul uses the word in his Second Letter to the Corinthians, "But we all, with unveiled face, beholding as in a mirror the glory of the Lord, are being *transformed* into the same image from glory to glory, just as by the Spirit of the Lord" (2 Cor. 3:18, NKJV). In the English language, you have the word *metamorphose* which is used to describe a change of states. This word has its root in the same Greek word we have been discussing.

Therefore, in order for us not to conform we must be transformed. How are we transformed? Our minds must be renewed.

THE MIND AND THE BRAIN

The concept of the mind is not new to society and I am sure it was not new to Paul. Paul was an educated man and was familiar with Greek poetry and philosophy. This is why he could command the attention of the Athenians at Mars Hill. Democritus of Abdera (460-370 B.C.), a Greek philosopher, wrote extensively on the subject of the mind. He stated that matter was made up of invisible and movable substances. This concept is similar to our present concept of molecules. He saw that the brain was the place where all of the senses and perceptions dwelt. He believed that everything could be explained with more knowledge regarding this human organ. He thereby created a materialistic philosophy. Later, Plato rejected Democritus' philosophy as amoral and incomplete. If the whole world consisted only of matter composed of atomic particles, then man did not have will and could not be held responsible for his actions.

Paul was very much aware of this controversy and stated simply that the mind could be renewed. In doing so, Paul showed us that the mind was the center of concern. Our actions were to be guided by a transformation of our lives, which would be accomplished by a renewal of the mind. The mind was distinct from our physical brain which housed the senses and consciousness of men.

In order for us to greater understand the differentiation between our mind and brain, we need to know more about both. We are unique in God's creation: He created us in His own image. We are more than what we are physically. We are also more than we can understand about ourselves. Our potential is much greater than our experience. God, viewing man's ability at the Tower of Babel, said that man was capable of doing whatever he was able to envision.

If this is so, then even with our great advances in knowledge and technology, we have yet to see man's potential realized.

We have normally understood the verse quoted at the beginning of this chapter as a warning against the Christian remaining or becoming worldly. Yet we can also interpret the verse as a great challenge to the Christian. If this world is to be saved, we must be able to speak the Word of God in the power of the Holy Spirit. The mind of the Christian can not only be renewed for the purpose of not conforming to this world, but it also can be renewed for the sake of realizing our potential as human beings created in the image of God. We can then not be limited to the limits that this world is placing on our knowledge and understanding but we can transcend the limitations. Our ability is only limited by our own limits.

God said of man after the flood that he was capable of doing whatever he envisioned. Could it be that as our minds are renewed, we will have a greater vision? Could it be that the world's greatest problems are awaiting a renewed people who have been able to transcend the self-imposed limits of our present society? Before we address these important questions, let us look at the organ that houses our self, that is, our brain.

The human brain is the most intricate system in the explored universe. Without the protection of the skull, the exposed organ of the brain is the most vulnerable in the human body. It has the consistency of paste and can be severely damaged by only slight pressure. It can also survive severe damage having the ability to transfer crucial functions from damaged to undamaged areas. The combination of structural delicacy and functional ruggedness makes the brain a marvel to the scientific community.

THE BRAIN IN HISTORICAL PERSPECTIVE

Men have not always thought that the brain was the center of our mental and emotional activities. The early Greeks thought that thinking took place in the belly. Aristotle thought that the heart was the place where man thought. In Italy, at the University of Bologna in 1637, the first real ideas developed regarding the brain and its functions, using the pooled resources of men and women from all over the world. The information derived from dissecting human cadavers was used by early Renaissance artists such as Leonardo da Vinci.

From early times till today, the brain has been one of the subjects most studied by scientists, doctors and philosophers. Yet, although much is known, many questions are still to be answered.

HOW DOES THE BRAIN FUNCTION?

The human central nervous system consists of the brain and the spinal cord. From these two structures branch out a network of fibers, similar to a telephone network, which link the entire body together. The fibers are called nerves. These nerves are one-way paths which either feed information to the central nervous system or carry commands from the system to the whole body. The command-carrying nerves are called the efferent system. These are broken down into two categories: one is voluntary and the other is autonomic. The voluntary nerves control those parts of our body that we can consciously move, such as our muscles. The autonomic nerves control those parts and functions of our body that we do not consciously control, such as the heart, glands and body temperature.

Although the body has many parts and performs many functions, it has only one control center. The fact is that we are only conscious of ourselves as one. We never think of ourselves as primarily a heart, arm, leg, brain or any other distinctive part. This is one reason God has linked our relationship to each other and to Himself in terms of a body. The Body of Christ has only one consciousness; we, as each part, can only function as we function under the direction of our head, Jesus Christ. The whole Body is linked together by one system which is the person of the Holy Spirit. He feeds our head the information we send in prayer and then He carries the commands to the several parts of the Body. Some of the commands are voluntary requiring our obedience, but many are automatic, such as His function as the convictor of sin, righteousness, and judgment.

WHAT IS THE BRAIN LIKE?

Approximately 83 percent of our brain is the neocortex, also known as the cerebral cortex. The brain is divided roughly into two hemispheres, the right and the left. The composition of the brain is made up of cells called neurons. The two halves of the brain are linked through a thick band of axons (the fiber through which neurons communicate) called corpus callosum. The top portion of the neocortex is called the grey matter and the portion underneath is called the white matter.

My purpose is not to give an exact description of the brain's composition. This would be both tedious and cumbersome to many readers of this book. However, a simplified understanding of what the brain is like will help us to understand what I will be describing later.

HOW DOES THE BRAIN COMMUNICATE?

The brain communicates through the nervous system by the means of small electrical impulses of about .10 of a volt. The neurons have an ability to not only receive information through these impulses but also to pass along the information throughout the entire system directly to the organs, muscles and senses involved.

THE BRAIN AND BLOOD

Recent studies have provided some new information about the living human brain. It has been observed that blood flow to different parts of the nervous system is delicately and carefully controlled by the vascular system. Neural activity consumes energy just as muscular activity does. An active section of the brain demands more oxygen than does one which is inactive. Therefore, more blood needs to be rushed to that part of the brain which is engaged in activity.

Scientists in Sweden have observed that, by using a radioactive substance in a person's bloodstream, they can observe the gamma rays coming from the brain. When the patient was at rest, most of the blood was in the frontal cortex. This part of the brain is believed to control our reflections on the past and the ability to creatively plan for the future. This means a great deal to us in understanding the function of our brain. When the same patient was speaking or acting in some way, the blood was more evenly distributed.

Learning how to rest and wait upon the Lord is one of the most important and difficult things that Christians need to learn. Hours spent quietly and prayerfully not only give us perspective and direction but they are now understood to allow the most creative aspect of our brains to work as well.

WAITING ON THE LORD

Thousands of years before these observations were made, the prophet Isaiah revealed, "Even the youths shall faint and be weary, and the young men shall utterly fall, But those who wait on the LORD shall renew their strength; They shall mount up with wings like eagles, They shall run and not be weary, They shall walk and not faint" (Isa. 40:30, 31, NKJV).

The message of the preceding verses is very clear. Natural strength as exhibited in youth is not capable of overcoming extreme difficulties. But there is a strength which does not depend on being young. This strength comes from learning to wait upon the Lord.

I have learned that an idea is more valuable than material resources. Obstacles which cannot be overcome by natural resources can be overcome through a creative idea. The problems which humanity has faced in the past have resulted more than anything else from a lack of ideas.

Years ago, in the beautiful city of Helsinki, Finland, the State Church desired to build a church in the downtown area. However, there was no land that could be purchased for this purpose. The only place where there was an open space was in one of the most strategic downtown locations. Yet there was an enormous rock which dominated the area. There was no way to eliminate the rock and the situation seemed hopeless. But two Christian young men waited and got an idea.

"Why not make the church inside the rock?" they thought. Now there exists one of the most beautiful church structures in the entire earth: the Rock Church. Anyone looking from the outside can only see a large boulder, but as you go through the doors you enter into a marvelous church which has also become an important tourist attraction. The solution did not come from trying to remove the obstacle, but digging through it with a creative idea.

Problems which eluded us in the past can be overcome through creative thinking, if we can learn to wait upon the Lord. Isaiah shows us how waiting works. He uses a Hebrew word translated "renew" but which can be better translated "exchange." This means that, by waiting upon the Lord, we actually exchange our strength with God's strength. Now this strength does not only have to be physical. It can be mental as well. Therefore, as we wait upon the Lord, we can have His creative strength work upon our minds to give us the answers to questions we have not been able to resolve.

Since the physical world is a shadow of the spiritual world, what we know scientifically of the material helps us in understanding the spiritual. Jesus revealed spiritual truth by using material examples. The regeneration which is done by the Holy Spirit at conversion was referred to in a physical way as being born again. When describing the spiritual implications of the kingdom of God, Jesus used the material mustard seed which is small yet grows into a large plant. Paul reveals the same principle when teaching the Corinthian church the importance of the physical resurrection of Jesus Christ. "Howbeit that was not first which is spiritual, but that which is natural; and afterward that which is spiritual." Therefore, our understanding of the creative thinking in our brain during times of inactivity only points to the spiritual implications of waiting upon the Lord.

SCIENTIFIC DETERMINATION VERSUS RANDOMNESS

One of the most significant arguments within the scientific community is the argument between the determinists and those that hold to the random theory.

Men like Harvard's Sanford Palay that hold to the determinist point of view have pointed out that the nervous system is not a random net. It is redundant. Its organization is highly specific, not merely in terms of connections between the neurons, but also in terms of the number, style, and location of terminals upon different parts of the same cell and the precise distribution of terminals arising from that cell.

In order for us to understand this position, we must first examine what gives each of us individuality. Each of us has inherited a specific blueprint which is unique to ourselves alone. The blueprint is contained in molecules called DNA (deoxyribonucleic acid). The blueprint is followed not only in our body features, but also in our emotional make-up. We also have other proteins (histocompatibility antigens) which give each of us a distinct selfhood. This genetic selfhood makes up our immune system, which protects us from invasions of foreign bodies. (This is not to be confused with the selfhood we have which is experienced in our consciousness.)

We often have heard of people being given organs from donors to replace organs that have become defective. The greatest difficulty after a successful operation is the natural tendency of the recipient to reject the foreign body because it does not have the same antigen or code. It is as if each of us has been given a code similar to the ones used by banks in order for us to draw money from automatic tellers. If someone tries to make a transaction within your account and they don't have the secret code, the transaction is automatically cancelled.

The wide range of individual codes (if we can continue with the same metaphor) is very large. We see this by looking at identical twins. We know that their genetic blueprints are identical. They may have the same eyes, noses and hands, but their fingerprints will be different. What gives the difference that protects each person individually and causes such a wide variation in the human species?

The determinist believes that there is a reason for the great variation. Although the reason may not be clear at the time, there are physical causes which can be understood in the future. The people that follow the random theory believe that the variety is caused by chance. We will understand this better as we go along.

A question which is of particular interest to us as Christians is how we can all be different and still all be in the image of God. There are several spiritual principles that give us understanding regarding this important question.

1. Within unity there is diversity.

God is one God yet He is three persons: Father, Son and Holy Spirit. His completeness is manifested in the Son who came to this world in the person of Jesus Christ. Yet Jesus depended completely on the Father who gave Him power through the Holy Spirit. Although the complexities of the Trinity cannot be exhaustively understood, we can understand and know Him by faith.

2. God has a definite will, yet His ways are beyond our finding out.

This does not mean that we cannot know the ways of God, but we can never know them exhaustively. Moses knew His ways, but he did not know them all.

3. God's creation reflects His nature.

Within all entities there are parts. We are only conscious of ourselves as one. We do not recognize the left and right hemispheres of our brains as distinctive. We only recognize that we are who we are. Yet, experiments have proven that there are two distinct levels of consciousness in the two hemispheres of our brains. Each one has different functions. For example, the left hemisphere has the ability to speak and articulate its thoughts. Yet, everyone has only one identity.

4. Even matter reflects the principle of unity and diversity.

As you hold the book you are reading in your hand, you are taking for granted the stability of the paper which has been bound together. Your book is not moving at random in your hands. If you put it down and go to the kitchen to get a cup of coffee, you can be sure that when you come back it will be at the exact location where you placed it, barring an earthquake or an intruder.

Yet you are taking too much for granted! As you look at the paper you are now reading, you are not conscious of the fact that the paper is made up of certain molecules. Each one of those molecules is made up of atoms. And you probably don't realize that the atoms are made up of subatomic particles which are in a constant state of motion. Thanks to quantum mechanics, we now understand much more about the microuniverse which makes up all matter. It is important for us to understand our universe because God created it. The more we know about His creation, the more we appreciate the manifold wisdom of the Creator.

What is quantum mechanics? This new system grew out of observing light waves and X-rays. Scientists saw that they had characteristics of particles under certain circumstances.

In 1925, the French physicist De Broglie stated that particles, like electrons, had characteristics like waves. Soon, Erwin Schrodinger proposed a new type of mechanics which was able to analyze waves and particles. Niels Bohr proposed that electrons move in an uncertain pattern and their exact location could not be exactly predicted. Therefore, only the probability of where the electrons could be at a certain location could be predicted. For example, we could say that there was a 60 percent chance of it being at a certain place. This poses a serious problem for many scientists in that they try to understand and predict something exactly. But the conclusion now exists that in the world of the subatomic particle, nothing can be predicted exactly.

Some have said that this world exists in a chaotic state. This view holds that nothing can be predicted exactly and that events are guided by chance. However, how can a material universe so exact in so many ways, and so stable, be essentially chaotic? This is a mystery which is still puzzling the scientific world.

Yet when we understand that the universe reflects its Creator, we can have some appreciation for this puzzling phenomenon.

One thing that mathematicians and physicists find difficult to understand is that there are things that are beyond our understanding. Although man has the ability, given by God, to understand, his understanding is only finite and not exhaustive. "The secret things belong unto the LORD our God: but those things which are revealed belong unto us and to our children for ever, that we may do all the words of this law" (Deut. 29:29, KJV).

Another aspect that is of interest to every believer is the power of the Word of our Lord and Savior, Jesus Christ. His Word brought order out of chaos in the beginning. It also holds all things together. This means that the whole material creation is held together not by a mystery, but by His Word. When God said, "Let there be!" . . .

that Word not only worked once, but it is still at work. Therefore, randomness may be better understood as unlimited variation. Also, the book that you are presently holding is stable due to a force which is at work making the chaotic subatomic particles into a stable material product. This force is the Word of the Lord and will be explained in the next chapter.

I further understand that to some this answer may seem simplistic in that it is based on faith. Yet faith cannot take the place of knowledge and knowledge cannot take the place of faith.

Scientists have faith in their rational power. We have faith in the Word of God. The two are not necessarily in conflict. We, as Christians, have the distinct ability to understand knowledge within the context of faith. We, therefore, can conclude that there is a difference between two levels of the material world (the perceptible world of matter and the imperceptible world of the subatomic). These two levels are not necessarily in conflict, for the unity of the Creator can overcome the diversity of the smallest level of the creation.

THE MIND AND CONSCIOUSNESS

We are more than our physical parts. We are more than merely a machine. We are conscious of being a person. We have the ability to see, feel, taste, smell and be concerned. Machines don't concern themselves with worrying about whether they will be kept in good repair or not. They do not have consciousness. Our consciousness is quite complex; it will not serve our purpose to try to go into too detailed an explanation in this section. However, understanding who we are will give us an idea of what and who we are able to become under the Holy Spirit's influence in the fourth dimension.

It is my intention to try to understand with you, my reader, the newest neuroscientific developments as they relate to our sensory perceptions and consciousness, then relate what we are now learning to the truth about us derived from God's final word, the Scriptures. I must state in this section the fact that I am not a neuroscientist; as a preacher of the gospel, however, I keep abreast of what is happening in the world of science. The reason for this is that I believe that we who proclaim the Word of God have an opportunity and responsibility to unveil reality to the world in a way that the world can understand. I am also a man who enjoys learning more about God and His creation. In doing so, I can help others learn more as well.

OUR SENSES

Most of what we know consciously comes to us by what we see. Yet our seeing is more than what we actually view with our eyes. We not only see, we also perceive.

For example, suppose you are taking a walk on a lovely day in the fall. You look up at the sky. What do you see? Well, what you see depends to a great deal on your perception, based on what you have learned and experienced in the past. What you are actually seeing is light coming into your eyes. This light is focused on your retina where a neural pattern is created and transmitted to the visual cortex. There the neural code simply reports a message to your brain. You are seeing white, irregular shapes slowly drifting across a blue background. Yet when you look at the sky you are perceiving much more than just that sensory information.

If you are an artist, you might view the formations of clouds as a beautiful picture worthy to be reproduced on a canvas. If you are a poet, you may be inspired to reflect on a sheet of paper your emotions regarding the scene that you have just witnessed. If you are a weatherman, you may look for signs within the clouds which might foretell a changing weather pattern. Yet no matter what your background may be, you are still looking at the same thing. Perception, therefore, is a vital part of what we call our consciousness. Perception involves not only the gathering of information from our physical senses, but also the integration of the information into logical mental patterns that we can understand and relate to others.

The eye is more than an organ which gives visual information to the brain. In 1975, scientists at Northwestern University tested subjects for what are known as blind spots. Basically, they showed that visual patterns surrounding blind spots are extended through the non-seeing area by the perceiving brain. They also showed that these could also appear in portions of the visual field that are served by a healthy, functioning retina and visual cortex (within the brain). The subjects were able to complete and see visual patterns that were not actually complete. The eye in conjunction with the brain was able to make up the difference. This is also true when we study our sense of hearing. Subjects can listen to a tape and hear a missing word in a sentence. For example, they might hear, "John, please pick up the laundry!" as a complete sentence, while actually the word "up" was left out. Scientists concluded that the brain works with the senses to supply information which is left out. In this way it can present a rational conception of a fact or an event.

This is not to detract from the fact that senses can receive direct stimuli from the objects being perceived. For example, when one sees water and one is thirsty, the water can produce enough stimuli to cause the person to want to drink it. But the fact still remains that our previous experience and knowledge has a great bearing upon what we know through our senses.

For this reason it is difficult to learn something totally new. We have a tendency to know what we have known because we can relate to it easily from our previous experience. This fact about us has a very important spiritual bearing.

There is an account in Luke 9 which illustrates this very principle. The disciples had just experienced two very remarkable events in the life of Christ. They had seen the Transfiguration of Jesus, heard the voice of approval from the Father and then they saw Christ rebuke unclean spirits from a child. They were very impressed with the Master they had chosen to follow. It was at this time of heightened expectation that Jesus said something very remarkable to them: "Let these sayings sink down into your ears, for the Son of Man is about to be delivered into the hands of men." However, Luke tells us," But they did not understand this saying, and it was hidden from them so that they did not *perceive* it; and they were afraid to ask Him about that saying" (Luke 9:44, 45, NKJV).

The disciples *heard* what Jesus said, but they did not *perceive* what He said. Their perception of Christ was one of victory, not death. They could not integrate His statement with their experience of seeing Him heal and being glorified. This was why they still did not believe until Christ was resurrected, although He had explained everything to them very clearly.

The Pharisees saw the miracles of Christ, yet they did not perceive them. If Christ had come from better circumstances, if their mind-set had been different regarding the possibility of His being the Messiah; then they would have not only seen, but they would have perceived.

Our attitudes have much to do with our perceptions. If we have no desire to see or to hear, we can often not see and hear, although both of these senses may be otherwise working properly.

Jesus said, "Ye shall know the truth, and the truth shall make you free" (John 8:32, KJV). If we desire to have our minds delivered from the preconceptions that keep us from perceiving reality, then the way has been made. We need to know the truth of the Word of God not only in our minds but also in our experience.

By allowing God to cause us to grow experientially into fourth-dimensional living, we can then have the capability to see and hear what we may have missed, if we did not know His truth.

An example which can make this point clear to us is an experience that a man had in a European museum. This gentleman was knowledgable in the area of art. He walked through the museum in Florence and was amazed at the beauty of a Michaelangelo sculpture. As he stood away to get a better perspective, another gentleman walked up to the sculpture, looked at it and said to his friend, "Isn't that pretty?" With that, he moved on to see something else. The first man was shocked at the other man's lack of appreciation. When my friend told me the story, I simply asked, "Which one of you saw the work of art?"

The priceless truths of the Word of God have been written for thousands of years. Men from all backgrounds have glanced through the pages or tried to memorize the words, but not many have seen the truths that are in the Scriptures. Why not? Because what we see as well as what we hear is based not only on our ability to read and study the language, but it is based on our mental preconceptions, desires and experience. Jesus said, "For judgment

I am come into this world, that they which see not might see; and that they which see might be made blind" (John 9:39).

Therefore, our minds can be renewed by allowing the Holy Spirit to change our preconceptions, attitudes and desires. He also guides us in our lives towards experiences which will cause us to have a basis from which we will be able to see. This is the process of maturity in the Christian. We cannot add any more to this subject than the explanation that is given in Hebrews: "For though by this time you ought to be teachers, you need someone to teach you again the first principles of the oracles of God; and you have come to need milk and not solid food.

"For everyone who partakes only of milk is unskilled in the word of righteousness, for he is a babe. But solid food belongs to those who are of full age, that is, those who by reason of use have their senses exercised to discern both good and evil" (Heb. 5:12-14, NKJV).

MENTAL SIMULATION

Before an artist begins to paint, he first forms a mental image which he draws upon a sketchpad. If we follow the idea carefully, we notice certain important facts. The idea begins in the mind of the artist and is then projected upon the pad. However, the same mind that thought of the idea and was able to sketch the idea on the pad is also able to examine it and make additions or deletions. The artist may like or dislike the idea, but he has the capacity to judge and improve it because he has sketched it out first.

In the same way, Bach needed a musical instrument to play the composition before he could judge it, all those who create in any medium need to create a simulation of thought in an external way in order to judge that thought.

Language has a similar function. When we talk to ourselves or think out loud, we may not be crazy, but we may actually be clarifying our thinking, which cannot be analyzed while it still remains silent in our mind. Psychologists now believe that children develop language skills not so much by speaking to others, but by talking to themselves.

The mind has the ability to hold and analyze thought only for a relatively short period of time. We can examine thoughts and images in our minds. But these do not last; therefore, protracted contemplation is not possible. The mind's ability to do this is called mental simulation.

Where and how are these images stored and analyzed? The answer to this question is still not completely known. However, it is now believed that this is done in the part of the brain which controls our sight. It seems that the mind has an internal mechanism in which images are produced as thoughts. In the next chapter we shall see that a proper exercise of language can be to use words to produce the same image within the person's mind that you may have in yours. This principle has rich spiritual meaning for us in this book.

As we discussed in the previous chapter, one of the principles of fourth-dimensional life is learning to speak the language of the Holy Spirit, which is visions and dreams.

How does the Holy Spirit use visions and dreams in communicating with us? We saw in the previous chapter examples of Abraham, Joseph and others using this principle. But here our desire is to try to understand how this principle actually works.

If our thinking is a series of pictures which take place in the area of our minds that is involved in our speech, and if the Holy Spirit works within the Christian to communicate to him the will of God, then He communicates to his mind in the area where he thinks. If we have an internal sketchpad which we use as a reference point to write, play an instrument or speak, then this same sketchpad can be used by the Holy Spirit to give us God's direction.

The problem exists of distinguishing the voice of the Holy Spirit from other voices. For this reason we need to rely solely on the Word of God, which gives us the will of God. However, the sketchpad is also available to be used by the believer in developing the mindset which will guide his future actions.

I have often said that to accomplish something we have to see it first. This is because our bodies will fall into line with that which is going on in our minds. We can actually participate in the fulfillment of the will of God communicated to us by the Holy Spirit by taking the paint brush of the will of God, dipping it into the ink of faith and beginning to draw pictures of His will on the canvas or sketchpad of our imagination. Our imagination is then that sketchpad that plays such an important role in our lives and is such an integral part of our conscious actions.

Athletes claim that they have to first picture the accomplishment of a certain play before they actually can perform it properly. This is mental simulation at work. Therefore, the same principles which neuroscientists are now studying have been in the Word of God for thousands of years. Remember the previous chapter when we spoke of Abraham looking at the stars in response to the command of God? He pictured his children as a countless number. He used mental simulation to draw a mental picture in his imagination which eventually was able to control his ability to produce a child with his wife Sarah.

VOLITION

Nothing is more precious to man in his conscious state than his ability to exercise his will. The freedom to exercise his will has been something that man has been willing to die for.

Nineteenth-century materialists believed that since man was only a highly complex machine, his free will was only a mental delusion. All that was happening when he thought that he was acting was that the machine was responding to external stimuli along with his own chemical and physiological state. Fortunately, that view is today in decline.

Yet what is free will? What is really happening when we decide to do something? These questions are at once very complicated and very important.

When a man does something or desires to do something, he has to be motivated. That motivation may not be rational but it is certainly actual. If something or someone is restricting his ability to act freely, he then focuses on that restriction and has to decide either to fight it, try to remove it or just submit to the restriction and possibly wait until he is able to act freely.

There is also another aspect of volition which is part of our state of consciousness: we have a feeling of being free. Man has known little that lifts his spirit more than the ability to walk outside and feel free. In the 13th century Dante said, "The greatest gift that God in His bounty made in creation, and the most conformable to His goodness, and that which He prizes the most, was the freedom of the will, with which the creatures with intelligence, they all and they alone were and are endowed."

I recently read of an interesting study which related to this subject. This study was conducted in 1976 by a group of scientists in Germany. They placed electrodes on the brains of a group of volunteers and traced the impulses coming from the brain as the subjects were asked to voluntarily move their fingers. Amazingly, there were impulses in the brain as much as one second before the subjects voluntarily and freely moved their fingers. Was something triggered in their minds that they were not conscious of before they exercised their freedom to move their fingers? Apparently. If, when we act freely, we are actually doing something without being caused to do it by an external force, then, perhaps we may not be as free as we have been led by our feelings to believe.

The subject of freedom is still a mystery to many who have not trusted the Word of God. Even in the believing community we have had controversy concerning our freedom. Since the beginning of the Church people have wondered whether we accepted Christ because we wanted to or we simply did what we were predetermined, by God, to do. Obviously, this question will not be resolved in this book; however, we can understand something about our freedom from Paul's Letter to the Philippians: ". . . work out your own salvation with fear and trembling; for it is God who works in you both to will and to do for His good pleasure" (Phil. 2:12, 13).

Paul commands the church at Philippi to work out their own salvation with a deep sense of responsibility. We cannot consciously blame someone or something else for our actions. If we act, we are then responsible for our actions. When, however, you examine your actions further, you see that many times things seem to happen beyond your understanding. We seem to act freely, but our actions fall into a perfect pattern we could never know naturally.

God is at work in us both in our actions and, more importantly, in our motivations. The Holy Spirit, when He enters into our lives, begins to motivate us to do the will of God. Yet, even before we are Christians, the Holy Spirit is arranging the circumstances under which we will hear the gospel and believe. Remember that the Holy Spirit was sent to the world to convict of sin, righteousness and judgment. He was working on us before we ever allowed Him to enter into us. This does not mean that we are not responsible if we disobey. God holds us responsible for our actions. But we have been given all of the stimuli necessary for us to do the will of God.

Other experiments in this area have shown that we are not always conscious of what is going on inside our minds and what our senses are telling us. Therefore we must rely on the Word of God which never changes.

Finally, we seem to have two levels of actions. One level of acting freely is the conscious action. That is, we act knowing exactly why we are acting. The other is the act in which we do not know exactly why we act, only we feel like performing that particular act. We may call one rational, and the other emotional. However, both, if we are able to perform them without outside stimuli or restriction, are free acts of will. Yet, we have been made from two parents from which we have inherited not only looks but also personality and predispositions. We are also products of our environment, which influences our behavior. But for the Christian, the most important thing is to recognize the importance of filling our minds with the Word of God, so that our natural predisposition for action will be in accordance with the truth of the Scriptures.

"Thy Word have I hid in mine heart, that I might not sin against Thee" (Ps. 119:11, KJV). If it is true that there are motivational forces at work in our minds which trigger actions which we feel are totally free even for impulsive acts of our will, then it is extremely important to let that motivational force be the Holy Spirit. The Holy Spirit will then trigger responses in our minds that have been predetermined by the Word of God. In this way we may be able to lead lives that are both pleasing and productive.

The renewed mind is a mind that will be able to discern the will of God which is pleasing, acceptable and perfect. We will not feel like accidents waiting to happen, but our lives will be ordered and directed to the goals that we know are the will of God. Our energies and resources will not be sapped by irrelevant activity, but our resources will be trained upon the perfect will of God in our lives.

A renewed mind will change our lifestyle. We will no longer live meaninglessly, but the purpose which we are geared to accomplish will cause us to be happy, healthy and productive Christians. Our minds can then guide our words and our words will have a great effect on our actions. This is why you need to read the next chapter.

CHAPTER 10

The Creative Ability of Your Words

Did you know that your words are creative? They are either creative in a positive or negative way. They can produce life or death. Words have a power much greater than most of us can understand today. Psychologists, medical doctors and philosophers are just starting to understand what the Bible has been telling us for thousands of years: "For we all stumble in many things. If anyone does not stumble in word, he is a perfect man, able also to bridle the whole body" (James 3:2, NKJV). The truth given to us in this verse is very important; it enables us to see the impact our words have upon our whole being. James gives us three basic facts about the power of our words:

1. Words can be uncontrollable.

How many times have you said something only to later regret having said it? So often our emotions have more control over our words than our logic. We have a tendency to react to someone who has gotten us upset and we say something back that later we feel terrible about. Therefore, James tells us that we stumble over our words.

Our words also can be motivated by our insecurity. Many ministers are guilty of exaggeration. This is due to the fact that preachers receive their approval not from monetary remuneration, but from crowd acceptance. Therefore, by embellishing a story, fact or event, they stand to gain even greater approval from the crowd.

Our words can be greatly influenced by our associations. If we associate with negative people, we will find our words becoming more negative than normal.

Our words can be controlled by our imagination. Whatever we dwell upon, we will speak. If we daydream about things that are of the flesh, then out of our mouths we will find words coming that will refer to fleshly things and which will be beyond our control.

2. What indicates a perfect, or, more accurately stated, a mature man?

A mature person is one who is able to control his words. This, of course, does not justify those people who find it easy to say nothing. However, James tells us that if someone is so disciplined that he is able to control his speech, he is then mature. The Greek word *teleos* (perfect) means mature or fully tested. But the word translated man is not the more common *anthropos*, but the word *aner*. Kittel states that in classical Greek, this particular use of the word signifies man as opposed to woman.[1] He also states that in the New Testament the word signifies husband.[2] Robertson agrees with Kittel and translates the verse as "perfect husband."[3]

Those who have been married understand perfectly what James is implying in this verse. If your words are not going to be cautious, they will be so with your spouse. However, the general principle is also true for all people.

3. The way to control your body and to avoid its misuse is to control your words.

James likens the proper control of the tongue to the control of a horse. He uses the word "bridle." In a well-trained horse, a bridle can serve to either start, stop or change a horse's direction when it is used to exert a small amount of pressure in the horse's mouth. The part of the bridle that is doing the work is not easily visible, but it can dramatically affect the horse's behavior. So too our words. They seem so insignificantly uttered, but they have such great consequences upon us physically, emotionally and spiritually.

James uses the metaphor of a ship's rudder in the fourth verse. Winds,currents and sails do not ultimately determine the direction that a sailing vessel will go. The direction will be determined by a small rudder which is not seen but which nonetheless exercises great influence.

The point that James is making by using these two powerful examples is that whatever is in control of your words will control you. If you do not bring your words under your control, your life will be lived as a stumbling horse, directionless and accomplishing very little. Yet a mature spiritual man will make sure that his words are positive and creative. He will not allow himself to be controlled by circumstances, but will control his circumstances because he knows where he is going. He will use his words wisely.

WHAT ARE WORDS?

Although we accept the importance of our words, we have to have an understanding of what words are. After all, as Christians, we are people who are verbally oriented. We believe in the Word (Jesus

Christ) according to John 1:1-3. We also accept that the basic force that keeps everything in the physical world together is a word from the Word, "who being the brightness of His glory and the express image of His person, and [upholds] all things by the word of His power . . ." (Heb. 1:3, NKJV). Our faith is based on trusting in a God who is revealed to our hearts by the Holy Spirit. We accept the truth of a book (the Bible) which is full of words. Yet these words are more than ink on paper; they are the Word of God. Christ challenged us to go into all the world and preach the good news. Therefore, we are people who believe in propagating our faith through the use of words. No other group of people on earth should be more interested in understanding what words are and how they can be used more effectively.

Within the past hundred years many people have been challenged to understand exactly what words are. One of the fathers of modern linguistics, F. de Saussure (a French-Swiss) stated, "The function of language builds on the complex interplay between objective (physical) and subjective (mental) elements. Sounds, such as physical activities, are employed as symbols of meaning which is what ultimately establishes language as a mental rather than a physical phenomenon."[4]

Saussure continues, "Everything in language is basically psychological."[5]

What Saussure is basically saying is that words are more than what we say. They begin in the mind as thoughts. This is why people who are mutes can use words in sign language. Although they cannot speak, they can communicate ideas by using physical actions which signify understandable words.

Psychologists have been interested in this subject ever since Wilhelm Wendt (1832-1920) coined the term "psycholinguistics." Believing that by understanding the psychological aspects of words, they might be able to understand the way man's mind functions, he tried to use methods by which he could understand the relationship between ideas and phonomes (words as physical sounds).

Interest in words is not new. Plato gave his ideas concerning the nature of words in his dialogues. St. Augustine stated that every word had a meaning and that sentences were merely a combination of these meanings. However, the study of the psychological, physical and emotional impact of words is basically new to scientists. Much of the philosophy of the West has concentrated on defining what words mean. Ludwig Wittgenstein, however, became skeptical of this practice and stated that objects could never be defined too specifically because of the nature of change within language. The inability to give exact definitions of words caused him to want to understand what words were in essence. "What really comes before our mind when we understand a word?" he asked. "Isn't it something like a picture? Can't it [the word] be a picture?"[6] What Wittgenstein believed is that our understanding comes in the area of our imagination. When we picture something in our mind we understand it. That, in essence, is the definition of that thing. The word sound which is uttered may not be able to fully communicate that picture, but the purpose of communication is to convey the picture to someone else as completely as possible.

Therefore, we understand that words begin in the mind. We visualize something and we associate a phonome with it. The word exists in our mind before it is ever spoken. When we speak, there is a dynamic added to the concept we visualize, for the sound of the word may also add meaning to the word spoken.

In Chinese the same word can have different meanings, depending on the way the word is spoken. The tone that is used and the inflection of the voice lend an added dimension to what is said.

Children understand this concept very well. Having three children, I have learned much from being a father. One of my three boys was still getting dressed as we were on our way to a church dinner. The rest of us were dressed and still waiting for him. I went into his room and yelled, "Hurry up!" He, being quite young, began to cry. I could have used exactly the same words with a different tone and his reaction would have been much different. He knew what I was trying to communicate to him. My words stated a command; I wanted him to hurry. But the tone of my voice stated, "Hurry up! You have made me upset and you are going to be spanked!"

Words are described by John William Miller as symbols to grasp understanding. Words therefore reproduce the picture that the speaker is conveying in the mind of the hearer. He states that art is also a symbol in that it too tries to communicate ideas or pictures in the artist's mind by the use of a symbol (a work of art).

THE WORD IN THE NEW TESTAMENT GREEK LANGUAGE

The word translated "speaking" (*lego*) and the word translated "thinking" (*logismos*) both, according to Kittel, have their roots in the Greek word *logos*.[7]

Therefore, what we have previously discussed concerning the psychological aspects of words were already in the minds of the Greeks; the idea of the relationship between thinking, speaking and writing is not new.

The word *logos* in the Greek language has a rich meaning and history. It originally had several nuances which were used by John to describe our Lord.

Some of the developmental meanings of the word *logos* are:

- the collecting of information
- the counting or reckoning of something
- mathematical calculations used in accounting
- the evaluation of facts

From the previous meanings the word developed into: the assessment of things in general and their correlation. (This is where we get the word "catalogue" in English.)

During the time of Homer the word had the meaning of the reasonable explanation of something.

After the ancient Greek poets, *logos* takes on the meaning of speaking, replacing the previous word, *epos*.

The reason the word changed was because the people changed. As philosophers took a more important role in the lives of the Greek people, they in turn affected the language. Since reason and logic were important to the Greek people, the word signifying "speaking" was then developed from a word whose previous meanings included "the gathering of information" and "the presenting of facts." This had a different nuance than other words such as *epos* and *rama*, which described speech. These two were concerned more with the phonetic implications rather than the reasoning of the philosopher. "The causing of something to be seen for what it is, and the possibility of being oriented thereby is the meaning of logos," Aristotle stated.

Later on, the word *logos* is used in relation to the mythological god, Hermes. Hermes, in mythology, was the mediator between all the other gods. He was the revealer of truth. Therefore, during the Hellenistic period, *logos* took on a significantly religious connotation. The secular Greek use of *logos* was quite different from the New Testament use of the word, specifically as it refers to Jesus Christ in John's Gospel.

WORDS CARRY THE WEIGHT OF THE SPEAKER

H. Meyer, a New Testament scholar, believes that the Greek word *logos* had an implied meaning based on the importance of the person speaking. The more important the person, the weightier his words. The principle which Meyer states is true today. If the president of a country makes a speech, his words will carry more weight in that country than if an ordinary citizen states the same thing.

Jesus Christ, being the Son of God and the Redeemer of the world, spoke with such weight that His words produced life. If what was spoken by Jesus was repeated by anyone else, in another name, then his words would not be as powerful. The implication of this principle is that words not only convey meaning, but they also convey the character and personality of the speaker.

Since our words come from within our heart, they divulge the very intent of our thinking. This is why it is not what goes into a man's mouth that defiles him, but what comes out of his mouth. The person speaking a word, or words in a sentence, has to understand the importance of what he is saying, especially if he is a prominent person. People who are highly regarded are going to be heard.

In Korea, I am well known by almost everyone in the whole nation. When I speak, people listen and take what I say very seriously. Since I have never thought of myself as being better or more important than anyone else, I have had a difficult time adjusting to the fact that people are closely listening to my words, especially those words which I speak casually. I have learned that I cannot jest openly. I have to watch what I say. If I were to say something casually in jest, people would take me seriously and spread it all over the country. So I have learned to watch my words for I know that other people are listening to me intently.

The speaker's importance is an additional factor in his word because of the dimension of the speaker's authority. The masses in Israel listened to Christ by the hillside and by the lake and they also listened to the priests in the temple. The comparison that they made was that Christ's words were different, for He spoke as one having authority.

When someone says something, the authority of the individual will determine the degree to which what he says will be obeyed and remembered. The Roman centurion told Jesus that he understood military principles. He was not worthy that Christ should come under his roof, knowing that a Jew could not defile himself by going into the home of a Gentile. But he said that he was under authority and therefore he exercised authority. Taking for granted that the spiritual kingdom of Christ functioned under the same principles as Rome, he then told Christ to simply speak the word and his servant would be healed (Matt. 8:8). Jesus marvelled at the Roman's understanding of spiritual reality, for He had offered to go to his home and had promised the healing. What greater honor could be bestowed on anyone? Yet the centurion knew that only a word (*logos*) was needed for the miracle to take place. He recognized the authority with which Jesus spoke. This does not mean that Jesus spoke in an overly loud voice. At times, those with the least authority speak loudly because of their insecurity. But when someone has authority, that authority is transmitted by the way in which he speaks. Those who hear one who is speaking in such a manner will comprehend the weight of what is spoken, although additional language may not be added.

THE WORD OF GOD

In Acts 6, we learn that the Apostles realized that they were not to be involved in the daily administration of the needs of the saints, but their job was to study and teach the Word (*logos*) of God. This truth seems to be lost to much of the ministry today. So many preachers spend more time in their offices doing administrative work than in the Word of God. The fact is that the Word of God has many dimensions which cannot be comprehended by only a single reading. The Bible (God's Word) is not just a piece of literature. It cannot be read once, understood and then taught to others. The Word of God is many-sided and must be studied over and over again.

The Spirit of Truth has come to lead and guide us into all truth. How does He guide us? He, the Holy Spirit, knows the mind of God. He is, therefore, able to explain what was in God's mind when God spoke, both in the Old Testament (through the prophets) and in the New Testament (through the Apostles). If we understand that words do not fully and exhaustively explain the mental picture, then it is helpful to have someone who knows the inner working of the mind of the person who spoke. Therefore, it is imperative that we have the Holy Spirit leading and guiding us through the study of the Scriptures.

If the word which is spoken carries the weight of the speaker, then the logos of God has a spiritual as well as an intellectual dynamic which makes that word special. If God has told us (in James) that we should be careful in our use of words, then it is certain that God has been careful in the use of every word which has been written in the Scriptures. If words are to convey a mental picture, then we should learn how to visualize the Word of God and try to understand what He sees. We most assuredly need the Holy Spirit in order to do this. Since the Holy Spirit was the one who caused the prophets to speak ("For prophecy never came by the will of man, but holy men of God spoke as they were moved [borne gently] by the Holy Spirit"—2 Pet. I :21, NKJV), He then is able to interpret best what they said.

Jesus said that the Holy Spirit came upon the prophets as they spoke in the Old Testament. These prophecies were spoken as the Holy Spirit moved the prophets to speak. And these very words are called the Word of God or Scripture (Mark 12:10; 15:28; Luke 4:21; John 7:38; Acts 8:32, etc.). Yet the Word of God found in the Old Testament and the Word of God spoken by our Lord are not the only words called Scripture; the New Testament also is the Word of God: "Therefore, beloved, looking forward to these things, be diligent to be found by Him in peace, without spot and blameless; and account that the longsuffering of our Lord is salvation—as also our beloved brother Paul, according to the wisdom given to him, has written to you, as also in all his epistles, speaking in them of these things, in which are some things hard to understand, which those who are untaught and unstable twist to their own destruction, as they do also the *rest of the Scriptures*" (2 Pet. 3:14-16, NKJV). Therefore, the same Holy Spirit that came upon the prophets and moved them to speak also moved the writers in the

New Testament, but from a different location. Jesus promised that the Holy Spirit would be inside the believer.

As the Holy Spirit has invaded human beings who believe in the Lord Jesus Christ, He is not occasionally coming upon us, but He lives the life of Christ in us. This Holy Spirit can cause us to see what was not seen, even by the prophets who heard God speak and faithfully spoke for God, as recounted in the Old Testament. Therefore it was imperative that Christ depart so He could send another Comforter, the Holy Spirit. This is why it is so important for us to depend upon the Holy Spirit as we endeavor in a deeper way to understand God's Word. Paul said," But we speak the wisdom of God in a mystery, the hidden wisdom which God ordained before the ages for our glory, which none of the rulers of this age knew; for had they known, they would not have crucified the Lord of glory. But as it is written: 'Eye has not seen, nor ear heard, nor have entered into the heart of man the things which God has prepared for those how love Him.' But God has revealed them to us through His Spirit. For the Spirit searches all things, yes, the deep things of God" (1 Cor. 2:7-10, NKJV).

Although the Old Testament is full of the Word of God coming to the prophets, there are only two instances in the New Testament that the Holy Spirit came in the same way (to Simeon and John the Baptist). We are told that the Holy Spirit directed Simeon to the temple at the same time that Jesus was to be presented before the Lord God. (See Luke 2:25-30.) As he saw the Christ child, he was moved by the Holy Spirit and began to prophesy. John the Baptist was also moved by the Holy Spirit in the wilderness to begin his prophetic ministry. The term used in the Greek is *rema Theon*. The Word of God came upon him. These are the last two times in the New Testament that God spoke to man in this way.

Kittel says, "The phrases *logos tou Theou, logos tou kuriou* and *rema kuriou* (Greek for 'the Word of God' and 'the Word of the Lord') are very common in the New Testament, but, except in the case of these introductory figures (Simeon and John), they are never used of special divine directions. It is not that these do not occur in the New Testament. On the contrary, the apostolic age is full of them. But they are described in many other different ways."[8] The conclusion can therefore be drawn that since the coming of the Lord, who is the Word of God, the Word of God would never come again in the same way. Jesus never received the Word of God because He was the Word of God. Everything that had ever been said by God through the prophets in the past represented only a partial revelation of truth; with the coming of Christ, however, the whole of truth was revealed in a Person. The only times God spoke from heaven (at the Mount of Transfiguration and at Christ's water baptism), the audience was not Christ, but those who were watching God bear witness of Him.

It is not that God would not speak prophetically through His servants in the New Testament, but that there would be a difference in their prophetic ministry. Therefore, Jesus spoke the Word of God as the Word of God. The prophetic realm is a limited one: "For we know in part and we prophesy in part. But when that which is perfect has come, then that which is in part will be done away" (1 Cor. 13:9, 10, NKJV).

How can we speak the Word of God in a complete way? Peter gives us the answer: "For we did not follow cunningly devised fables when we made known to you the power and coming of our Lord Jesus Christ, but were eyewitnesses of His majesty. For He received from God the Father honor and glory when such a voice came to Him from the Excellent Glory: 'This is My beloved Son, in whom I am well pleased.'And we heard this voice which came from heaven when we were with Him on the holy mountain. We also have the prophetic word made more sure, which you do well to heed as a light that shines in a dark place, until the day dawns and the morning star rises in your hearts; knowing this first, that no prophecy of Scripture is of any private interpretation" (2 Peter 1:16-20, NKJV).

Words which are written have a more permanent nature than those that are spoken. My people have learned that misunderstandings can arise when they communicate by phone only, but when they write a letter, which can be answered by a letter, then there is a permanent record of the communicated information. Our faith does not depend on an oral tradition, as many other religions have. God spoke in the Old Testament and what God wanted us to know was written down. God speaks to us today through the Scriptures, both Old and New Testaments. Peter states that this record is more reliable than actually hearing the voice of God personally. He compares the voice he heard at the Mount of Transfiguration with the record in Scripture and says that the record is a more sure Word of prophecy. This does not mean that man cannot prophesy today. But it does mean that when we speak the Word of God from Scripture, that Word is complete and not partial.

WORDS HAVE POWER

Solomon said: "Death and life are in the power of the tongue" (Prov. 18:21).

In Volume One I wrote about a neuro-surgeon who told me about a new discovery in his field. By now, that principle is a well-established fact. The speech center in the brain has direct influence over the entire nervous system. Solomon, thousands of years before the discovery which science has made in recent years, stated the very same fact. In surgery, the will of the patient to pull through his operation will have as much to do with the success of the operation as any other external factor. The will of the patient will not only give the body of the patient the ability to stay alive during the operation, but will actually aid in the healing process. That will is affected by what the patient confesses. If he confesses death, then death will begin to work in his system. If he confesses life, the body begins to release the natural forces of healing to make that confession true.

This truth is especially important for older people. One of the most debilitating factors in contemporary society is forced retirement at what is frequently the still productive age of sixty-five. This is just when a person begins to learn about life, just when the cumulative experiences of a lifetime can be most useful. To be forced to go out to pasture at such a time can be disastrous. The mind then starts to think of itself as old and will begin to confess, "I'm retired now. I am too old to do anything productive." The body will respond to those words and begin to age more rapidly. This does not mean that all retired people are unproductive or are forced to retire because they are no longer of use. But it does seem like that to many retired people. They miss years of being useful to God and their society because they feel that they are "too old" and ineffectual. Age is more than chronology; it is a state of mind. That mind is influenced by the words which are spoken.

Poverty is a curse from Satan. God desires that all His people prosper and be healthy as their soul prospers (3 John 1:2). Yet much of the world has not really seen poverty as I have seen it. Especially in the Third World, people live their lives in despair, struggling to survive for one more day. I am from the Third World. I know first-hand what it is not to have anything to eat. My country was ravaged by the Japanese for many years; then we suffered through two wars. Korea is now rising up economically. Why? One of the reasons we are succeeding and prospering materially is because we are changing our self-image as a nation. While under Japanese colonial rule we found it difficult to have a good self-image and national dignity. But, against great odds, we were able to maintain our language, culture and national identity.

When I started my church, we had just seen the end to the Korean Conflict. Our people struggled just to eat. I then saw that God wanted to bless us materially as a testimony to His grace and power. This does not mean that economically underprivileged Christians are second-class citizens. But it does mean that we have to believe that the blessing of God is part of His redemptive provision.

I then started to see the importance of teaching my people the power and substance of their confession. If we confessed we were poor and created a poor self-image by our confession, we would always be poor and in need of material help and handouts from the West. But by trusting in God and working very hard, our people were able to lift themselves from the depths of poverty into a place where they could bless the work of God in our country and throughout the world.

Last year, I spoke at our Church Growth Conference in Sri Lanka. Previously called Ceylon, that nation is one of the poorest countries in the world. The bulk of my ministry was spent teaching them how to change their self-image. They had to realize that God is their source, not America and Europe. The main way a group of people can change their self-image is by carefully using words which are positive and which produce dignity within both the speaker and the hearer. Reports are still coming back about the results of that conference which brought together about five hundred Christian leaders from all Christian denominations.

In Mark's Gospel, we have a very beautiful and interesting narrative which reveals the potential power of our words as Christians. After Jesus had returned from His triumphal entry into Jerusalem He went directly to the temple. He saw what was going on but said nothing. He left Jerusalem to spend the night at the home of friends in Bethany. The next morning, He was hurrying and approached a fig tree that had large lovely leaves. Looking under the leaves for the fruit He saw nothing. The tree looked productive, but had produced no fruit. Jesus then cursed the tree and went on back into Jerusalem to cleanse the temple.

Since no action taken by Christ in the Scripture is without meaning, the tree, of course, symbolized Israel. Upon the disciples' return to the area where the tree was, however, Peter looked at the tree and said, "Rabbi, look! The fig tree which you cursed has withered away." Rather than dealing with the symbolic significance of the tree withering, that they could know the principle that that which cannot bear fruit shouldn't make the appearance of health, Jesus dealt with Peter's surprise at His ability to produce a miracle. This should be surprising to us because Peter had seen Christ perform many more spectacular miracles in the past. However, Jesus used this occasion to reveal the potential power of our words as Christians.

"For assuredly, I say to you, whoever says to this mountain, 'Be removed and be cast into the sea,' and does not doubt in his heart, but believes that those things he *says* will come to pass, he will have whatever he *says*" (Mark 11:23, NKJV). Merely *thinking* our words does not produce the miracle; the miracle is produced by *saying* what you believe. Christ promised that we could only have what we confessed. The story of the mountain being physically removed is only to add emphasis to the ability of the spoken word. If we as Christians only knew what power we can release when we speak in faith, we would be using our words more effectively.

Our words are important. Malachi tells us that God keeps a book of remembrance. Daniel was told by the angel Gabriel that he had come for his words. Paul tells us that God's redemptive word of salvation climaxes when we confess Jesus Christ as our Savior. The heart believes unto righteousness. You can be righteous in your heart, but words are necessary for you to be saved. Only thinking in faith will not release the power of God; we must learn to speak in faith. Our words are creative either for good or for evil. God has given all the grace necessary for us to learn to use our words creatively for the purpose of seeing His kingdom established in this earth.

HOW TO DEVELOP A CREATIVE WORD

As we look at the Genesis account of the creation, we can understand how God used His words creatively. Before God said, "Let there be . . . ," He had a clear goal and objective. As we understand by looking carefully at the story of the creation in Genesis, everything was created from the earth's perspective. But why should God create from this perspective since the universe is so vast, with many billions of stars larger than our own sun?

The reason for choosing the earth was that this planet was the place where man would dwell. If it were not for this goal, that is, creating a perfect place for man, the earth would be like any other planet, incapable of supporting human life.

Paul shows man's central purpose not only in the earth but also in the universe. He says in Romans 8 that the whole of creation was placed in a decaying process by the sin of Adam, but when man finally comes to the place of total victory and redemption, the creation, which has been waiting in hope, will be set free. The physical law, called by science "entropy," will be reversed even as we see our bodies overcome the process at the end of the age.

In the Letter to the Colossians, Paul reinforces the fact that Christ was the means by which everything, either visible or invisible, was created. Yet Paul immediately links Christ to His physical body on earth, the Church. In Ephesians, Paul states that we were in Christ before the worlds were founded. He then closes the first chapter by stating that we are His fullness which fills all in all. In the Greek text, this passage has even more significance than is obvious in the translation we are using. A more literal translation can be, "fills all that is capable of being filled." The obvious inference is that the Church, filled with Christ's glory, then fulfills His ultimate purpose of having the whole of creation filled with His glory. Our ultimate influence, therefore, is not just limited to this earth, but is intended for the whole of God's creation.

Seeing that we were in God's mind before the world was created, we can then understand the purpose of God choosing to create this planet capable of sustaining human life.

In learning to use our creative words, we must take our lesson from God. So often we speak in faith, but we don't have a clear objective. We don't know where we are going because we live from day to day. You may ask, didn't the Lord tell us to live like this? This is true, but He was dealing with those who worry. I am not speaking about worry. I am speaking about having a clear objective and goal for the future which you have received from the Holy Spirit.

When God said, "Let there be . . . ," He already knew the end of the matter. He saw clearly all of us, not as we are, but as we will be in Christ. He then had a clear objective: He would create a planet for the purpose of having a perfect place for man to inhabit.

Yet before God ever spoke, the Holy Spirit was working in the area of His desire. The Holy Spirit was creating the circumstances which would bring about what God would say. This fact must be very clear if we are ever going to learn how to use our creative language. We must learn to walk in the Holy Spirit and have Him direct us in what God desires. Once we get our instructions from the Holy Spirit, we can speak to our chaotic situations and circumstances with authority and we will see things begin to happen.

I was once invited to a church banquet and at this lovely dinner I used this very principle. One of our elders had a son who had an incurable paralysis which was getting progressively worse. As I was sitting at the table, the Lord spoke to me: "Get up and go to your elder and tell him that tonight his son will be completely healed!" I then began to be fearful in my heart. My wife turned to me and said, "What is wrong with you?" When I told her, she put her hand on my arm and said, "Don't you dare do that! You know that he has been prayed for many times. What if nothing happens? You will be ruined in this church." I agreed with her wisdom but got up anyway. (I have learned that it is better to obey the Holy Spirit at the risk of failure than never to try to see the glory of God manifested.) As I approached the elder, I smiled as he asked me, "What can I do for you, pastor?" I then breathed deeply and plunged into my statement: "The Holy Spirit just told me to tell you that tonight your son will be healed." Once I had obeyed, I felt total and complete relief. He then told his wife and the two of them began to cry out thanksgiving to God. Before long, everyone knew what I had shared with the elder and they too were praising God.

Once I sat down, my heart sank. What would be the consequences if nothing happened? But it was too late.

That night, the couple went directly to the boy's room and told him what I had said. He tried to get out of bed, but could not. They prayed and he tried again, but still his condition remained the same. Finally, the father said to God, "Lord, you told our pastor tonight that our son would be healed. He is a man of God and we believe him. We know that you would not ask him to say that unless you meant to perform a miracle." With that, the father took his son's arm, pulled him out of the bed and said, "In the name of Jesus, rise up and walk!"

As the child stood on his legs, his limbs were strengthened. He stood up and began to run all over the room. The news of that miracle spread all over their community; because of that testimony many families were saved.

In our society we are faced with chaos all around us, just as the earth was chaotic (without form and void) before God spoke. As we learn to walk in obedience to the Holy Spirit, we will learn to use the creative ability of our words to bring order out of chaos.

Our words can make the difference if we learn to use them effectively. We can either spend our Christian lives without proper control over our words, or we will see their importance, power and creativity and use them for the purpose that God originally intended. Let your words be positive and productive. Meditate upon positive and creative things. Fill your mind with the Word of God and you will be able to see the Word of God coming forth from your lips naturally. "Let the words of my mouth, and the meditation of my heart, be acceptable in Thy sight, O LORD, my strength, and my redeemer" (Ps. 19:14, KJV).

CHAPTER 11

Love: The Motivational Force

What motivates you to do what you do? This is an important question which Christians need to explore. Psychologists have been interested for many years about what basically motivates human behavior. We understand that our actions are motivated by differing forces. Some are motivated by power, others by the need to have money, and still others are driven by their creative instincts. This is particularly true of artists who are willing to sacrifice materially in order to create within the areas of their interest. But, what is it that motivates us as Christians to break through the usual into the unusual, the natural plane of life into the supernatural, the three-dimensional lifestyle into the fourth dimension? What will cause us to put into practice those truths which I have previously shared in this book? This is what we are going to explore in this chapter.

Before we explain how we are motivated, we need to understand what motivation is. "Motivation is a term used to cover explanations of why a person behaves as he does. It is not synonymous with 'causation' because it is generally restricted to only one class of events determining behavior. For example, it is commonly contrasted with ability, another determinant of behavior: a person may be able to play a game of tennis, but he may not want to; i.e., he is not motivated to play. Or on the other hand, he may want to and not be able to. Both ability and desire jointly determine what he actually does. Motivation is ordinarily indicated by such words as want, wish, desire, need and strive."[1]

In classical Greek thinking, the soul of man was divided into three parts: reason, and then two other parts which controlled his motivation. These two parts were his will and desire. Sigmund Freud taught his pupils that man had three parts. The three parts of man all worked together to form his personality and govern his actions. These were the id, the ego and the superego. Freud believed that the superego motivated man to perform his most noble acts, the id was the opposite force working against the superego and the ego was that balancing force which mediated between the other forces so that the person would act in a rational manner. C.G. Jung did not agree with Freud because he felt that Freud's concepts of man did not explain in enough detail the motivational forces of an artist's creativity.

Today, both sociologists and psychologists are more interested in practical aspects of motivation. Studies have been made to try to understand what causes some people to perform better than others of equal ability. If industry can understand what motivates people most effectively, an individual's productive capacity can be increased dramatically. Recent books have noted that the reason for low productivity within industrial nations can be attributed to the change of incentives within their economies. In the past, when most people lived on farms, a man was motivated to plant crops because he was able to reap his own harvest. The fall harvest made the work in the spring and summer worthwhile. Then there was a mass migration into urban areas in which men were no longer rewarded by harvests, but instead by paychecks and fringe benefits. With increased industrial specialization a worker would often not see the finished product, which he had only a small part in creating. The pride which a worker could take in his work was replaced by money. With increased leisure time available in the form of longer vacations, a person who previously had an investment of ego within his work, came to look at his job only as a means of earning money to do other things. Increased salaries and benefits did not produce greater productivity because of the loss of motivation. Now, industry is trying to understand what really motivates workers to produce better products. The answer is not money.

Educators are also vitally interested in trying to understand motivation. It is now understood that an important relationship exists between motivation and cognition. Students will learn and retain to a greater degree those things that they feel will be of practical use to them. Therefore, new techniques are being introduced into early school years which will seek to understand a child's motivational pattern and then provide specialized training in that area along with the liberal arts necessary to complete his education.

Although we as Christians are affected by the same motivational forces which affect the world, we have a greater and more powerful force at our disposal. We are not just citizens of this world. Our citizenship transcends the kingdoms of this world and brings us under the rulership of the kingdom of God. The Apostle Paul said, "He has delivered us from the power of darkness and translated us into the kingdom of the Son of His Love" (Col. 1:13, NKJV). We are not limited to this world's resources, but we are joint heirs with the Christ of eternal resources. Through the eternal motivational force of the kingdom of God, we are capable of doing more and enduring more than those who are depending on the limited resources of this world. This unlimited force which can and should motivate all of our behavior is the Love of God.

THE LOVE OF GOD: HIS MOTIVATIONAL FORCE

Probably the most familiar verse in the New Testament is, "For God so loved the world that He gave His only begotten Son, that whoever believes in Him should not perish but have everlasting life" (John 3:16, NKJV).

W. Frank Scott in his "Homiletical Commentary" states concerning this verse: "John is veritably the apostle of love. He alone of all the apostolic band seems to have been chosen to understand somewhat the depths of this divine love, so that he might tell it to men. The spirit of inspiration chooses fitting instruments; and we must assume that by nature and grace St. John was best fitted to make known the gospel of this eternal spring. Its presence had been implied before, when the revelation of Christ was spoken of; but now it is clearly made known."

The eternal spring that Scott refers to is the motivational force that caused God to sacrifice His only begotten Son, Jesus Christ. Why would the Father give His all not only for Israel, the Church, but the whole world? The answer is His Love. In order to understand the motivating force which caused God to sacrifice His Son, we must look carefully at His love. What is the Love of God? It is His essence. God does not love as an act, He loves out of His own essence. He does not try to love; His love is natural. "He who does not love does not know God, for God is love" (1 John 4:8, NKJV). His actions are not motivated by sentiment but by His nature: God is Love.

During the time of Christ, the Old Testament was the subject of much controversy. Daily there were arguments concerning the finer points of the law. The Pharisees had one point of view, the Sadducees another. At one point, a lawyer, who was also a Pharisee, asked Christ a question which he did not think had an acceptable answer. "Teacher, which is the great commandment in the law?" the lawyer asked, knowing that Christ could be stuck if He merely tried to answer the question. After all, if all the commandments were from God, who could put a value judgment upon them? By choosing one, he would reduce the others to a lesser position. But Christ had no difficulty with the answer and did not hesitate: "You shall love the Lord your God with all your mind; this is the first and great commandment. And the second is like it: You shall love your neighbor as yourself. On these two commandments hang all the Law and the Prophets." Instead of placing a value judgment on the commandments which God had given to Moses, Christ summarized all of them by giving the essence of what God desires His people to do: love Him and love others. Jesus also summarized and condensed the entire Old Testament into these two commands, which John reveals later are really one. John asks, "How can you love God who you can't see and hate your brother who you can see? Therefore, it is impossible to love God and hate your brother."

Since the great commandment was given by our Lord, men have been trying to divide the one into two. In some liberal churches, the great emphasis is on loving people. In some conservative churches, the command is to love God. History records horrors against groups of people, who say that they love God, against groups of people who believed differently. Yet some of the people that do most for other people often fail in their personal devotion to Jesus Christ. Jesus Christ taught that to truly obey God, one must do both. I have discovered in my twenty-seven years of ministry that when I am most loving to God, I am also most loving to His people.

Seemingly, some liberal groups have left the preaching of the Scriptures and have become little more than social welfare agencies. People come to these churches to be fed self-justifying platitudes. It seems that their only reason for meeting and collecting offerings is to do social work. This is not the Love of God. Human love is motivated by a sense of duty and sympathy; the love of God is motivated by the Holy Spirit. But some conservative Christian churches are preaching the gospel of salvation from sin, but are not too concerned about the people's physical needs. They may spend hours praying and worshiping God, yet are oblivious to those that are needy. The love of God brings balance! It causes us to serve God and love Him faithfully, but does not ignore those who are in need. The New Testament church is revealed to us through the Book of Acts. Luke shows how the early church loved God faithfully, and were also willing to sacrifice their material possessions to meet the needs of those in their group who were suffering materially.

Studying church history reveals that every great revival has been followed by a change in the social order of the people affected by the revival. For example, the revival which brought into being the Methodist church saved Great Britain from the revolutionary upheaval suffered in France. With the genuine spiritual renewal of the church came a greater awareness of the suffering of the English masses. New organizations designed to help the needy were founded. An example of such an organization is the Salvation Army, founded by William Booth in 1865. This organization was founded as a result of a new social awareness created by a spiritual awakening which previously swept Great Britain. Organizations such as the Red Cross were started around the same time. Once the love of God flows into us, it must naturally flow out to others!

WHAT IS LOVE?

Everyone thinks they know what the word love means, but it is widely misunderstood. In our culture, the word is thought of as an act rather than an attitude. We have perverted the word from its original biblical concept and returned to the Greek concepts of love which are foreign to Scripture. For us to understand the love of God, we must look at the difference between the Greek and the scriptural concept of the word.

1. Love's intensity.

"You shall love the Lord your God with all your heart, with all your soul, and with all your might" (Deut. 5:5). Modern man says, "I love you because you are now doing good things for me." But this type of love involves little permanence and only temporary commitment. God revealed the intensity of love when He commanded Israel to love Him. There are several implications which can be derived from the verse which I just quoted:

a. The Love of God can be willed.

   God will never require His people to do anything which they are incapable of doing. If God said, "You shall love," that means that we are capable of loving by choosing to love. Western culture's concept of love has been affected by the Romantic Era. During this time people thought that loving was something that was purely emotional and had nothing to do with an act of the will. As we shall see later, the Love of God is not emotional, although it can be felt emotionally. Therefore, we can choose to love as an act of obedience to God.

281

b. Love is complete.

God commanded Israel to love Him with all, not some, of their heart. Israel could not save a bit of love for some other god; God required everything.

c. Love is an act of the heart, mind (soul), and will (might).

Although love begins in the heart as a response, it also includes the mind. We are given many instances in Scripture where God reasons with the people of Israel and gives them logical reasons why they should love Him. Circumstances change, misunderstandings arise, yet love is also kept alive by an act of our might. Sometimes loving someone is inconvenient, but when we choose to love, we love regardless of the circumstances. Using might in love is not common within human relationships that are founded on emotional responses. But the love of God is more than emotional; it is eternal.

Our natural inclination is to love someone when they produce for us. I often say that we have a natural tendency to write good things others do for us on tablets of water, but bad things are written on tablets of stone. In baseball the saying is true that the crowd forgets the last home run after you strike out. Yet God has commanded His people to a higher level of love. Jesus took love a step further when He gave us a new commandment. He said that it was nothing special to love our friends. After all, this is a common response. He commanded us to love our enemies. This kind of love is not common because it is not natural. God has set the example by loving the world. The world is at enmity with God, Paul reveals. Therefore, the natural world is actively fighting God. It is the world that God loved so much that he gave His Son. God did not wait until the world started loving Him before He sacrificed His Son. He took the initiative.

LOVE AND COVENANT

The basis for love in the Scriptures is the covenant relationship between God and His people. A covenant is a legal agreement between two parties. Each party promises to perform a certain duty in exchange for something from the other party. In Deuteronomy, Moses retells the story of the covenant God made with Israel at Sinai. Basically, God promised to give Israel the land which had been promised to their fathers if Israel would keep His commandments. Along with the land was to come protection from their enemies, material blessings and prosperity, and physical growth and standing as a nation. Since the great commandment was to love God unconditionally, eternally, exclusively and intensively, they made an agreement that both could and would keep. God then became their God, and in turn, Israel became His people. Based on this binding agreement, we understand the essence of God's love. Choice is not involved. Feelings and emotions are peripheral aspects of the relationship. God loved us because He chose to. Our response is not based on anything else but an act of obedience. This does not mean that emotional responses to God cannot be involved, but it means that with or without them, our actions are to be loving.

God has made a covenant to love us. This covenant is natural since He is love. Although mercy, pity, kindness, charity and forgiveness are all aspects of His love for us, His primary determination comes out of fulfilling His covenant to love us. This concept of love will become much clearer to us as we understand the Greek word *agape*, which is the word chosen to distinguish the love of God from all other forms of human love commonly understood when the New Testament was written.

LOVE AND FIDELITY

Not only is the love of God experienced and known in a juridical way, as in the covenants, but it is also known from a basis of commitment and fidelity. The obvious example of this aspect of the love of God is the fidelity which is commonly expected in marriage.

Being loyal and faithful is something which is still expected in a marriage. Although our worldly age has experimented with what is called "open marriages," these experiments have proven to be total and complete failures. Man is created in the image of God. Marriage was instituted by God Himself. Even the non-believer has to look to the Scriptures when he desires to understand the normative behavior expected in a marriage. A man leaves his father and mother and cleaves unto his wife. This principle is as true today as it was when Moses first wrote it. But, the faithfulness which is expected in marriage universally is only a shadow of the relationship of love which God has chosen to have with His people.

"And it shall be, in the day," says the Lord, "that you will call Me 'My Husband,' and no longer call me 'My Master'" (Hos. 2:16, NKJV). Paul gives us the fulfillment of that promise when he states, "For this reason a man shall leave his father and mother and be joined to his wife, and the two shall become one flesh. This is a great mystery, but I speak concerning Christ and the church" (Eph. 5:31, 32, NKJV). The example for the husband is Christ. He loves, protects, supports and gives himself to His people. The example for the wife is the church. She is to love, obey, respect and give herself only to Him. The love which the two share can be maintained by the faithfulness which they have with each other. The relationship is more than emotional. It is legal. They have rights to one another and those rights are protected by a covenant made within the marriage vows. When the heat of their emotional love wanes, they can still maintain their relationship because it is based on a commitment that is eternal. Moses said that writs of divorce were given to Israel because of their unbelief. However, in the love relationship between Christ and the church there is no divorce. Their relationship is eternal.

THE THREE GREEK WORDS TRANSLATED LOVE

In pre-biblical Greek, there were three words which were used to convey the meaning of love. These three words are *eros*, *phileo*, and *agape*.

1. Eros: *This word simply means strong passion.*

What many are calling the sexual revolution is not new. The Greeks lived for passion. This can be seen in the writings of Plato in which he spent a good deal of time discussing love as passion. Many of the Greek poems and stories dealt with the intoxication of *eros*. Even the Greek gods fell in love with each other and passionately desired humans. These gods were not served out of devotion but out of fear. They were not perfect examples of purity and chastity, but were subject to the same frailties which were so common to humans.

Eros was so unlike the love which God expects from His people that the word is never used in the New Testament. This does not mean that passion has no place within the marriage relationship, but the concept of passion as an ungovernable intoxication with another person is strictly foreign to the Bible. It is no accident that the Scriptures ignore the most common word for love in classical Greek writings. No! The writers of the New Testament were only too aware of the Greek concepts of love. They were repugnant and repulsive to any believing Jew. This is why there was such an aversion to preaching the gospel to the Greeks. This is why it took a special call to a special apostle to first bring the message of Christ into Macedonia.

Paul had to write to the Corinthians that they should not allow the popular attitudes of the world to affect them in any way. Those who had accepted Christ and His teaching had to purify their lives and avoid the behavior characteristic of contemporary Greek society which practiced things that Paul states are not even to be mentioned among God's people.

2. Phileo: *a genuine friendship or kindness based on a relationship of fondness.*

Another common word, which is also used in the New Testament is the word, *phileo*. It is often translated as brotherly love. The word was used when Plato wished to describe the attitude that one should have towards his community. The word described what was considered the most noble of feelings. It did not carry the intoxications and excesses of *eros*, but described the attitude that would bring the most admiration from others. In classical Greece, men were challenged to open themselves up to others so that they could develop their personality; this was called *phileo*.

During the exchange between Christ and Peter after the resurrection, both *phileo* and *agape* are used. When Christ challenges Peter by pointing to the other disciples and asking, "Do you *agape* me more than these others?" Peter responded, "You know that I *phileo* you."

3. Agape: *a particular word with an unusual background in classical Greek which has special significance as the love of God.*

The etymology of *agape* is not very certain in classical Greek. The word never carried the passion or emotion of eros,and it also never carried the nobility of *phileo*. Originally used to express a preference for something or someone, the word developed in an unusual way. *Agape* was used to express a determination of the will to prefer something. With little exception, the word was not used a great deal by Greek poets, who were more interested in exploring subjects of more popular interest. When Plotinus used *agape*, it was used in reference to an act of kindness more than to a strong feeling of emotion.

Therefore, it is not surprising that the Holy Spirit would take an obscure Greek word and inspire the New Testament writers to use it so often and importantly in the New Testament. In this way, descriptions of the love of God would not carry by implication Greek concepts or practices. God could take a word and refine its meaning so that it would give understanding to His essence and His requirements.

LOVE AND THE MINISTRY OF JESUS

The life and ministry of Jesus Christ not only fulfilled the will of God by becoming the means and channel by which lost humanity could approach the Father, but He also revealed the Father. By looking at the life of Christ, we could understand what the Father was like. In the Old Testament, we see God the Father dispensing commands and requiring obedience. His justice had to be satisfied through sacrifice. Although God has not changed, the Old Testament only gives us a partial understanding of His nature. Christ came to give us a complete understanding of the Father. He reveals the Father's love and mercy.

It was unfortunate that those who knew His word most understood His nature least. This is why Jesus said, "You see me, you see the Father." Christ did not come to destroy the Law, but to bring it to fulfillment. In doing so, He satisfied the righteousness of God. Now man could have free access to His presence, for the way to His presence had been made clear through Christ.

Christ revolutionized the concept of love. By asking us to *agape* God, He was telling us to serve Him with actions of obedience based on our relationship and not just based on our temporary emotional feelings.

Jesus broke with Jewish tradition when He told the righteous young and rich man that he should sell everything and follow Him as a disciple. Jesus told him, "You cannot serve God and Mammon." The rich young ruler was faithful in following the Law. He paid his tithes and in the eyes of those who followed Christ was a perfect candidate for discipleship. Yet Christ knew that loving God demanded sacrifice. Not that having possessions was wrong. But it was a matter of priorities. To love God was to serve Him, and you cannot serve two masters. Material possessions would be acceptable as long as they were held loosely.

Jesus revealed in Matthew 6, the demands of *agape* love. The rich young man would have an opportunity which would bring him historical importance. If he had been willing to rid himself of his great possessions, he might have been greatly used by God, like Peter or John. But he could not understand the demands of *agape*. He became the only person to be given an opportunity to become a disciple by choice; all the rest were called without an opportunity being given to choose whether to follow or not. The important matter of this story is not the ability of a Christian to have wealth.

The main point of this story is the exclusive service which love demands when we decide to become His disciple.

It is God's desire for us to prosper and have a sufficient amount of all good things. But *agape* love demands total and complete service.

LOVE VERSUS PRIDE OR VAINGLORY

Jesus referred to the Pharisees in many places in the Gospels. He was most concerned about the religious piety which they practiced which was without the content of godly actions (see His admonition to them in Luke 11:43). They were generous in their giving in that they regularly paid tithes, but because they displayed their giving for all to see, they had no eternal reward.

James makes the point very clearly, "Whoever therefore wants to be a friend of the world makes himself an enemy of God. Or do you think that the Scripture says in vain, 'The Spirit who dwells in us yearns jealously'? But He gives more grace. Therefore He says: 'God resists the proud, but gives grace to the humble' " (James 4:4-6, NKJV).

The Apostle Paul makes the love of God clear in his letter to the Corinthian church. In the first letter, Paul is dealing with a major problem within the church. This was an overemphasis on spiritual gifts and an underemphasis on spiritual fruit. In chapter twelve, Paul reveals the ministry of the Holy Spirit through the Body of Christ. Since they were all members of one body, they should not concern themselves with questions of preeminence. After all, the foot is not jealous of the hand, etc. He ends the chapter preparing the church for "a more excellent way" (1 Cor. 12:31). It is important that we see clearly that at no time does Paul say that what is going to follow is a more excellent thing, just a more excellent way.

So many have misunderstood chapter thirteen (the love chapter). I have heard and read chapter thirteen being regarded as more important than chapters twelve or fourteen. This is not so. Love is not a better gift than faith, healing or tongues. After all, love is not a gift. It is the fruit of the Holy Spirit. What Paul is going to teach the Corinthian church is a better motivation for exercising the gifts of the Holy Spirit. This new motivation is love. When you love, you don't concern yourself with who is in the limelight. It makes no difference if you don't get to preach or prophesy. You are more concerned with the Holy Spirit ministering to the whole Body of Christ than whether you are seen, heard, or not noticed at all.

Paul makes very clear in this chapter that our motivation for exercising every gift including faith has to be out of love. Then he goes on to define love not as a dictionary would define it, but by describing how love behaves. Paul states fourteen facts about love in this chapter. There are five positive facts about love and nine facts which show how love does not behave.

The positive facts are that love:

1. suffers long
2. is kind
3. rejoices in truth
4. bears all
5. believes all

On the other hand, love:

1. does not envy
2. does not parade itself
3. is not puffed up
4. is not rude

5. is not self-serving
6. is not easily provoked
7. thinks no evil
8. doesn't rejoice in iniquity
9. never fails

If a Christian has these fourteen qualities in his ministry and in his lifestyle, he is then emulating the God that he loves, because God is love. That person is not only manifesting the nature, personality and essence of God, but he is also a person whom others will enjoy as well. How often have we met people who sounded spiritual, were gifted and educated in the Scriptures, but were not enjoyable, pleasant people? Although they may sacrifice all and be very dedicated, Paul states that it doesn't profit them anything, since they do not have love.

The motivation which the Christian should then have is the love of God which is shed abroad in our hearts by the Holy Spirit. This motivation will allow a person to break through spiritually as well as in their normal lives. Without the love of God, all the spiritual endeavors will profit very little.

Why should we be desirous of entering into a fourth-dimensional reality and learning how to speak the language of the Holy Spirit? First, we love God and desire to know Him. Paul expressed this motivation in his Epistle to the Philippians: "But indeed I also count all things loss for the excellence of the knowledge of Christ Jesus my Lord, for whom I have suffered the loss of all things, and count them as rubbish, that I may gain Christ and be found in Him, not having my own righteousness, which is from the law, but that which is through faith in Christ, the righteousness which is from God by faith; that I may know Him and the power of His resurrection and the fellowship of his sufferings, being conformed to His death, if, by any means, I may attain to the resurrection from the dead." Paul then continues: "Brethren, I do not count myself to have apprehended; but one thing I do, forgetting those things which are behind and reaching forward to those things which are ahead, I press toward the goal for the prize of the upward call of God in Christ Jesus" (Phil. 3:8-11, 13, 14, NKJV).

Not only did Paul express his personal motivation, but he reveals what he desires for those that are following Christ because of his ministry: "For this reason I bow my knees to the Father of our Lord Jesus Christ, from whom the whole family in heaven and earth is named, that He would grant you, according to the riches of His glory, to be strengthened with might through His Spirit in the inner man, that Christ may dwell in your hearts through faith; that you, being *rooted and grounded in love,* may be able to comprehend with all the saints what is the width and length and depth and height—to know the love of Christ which passes knowledge; that you may be *filled* with *all the fullness* of God" (Eph. 3:14-19, NKJV, emphasis mine).

Second, we are motivated spiritually because of our love for God's people." We know that we have passed from death to life, because we love the brethren" (1 John 3:14, NKJV). Peter also emphasizes the importance of being motivated to new spiritual heights because of our love for our brothers and sisters in Christ when he states, "Since you have purified your souls in obeying the truth through the Spirit in sincere love of the brethren, love one another fervently with a pure heart" (1 Pet. 1:22, NKJV).

In the past two decades we have seen clear trends in the way society has been motivated. In the sixties, there was a massive rebellion against established principles of behavior and governmental authority. Men thought that they could change everything and that change would be beneficial. In the seventies, there was a turning to the self, as men tried to concentrate on what was best for them as individuals. This period of time can be called the "what's good for me" generation. The great causes and concerns of the sixties were given up if they proved too costly to the individual aspirations which were thought to be important. World-wide, bookstores were filled with "how-to" books in improving and building self-confidence. The church was also subject to many of the forces of social change which took place in the world. Yet God's Word has not changed. What has been true in the past is still true! God demands love, not only for himself, but also for His people.

What motivates me personally to sacrifice my life for the sake of the gospel is the love of God. This love is directed towards God by the Holy Spirit and then directed outwardly towards His people by the same Holy Spirit.

I am now incubating in my fourth-dimensional visions and dreams half a million members in my church by the end of 1984. Why do I incubate these people in the realm of my imagination? Because I know without a doubt that the best thing that can happen to my community, my nation and the world is for the church of Jesus Christ to be strong and powerful. We are the salt of the earth and without the church, the world would have no hope at all.

OVERCOMING BY LOVE

As a young man, I was full of feelings of inferiority. I did not feel I was able to do anything significant in this world. I came from a poor area and was not highly educated. I had tuberculosis and therefore my body was not strong. I had little to hope for. Yet I was captivated by the love of God.

I discovered that one can take refuge in self-doubt and self-pity. Pride will keep a person with inferiority complexes from breaking out of his personal problems and beginning to dream great things. Once I fell in love with the Lord Jesus Christ, and His Holy Spirit started directing the love of God towards His people, I could no longer hide within myself. I had to step out in faith and believe God for greater things.

Now I am incubating half a million members in my church by 1984. If you had asked me ten years ago if I thought this was possible, I would have laughed. But I am highly motivated to believe God for what He has promised me. I am also believing for a greater outreach of our missions program all over the world. Not that I believe that God hasn't called other ministries into the world harvest at the end of this age, but I know that God has challenged us to work as if we were the only ones. In order for us to accomplish all of the goals that God has set before me, I cannot afford to feel inadequate or inferior.

It would be very easy for me to settle down now on the accomplishments of the past twenty-five years. I can rest because of the cell system. All of the thousands of members are well taken care of because the cell leaders give personal attention to each saint. Yet I am busier now than ever. I not only preach up to seven times on Sunday, but I also travel throughout the world in Church Growth Conferences. Why don't I rest at home and take it easy? The answer is the love of God.

I have learned to see the fields of harvest. I have talked to the Lord of the Harvest, the Holy Spirit. He has given me a love for each ear of wheat, each church that needs to be encouraged and strengthened. I cannot rest in complacency. I have overcome because of the love of God.

In this day, we see many of God's servants discouraged because they are not seeing what they were believing for. As I travel, I meet many of these people who have lost their hope. I recently received a letter from an American minister that said, "Pastor Cho, I was discouraged and had lost hope. My church was not growing although I tried everything. Then I saw your television program and started to hope again. Now I have changed, my ministry has changed and my church is growing." This pastor had lost his hope and had become discouraged. He did not know the importance of cultivating his hope in love.

Paul shares the key to hope with the Romans: "Now hope does not disappoint, because the love of God has been poured out in our hearts by the Holy Spirit who was given to us" (Rom. 5:5, NKJV).

The basis of discouragement for most ministers is the opposition and criticism they receive even though they are trying to do the best job they can. Once they react to their circumstances without the love which is shed in their hearts by the Holy Spirit on a continual basis, they lose their hope. Their ministry then becomes mechanical and the people who are hungry for truth and reality are not fed.

By understanding the love of God and being motivated by it, you and I can overcome discouragement and hopelessness. God's love causes us to act and not react. God's love causes us not to be satisfied with the approval ratings given by people, but the approval of the Holy Spirit. God's love causes us to love our critics. God's love causes us to see beyond the present trial and look at the goal of our faith. As we learn to walk in love, we rekindle the hope without which it is impossible to build anything.

When a farmer plants his fields, he plants in hope. When a builder lays a foundation, he does it in hope. When an artist prepares a canvas, he does so in hope. Therefore, when you do anything, either secular or religious, you must do so in hope.

The farmer visualizes the harvest even though all he can see is an empty field of dirt. Most of his work is done before he can see anything which will reward his labor. Yet when the first blades begin to break through the soil, he waits patiently until the fruit of his field is ready for harvest. There are many things that can happen to prevent a successful harvest. There may be a drought or a flood. Yet the farmer cannot worry about these possible problems; he must work as if all will work out well.

Therefore, hopelessness and discouragement can be overcome by the love of God. Paul was the subject of much criticism and had to defend his ministry on numerous occasions. However, when writing to the Corinthians he said, "For we do not commend ourselves again to you, but give you opportunity to glory on our behalf, that you may have something to answer those who glory in appearance and not in heart. For we are beside ourselves, it is for God; or if we are of sound mind, it is for you. *For the love of Christ constrains us.*" (2 Cor. 5:12-14, emphasis mine). Paul had learned that the love of God was the great constrainer against the natural reactions that he would have against his accusers plus the ambivalence which he felt at the time.

Since agape love is sacrificial love, and since it needs no reciprocation, the love of God constrains our natural reactions which cause so many of our conflicts. To love is to be set free. To love is to act as an agent of the Holy Spirit and not react to circumstances and people. To love is to enter a place of existence which causes us to be unshackled from the fears and frustrations which dominate this world.

OVERCOMING ANXIETY THROUGH LOVE

It is a fact of modern society that most people suffer from increased anxiety-caused pressure and stress. Every day, millions get in cars, buses or trains and head downtown to work. Traffic, noise and pressure of getting to work on time cause people to begin their day full of stress. Jobs are more complex and demanding. With our present economic changes, the fear of losing your job and joining the ranks of the unemployed looms as a large problem to many today.

Those of us who travel a great deal know the pressures of airline schedules. Plane connections can be missed if your plane arrives late and the connecting flight departs on time. I often see people at airports rushing, their adrenalin flowing, facial muscles tight, and obviously suffering from anxiety.

The American Academy of Family Physicians recently released the findings of a study which showed that two-thirds of office visits to family doctors are prompted by stress-related symptoms. It is believed that up to $75 billion a year is lost by American businesses because of lowered productivity, absenteeism and medical costs due directly to stress-related symptoms. Anxiety is now accepted by the medical community as a major contributor to coronary heart disease, cancer, lung ailments, accidental injuries and even suicide. Recent drug reports indicate that the three leading drugs sold in the U.S. are an ulcer medication, a drug for hypertension and a tranquilizer.

The change in society's value systems has been a major contributor to the epidemic we are facing in anxiety-related ailments. Psychiatrists have discovered that the unclear sexual roles caused by today's changing moral values are the main cause of problems between couples. Doctors have also discovered that the stress that anxiety produces and the adrenalin which the body secretes as a natural defense mechanism can become addictive. For example, children who enjoy racing their automobiles in a dangerous manner, students who have to wait until the last day before preparing for an exam, businessmen who purposely function on very tight schedules can be addicted to their own adrenalin.

Thoman Holmes of the University of Washington discovered that people who were anxious were more susceptible to disease than those who were not. He also noted that those who were about to face a situation which they feared, or were anxious about, were more likely to come down with a cold or some other illness. The body produces antibodies which combat germs that enter into its system, but when the body faces stress, the natural combatants are retarded and the body is less resistant to attacks by germs and viruses.

Anxiety and stress is not just a Western problem. In today's changing world, the problems that we face in our modern society are also increasingly becoming universal. Finding the answers to overcoming the anxiety and stress epidemic is important for all people in every part of the world. Increasingly, our present communications system has brought the world closer together than ever before. The world is facing a time when more people feel alone in the midst of a population explosion. People feel that they have less control over their lives. Computers and the numbers that we all have to memorize have depersonalized our societies.

A University of California study showed last year that a large number of people suffer from anxiety because they feel they have no control over the circumstances of their lives. Dr. Robert Karasek, professor at Columbia University in New York City has found that people who have little control over their jobs and face tight schedules suffer a greater risk of heart attack than those who have decision-making responsibilities.

How can we overcome anxiety and stress in a world that is plagued by both? The answer is found in the Scriptures.

Although we live in this world system, we are not of it. We have been given the power to overcome. God commanded His people Israel not to be partakers of the fears that the nations which surrounded them were plagued by (Isa. 8:12, 13). Israel was told by the prophet that natural alliances and the thinking which was common in Syria, the nation with which Israel was negotiating a treaty, was not going to help them if the enemy attacked them. Their safety was in sanctifying the God of Israel. By doing so, they would not have the worry and fear which then surrounded them.

University of Michigan's Louis Ferman found out that a man who had been laid off in 1962 and again in the early seventies and now again from Chrysler was able to overcome the fear and anxiety that has gripped many who are unemployed in the auto industry in Detroit. His secret was that he went to church every Sunday and was strengthened by his faith. What Dr. Ferman has discovered is not new to the Christian who knows the Word of God.

Jesus prophesied in Luke that men's hearts would fail because of fear. What Jesus prophesied in the first century is now medical knowledge. Fear is one of the chief causes of heart attacks. If we can overcome fear, we can overcome anxiety, stress and worry. The fear that our families will have to go hungry if we lose our jobs, the fear that we will be dishonored by not being able to provide for our own, has caused many in this time of depression and recession to turn to alcohol, pills and tranquilizers.

The Apostle John revealed the ground where fear cannot stand upon: the perfect love of God. "There is no fear in love; but perfect love casteth out fear: because fear hath torment. He that feareth is not made perfect in love" (1 John 4:18, NKJV). Therefore we have the way we can overcome fear.

As the lack of control over our lives causes us to fear that we are hopelessly alone and produces anxiety, so the love of God gives us the confidence that God is in control over all of our circumstances. The love of God gives us purpose and meaning beyond that purpose and meaning that is universally known. We know that because God loved us individually and died for our personal and individual sins, we are therefore significant and important. The love of God gives us the confidence that all things are working together for our good because we love God and are called according to His purpose. We are not accidents waiting to happen. We have a calling and a destiny which is significant.

Since so much of the stress and anxiety that the world suffers comes from interpersonal relationships. The love of God is the answer. By not only knowing the love of God toward us, but then sharing this love with others, we do not have to live lives that are confrontational. We can treat everyone as we would like to be treated. As we do that, we find that people will respond. So often people are just as afraid of us as we are of them. They are waiting for someone to break the ice. Warmth and friendship can come forth out of impersonal situations. If you are in a crowded elevator, you will find people just looking up and staring at the numbers. People are afraid to smile and act friendly. However, the love of God does not need reciprocity. You can be a committee of one to smile and say something friendly. More times than not, others will smile back and the nonpersonal situation can change for everyone.

In our urban centers, people often live in apartments next to neighbors for years before they get to know each other. As so much of stress and anxiety is related to a sense of alienation, this can be overcome by the love of God which can begin through you.

Love also causes us to walk in forgiveness. By not allowing resentment and anger to dwell in our hearts, we can build ourselves emotionally. Therefore, when the natural stresses of life affect us, we have the emotional resources to combat them successfully. If Christ told us to forgive seventy times seven each day, how often will He forgive us? We cannot allow ourselves to be kept back by thinking about the past and our previous mistakes. The past is forgiven by the mercy and grace of our Lord Jesus Christ and the future is in His hands, so the only time that we can concern ourselves with is the present. I have discovered that people who are guilty because of sin which they do not feel forgiven from, will have a difficult time forgiving others. Therefore, the first step to learning to forgive is knowing that we are forgiven.

As we are certain and secure in the forgiveness which Christ has given to us, we can then live out the rest of our lives practicing forgiveness. As we forgive, the tensions that can arise from others wronging us automatically disappear and we avoid the fear, anxiety and stress that comes from broken relationships. The love of God will cause us to realize with Paul that we have been called into a ministry of reconciliation. Again, Christ is our example. He became sin for us who knew no sin, that we might be made the very righteousness of God. The message of the cross is the message of reconciliation. Our lives should be lived reconciling men to God. When you realize that your job is only part of your responsibility and that you have the ministry of reconciler, then there is no room for fear and anxiety.

The love of God will not only cause us to be motivated to do the will of God, living as fourth-dimensional Christians, but it will also be the means by which we can live healthy and successful lives.

Notes

CHAPTER TWO

1. Altizer, *Oriental Mysticism and Biblical Eschatology*, pp. 11, 107.
2. Arnold Toynbee, *Civilization on Trial*, p. 262.
3. Albert Schweitzer, *The Philosophy of Civilization.*
4. Philip Schaff, *History of the Christian Church*, 2:109.
5. C.G. Jung, *Modern Man in Search of a Soul.*
6. D.T. Suzuki, *Selected Writings* (on Zen), p. 15.
7. Alan Watts, *Beyond Theology: The Art of Godmanship*, p. 115.
8. Ibid., p. 164.

CHAPTER FOUR

1. Gerhard Kittel, *Theological Dictionary of the New Testament*, 1:361 (section 3).
2. Ibid., p. 362.
3. A.T. Robertson, *Word Pictures in the New Testament*, 6:39.
4. F. de Sassure, "Course in General Linguistics" (translated from French) 1959, p. 69.
5. Ibid., p. 71.
6. Ludwig Wittgenstein, *Philosophical Investigations*, 3rd Ed., 1968, Part 1, p. 79.

7. Kittel, 4:282.
8. Ibid., pp. 113-5b.

CHAPTER FIVE

1. *Encylopaedia Britannica*, 15:919.

PURE GOLD CLASSICS

TIMELESS TRUTH IN A DISTINCTIVE, BEST-SELLING COLLECTION

An Expanding Collection of the Best-Loved Christian Classics of All Time.

AVAILABLE AT FINE BOOKSTORES.

FOR MORE INFORMATION, VISIT WWW.BRIDGELOGOS.COM

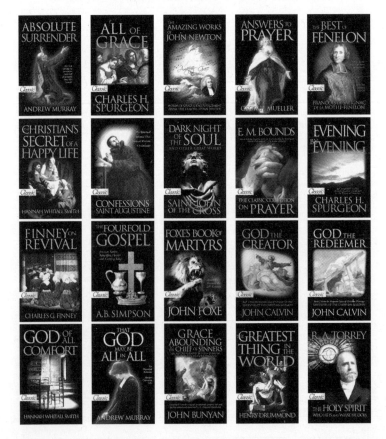

Prayers
That Change Things

by Lloyd Hildebrand

More than 160,000 copies have been sold in the series. These mass-market paperbacks contain prayers that are build from the promises of God and teaching that is thoroughly scriptural.

978-1-61036-105-7
MMP / 192 pages

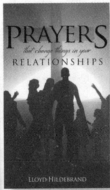

978-0-88270-012-0
MMP / 232 pages

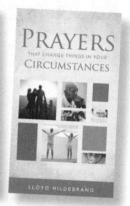

978-0-88270-743-3
MMP / 232 pages

978-1-61036-126-2
MMP / 216 pages

978-1-61036-132-3
MMP / 248 pages

978-1-61036-141-5
MMP / 256 pages

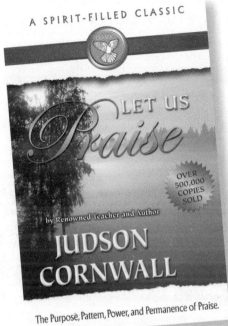

A SPIRIT-FILLED CLASSIC

OVER 500,000 COPIES SOLD

by Renowned Teacher and Author

JUDSON CORNWALL

The Purpose, Pattern, Power, and Permanence of Praise.

Let Us Praise
by Judson Cornwall

Let Us Praise has sold more than 500,000 copies through the years since Judson Cornwall wrote it. Its teaching about praise continues to minister to thousands of believers around the world who are learning about the power of praise in their lives. Judson writes, "May the ministry of praise that this book teaches find an expression in the Body of Christ far beyond the areas covered in **Let Us Praise**."

This dynamic book covers many important topics:

- *The importance of praise*
- *Why praise is vital in a believer's life*
- *How we should praise the Lord*
- *What does the Bible teach about praise?*
- *The purpose of praise*

These are only some of the topics that Cornwall covers in this Spirit-filled Classic. He answers the readers' questions about praise—its purpose, its patterns, its power, and its permanence.

The power of praise is a power that changes circumstances, personal perspectives, and the human heart. Yes, "It is a good thing to give thanks unto the Lord, and to sing praises unto thy name, O Most High" (Psalm 92:1).

ISBN: 978-0-88270-992-5
TPB / 168 pages

"The Consummate Apologetics Bible...

Everything you ever need to share your faith."

"The Evidence Bible is the reservoir overflowing with everything evangelistic—powerful quotes from famous people, amazing anecdotes, sobering last words, informative charts, and a wealth of irrefutable evidence to equip, encourage, and enlighten you, like nothing else. I couldn't recommend it more highly."

– Kirk Cameron

"Honestly, this is my very FAVORITE Bible of all..."	*"I have purchased roughly 30 copies of this Bible to give as gifts.".*
"Wow! What an awesome Bible!"	*"Amazing. Just amazing."*
"Love, love, love this Bible... I can't recommend it enough."	*"A fantastic study Bible! Very grateful to have it!"*

Compiled by Ray Comfort

This edition of The Evidence Bible includes notes, commentaries, and quotations that make it a comprehensive work of apologetics and evangelism that will be helpful to every believer. It covers a variety of practical topics, including the following:

• How to answer objections to Christianity
• How to talk about Christ with people of other religions
• How to counter evolutionary theories, while providing evidence for God's creation
• How to grow in Christ
• How to use the Ten Commandments when witnessing

There is no other Bible like this one. Every soul-winner who wants to lead others to Christ will want a copy of The Evidence Bible, because it provides springboards for preaching and witnessing, shares insights from well-known Christian leaders, gives points for open-air preaching, reveals the scientific facts contained within the Bible, and supplies the believer with helpful keys to sharing one's faith. The Bible is "the sword of the Spirit," and this edition of the Bible will motivate believers to become true spiritual warriors in their daily interactions with others.

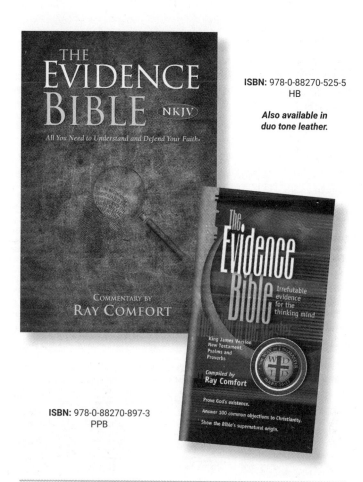

ISBN: 978-0-88270-525-5
HB

*Also available in
duo tone leather.*

ISBN: 978-0-88270-897-3
PPB

Also from Ray Comfort:

World Religions in a Nutshell

Ray Comfort

This book compares and contrasts
Christianity with various religions .
. . and includes sample witnessing
conversations and testimonies of
people from various faiths who
have turned to Christ.

ISBN: 978-88270-901-7
TPB